THE WRITING WOMEN OF NEW ENGLAND, 1630-1900
AN ANTHOLOGY

Edited by
Arlen Gilman Runzler Westbrook
and Perry D. Westbrook

"Another sign of the times is furnished by the triumphs of Female Authorship. These have been great and are constantly increasing."—Margaret Fuller, Woman in the Nineteenth Century (1845)

THE SCARECROW PRESS, INC.
Metuchen, N.J., & London 1982

Library of Congress Cataloging in Publication Data

Main entry under title:

The Writing women of New England, 1630-1900.

   Bibliography: p.
   1. American literature--New England. 2. American
literature--Women authors. 3. Women--New England--
Literary collections. 4. Feminism--New England--
Literary collections. I. Westbrook, Arlen Gilman Runzler,
1928- . II. Westbrook, Perry D. III. Title.
PS541. W7   810'. 8'09287   82-5459
ISBN 0-8108-1544-3   AACR2

TABLE OF CONTENTS

INTRODUCTION

Beginning in 1650, with the publication in London of Anne Bradstreet's The Tenth Muse, Lately Sprung Up in America --the first volume of poetry in English to be written in the New World--New England women have contributed vitally both in quality and in quantity to American literature. The list of such authors is long and impressive; the nineteen included in this volume have been chosen as representative, spanning a period of over three hundred years. They reflect, in both poetry and prose, the rural and urban values and ways of life of the region.

New Englanders of both sexes were in general more literate in the early days than inhabitants of other sections of the English-speaking world. Though formal, institutional education beyond the elementary level was available in Colonial times only to men, women of the more privileged families had opportunities for self-education aided by their parents and by home libraries.

Yet in the early Colonial period it was thought that women should be discouraged, indeed protected, from too much reading and studying. Governor John Winthrop clearly echoes the tenor of the times in his Journal. He describes the wife of the Governor of Connecticut as basically crazy because she spent time reading and even writing books. These things, he says, are clearly for men, who have "stronger" minds. The Governor's wife should stay in her "place." Colonial women who wrote did so despite this intellectual and philosophical climate. They deserve credit for their courage. Women writing after the middle of the eighteenth century found a somewhat more accepting attitude regarding their efforts.

After national independence, study in the excellent New England academies and so-called female seminaries came increasingly within the grasp of women with ambition and even moderate means. Moreover, the profound commitment of

many New Englanders up through much of the nineteenth century to their ancestral relation, the theological intricacies of
which they heard expounded in lengthy Sabbath sermons and
Thursday lectures, encouraged and indeed necessitated in both
men and women an agility and alertness of mind that would
be invaluable for any would-be writer. In the discussions
concerning religious doctrine that authors like Harriet Beecher
Stowe tell us occurred at family mealtimes we may be sure
that women were not silent. Even on the remotest hill farm
there would quite likely be intellectually challenging discus-
sions--albeit religiously focused--and the Bible and probably
several theological treatises would be regularly read. Access
to the printed record of the faith was thought by New Englanders to be indispensable to the spiritual life of every person, regardless of age and sex.

As evidenced by selections in this anthology from the
pre-Revolutionary period, the first writing in New England
by either men or women was either nonfiction or verse,
since the Puritans considered drama and fiction to be lies
and false representations, with which a pious Christian should
have no truck. Until after the Revolution no novels or short
stories and, with the exception of two satirical political plays
by Mercy Warren, no drama was written. Among the first
writers of fiction in New England, women predominated.
With some relaxing of the Puritan literary taboos, Susanna
Rowson (c. 1762-1824), in Charlotte Temple (1791), and Hannah Foster (1759-1840), in The Coquette (1797), wrote and
published moralizing novels with plots involving seduction.
More impressive are two novels by Catharine Maria Sedgwick
of Stockbridge, Massachusetts--A New-England Tale: or,
Sketches of New-England Character and Manners (1822) and
Hope Leslie: or, Early Times in the Massachusetts (1827).
Though no excerpts from the work of these three novelists
appear in this collection, they demand notice as standing at
the beginning of a long line of New England writers of fiction,
including among many others Harriet Beecher Stowe, Rose
Terry Cooke, Sarah Orne Jewett, Mary E. Wilkins Freeman,
and Alice Brown--all represented in this volume and all of
whom rank high among New England and American authors.

Concurrently with the writers of fiction other women
were writing nonfiction, much of it on the status of women
but also on other social and political subjects, such as abolition, temperance, education, and the conditions of labor.
Sarah Wentworth Morton, Harriet Beecher Stowe, Lucy Larcom, Margaret Fuller, Louisa May Alcott, Elizabeth Stuart

Phelps Ward, and Mary Ashton Livermore dealt with one or
more of these subjects, though the editors of this volume
have emphasized writings relating to the feminist movement,
which, with stirrings before the Revolution, became a matter
of deep and widespread concern in the nineteenth century.
Thus most, but not all, of the writings collected here have
been chosen because of the light they shed on the position of
New England women as seen by other women in the region.

New England during its first two hundred years was,
for America, remarkably homogeneous in its population and
was largely dominated by the way and view of life that had
its roots in Puritanism. The region, which sent forth a
steady stream of emigrants westward, has been called the
seed-bed of the nation. It was the seed-bed not only of people but also of ideas, values, attitudes, and character traits.
Along with their cattle and household goods, the migrating
Yankees, as Henry Ward Beecher pointed out, brought with
them their church, their schools, their town-meeting democ-
racy, and the respect for the individual that all these implied.
The "New England way" was transplanted far and wide, and
in many sections this became the norm. It is with such
thoughts as these that the editors of this volume have determined to draw their material from writers of a restricted but
intellectually and culturally influential area and period.

The authors represented in this anthology, chosen because their writing is important and has literary merit, have
a surprising amount in common. Though their viewpoints are
diverse and cover a wide spectrum, their backgrounds for the
most part are similar. They were born into educated, professional families, their fathers being ministers, lawyers,
doctors. All had relatively wide contact with the education
available to women in their day.

Another common factor was generally what Virginia
Woolf championed in A Room of One's Own. Literally speaking, we cannot know about a specific writing place; what we
do know is that these women had the time and freedom to
devote to writing in one way or another. Four of them--
Hunt, Jewett, Brown, and Alcott--never married and thus
were not burdened by duties to a husband who needed time
and attention. Phelps (Ward), Cooke, Freeman, Fuller (Ossoli) were not married until many years after their writing
careers were well established and not to be easily interrupted.
One, Hannah Crocker, was widowed at the early age of forty-
five. Others found free time because of their husbands' fre-

quent absences away at sea or on business. Perhaps this
made them, by necessity, assume more of the responsibilities
and decision-making in their families, made them more independent, and gave them an added element of self-esteem,
which enabled them to feel that their opinions had merit and
should be shared. Undoubtedly even Anne Bradstreet, though
the mother of eight children, had servants to care for them.

Those who were born into families of wealth and priv-
ilege--though they may, as women, have had no direct con-
trol over that money--possibly had more freedom and self-
confidence than the usual housewives of the time, whose husbands were dependent on others for employment.

There has not been room in the following pages for
many New England authors who deserve inclusion. Notable
among these are Catharine Maria Sedgwick, Elizabeth Palmer
Peabody, Helen Hunt Jackson, and Celia Thaxter. Most surprising to many readers will be the absence of any poetry or
prose by New England's greatest poet, Emily Dickinson. It
seemed to the editors that it would be impossible to do justice to her in the amount of space we could allot to even so
important an author as she. We trust that to most readers
Dickinson's verse is already so well known that its omission
will not constitute a serious deficiency. On the other hand,
the inclusion of a statement by Anne Hutchinson at her trial
before the General Court of Massachusetts Bay in 1637 may
need explanation, since she was not an author but a preacher.
Hutchinson is included because at that early date she asserted
her humanity rather than her womanhood, and did so in defiance of the magistrates and the clergy and on the strength
of her religious convictions, meeting her accusers on their
own theological ground. During the next two and a half cen-
turies in New England religious arguments and considerations
figured prominently in the gradual improvement of women's
status. Eventually Hutchinson came to be regarded as a
martyr ("sainted," in Hawthorne's phrase). The sampling of
her words in this anthology foreshadows much that was to
follow her ordeal.

THE WRITING WOMEN OF NEW ENGLAND, 1630-1900
An Anthology

ANNE HUTCHINSON

(1591-1643)

The first decade of migration to Massachusetts Bay brought to the colony two women of extraordinary talents and character. One was Anne Bradstreet, who, with Edward Taylor, was one of the two poets of real literary merit in pre-Revolutionary America. The other was Anne Hutchinson, whose religious convictions and power of argumentation became intolerable to the Massachusetts magistrates and clergy and caused her banishment from the colony. Hutchinson, the daughter of a Puritan minister, was born in Alford, Lincolnshire, England, in 1591. After some years in London she returned to Alford as the wife of a merchant of that place. In the nearby Lincolnshire town of Boston the Cambridge graduate John Cotton was vigorously preaching Puritan doctrine. When he migrated to New England in 1633 to avoid persecution for his beliefs, the Hutchinsons, who were among his admirers, soon followed him. In Boston, Anne began holding meetings of women in her house for the purpose of discussing religious matters and particularly the sermons of the local clergy. These men, with the exception of Cotton, she accused of preaching a covenant of works rather than a covenant of grace, branding them as unfit to be ministers of the gospel.

The distinction between the two covenants stemmed from the basic Calvinist tenets that only God's free gift of grace could save one's soul and that those who received the gift of grace had been irrevocably chosen from the beginning of time. The problem was, how could one tell if one were among the chosen? The clergy generally taught that the best evidence, aside from faith in Christ, was one's success in leading an upright and righteous life--in other words, engaging in "good works" or conduct becoming to a Christian. Anne, however, contended that "good works" were not significant as evidence of "justification," that is, of one's having received saving grace. Since the question of salvation was

3

extremely pressing to a true Puritan, Anne's teaching had a
wide appeal, maintaining as it did that assurance of having
received grace rested on a personal experience of conversion,
the inner signs of which would be unmistakable. Thus Anne's
meetings in her house were thronged, at first by women but
later by men; and herein she laid herself open to the discipline of the church and the magistrates, for it was thought
that the Bible forbade women from teaching, or preaching
to, men. Thoroughly alarmed at what they considered a chal-
lenge to their authority, the clergy and magistrates brought
charges against Anne and other antinomians (as she and her
followers were incorrectly called, since the word implies defiance of all authority). Cotton, who had been under a cloud
of suspected heresy, managed to clear himself, but Anne was
put on trial, in which she defended herself with great skill,
wit, and courage. Yet she made her condemnation certain
when she avowed that she had experienced revelations directly
from God. Excommunicated from her church and expelled
from the colony, she fled first to Rhode Island and later to
New York, where she resided in what is now the Pelham Bay
area of the Bronx. Here she and all but one of her family
were killed in an Indian raid in 1643.

None of Anne Hutchinson's writings, if there ever were
any, exist, but transcriptions of her examination by the General Court of Massachusetts and of her trial before her church
in Boston have been preserved. The brief excerpt that follows
is from the former, which may be found in Charles Francis
Adams, ed., Antinomianism in the Colony of Massachusetts
Bay, 1636-1638 (Boston, 1894). Despite some gaps, it re-
veals the strength of her character and convictions and her
calm self-trust, as she stood accused before the governor,
the deputies, and many of the clergy of Massachusetts Bay.
Like Anne Bradstreet she had engaged in activities considered
unsuitable for a woman, but unlike Anne Bradstreet her activities had not been the harmless (as many at the time conceived them) scribbling of verses. Hutchinson, instead of
confining herself to the only approvable sphere for a woman
--that of managing her husband's household and rearing his
children--had intruded into theology, an area in which only
males, and mainly those trained in divinity, were thought
competent. She had challenged officially accepted doctrine
and thus had posed a threat to the established order. She
soon became a symbol and her life a prophecy.

For accounts of Anne Hutchinson's life and her part
in the Antinomian Controversy, see Charles Francis Adams,

Three Episodes in Massachusetts History, 2 vols. (1892), and Emery Battis, Saints and Sectaries (1963).

From "THE EXAMINATION OF MRS. ANN [sic] HUTCHINSON AT THE COURT AT NEWTON"

[Governor John Winthrop presided. Present also were several clergymen, Deputy-Governor Thomas Dudley (Anne Bradstreet's father), and members of the General Court or legislature.]

Mrs. H. If you please to give me leave I shall give you the ground of what I know to be true. Being much troubled to see the falseness of the constitution of the church of England, I had like to have turned separatist; whereupon I kept a day of solemn humiliation and pondering of the thing; this scripture was brought unto me--he that denies Jesus Christ to be come in the flesh is antichrist--This I considered of and in considering found that the papists did not deny him to be come in the flesh, nor we did not deny him--who then was antichrist? Was the Turk antichrist only? The Lord knows that I could not open scripture; he must by his prophetical office open it unto me. So after that being unsatisfied in the thing, the Lord was pleased to bring this scripture out of the Hebrews. He that denies the testament denies the testator, and in this did open unto me and give me to see that those which did not teach the new covenant had the spirit of antichrist, and upon this he did discover the ministry unto me and ever since. I bless the Lord, he hath let me see which was the clear ministry and which the wrong. Since that time I confess I have been more choice and he hath left me to distinguish between the voice of my beloved and the voice of Moses, the voice of John Baptist and the voice of antichrist, for all those voices are spoken of in scripture. Now if you do condemn me for speaking what in my conscience I know to be truth I must commit myself unto the Lord.

Mr. Nowel. How do you know that that was the spirit?

Mrs. H. How did Abraham know that it was God that bid him offer his son, being a breach of the sixth commandment?

Dep. Gov. By an immediate voice.

Mrs. H. So to me by an immediate revelation.

Dep. Gov. How! an immediate revelation.

Mrs. H. By the voice of his own spirit to my soul. I will give you another scripture, Jer. 46. 27, 28--out of which the Lord shewed me what he would do for me and the rest of his servants. --But after he was pleased to reveal himself to me I did presently like Abraham run to Hagar. And after that he did let me see the atheism of my own heart, for which I begged of the Lord that it might not remain in my heart, and being thus, he did shew me this (a twelvemonth after) which I told you of before. Ever since that time I have been confident of what he hath revealed unto me.
[Obliter-⎫ another place out of Daniel chap. 7. and he
ated] ⎭ and for us all, wherein he shewed me the fitting of the judgment and the standing of all high and low before the Lord and how thrones and kingdoms were cast down before him. When our teacher came to New-England it was a great trouble unto me, my brother Wheelwright being put by also. I was then much troubled concerning the ministry under which I lived, and then that place in the 30th of Isaiah was brought to my mind. Though the Lord give thee bread of adversity and water of affliction yet shall not thy teachers be removed into corners any more, but thine eyes shall see thy teachers. The Lord giving me this promise and they being gone there was none then left that I was able to hear, and I could not be at rest but I must come hither. Yet that place of Isaiah did much follow me, though the Lord give thee the bread of adversity and water of affliction. This place lying I say upon me then this place in Daniel was brought unto me and did shew me that though I should meet with affliction yet I am the same God that delivered Daniel out of the lion's den, I will also deliver thee. --Therefore I desire you to look to it, for you see this scripture fulfilled this day and therefore I desire you that as you tender the Lord and the church and commonwealth to consider and look what you do. You have power over my body but the Lord Jesus hath power over my body and soul, and assure yourselves thus much, you do as much as in you lies to put the

Lord Jesus Christ from you, and if you go on in this course you begin you will bring a curse upon you and your posterity, and the mouth of the Lord hath spoken it.

Dep. Gov. What is the scripture she brings?

Mr. Stoughton. Behold I turn away from you.

Mrs. H. But now having seen him which is invisible I fear not what man can do unto me.

Gov. Daniel was delivered by miracle do you think to be deliver'd so too?

Mrs. H. I do here speak it before the court. I look that the Lord should deliver me by his providence.

Mr. Harlakenden. I may read scripture and the most glorious hypocrite may read them and yet go down to hell.

Mrs. H. It may be so.

ANNE BRADSTREET

(c. 1612-1672)

The daughter of Thomas Dudley, who was the steward of the Earl of Lincoln, Anne Bradstreet received an education far superior to that of most women of her day. In addition to being tutored in languages and music, she had access to the Earl's extensive library. In her girlhood she contracted rheumatic fever and smallpox--apparently without disfigurement--and all her life she suffered from poor health. When sixteen she married Simon Bradstreet, a graduate of Cambridge University and, like her father, a Puritan. In 1630 Anne with her husband and her parents set sail on the Arbella for New England, settling first in Boston, later in Ipswich, and finally in North Andover, where she lived until her death in 1672. Both her father and her husband served terms as Governor of Massachusetts Bay, her father during her lifetime and her husband (who lived to the age of ninety-four) long after her death.

By family and education a gentlewoman accustomed to the cultural and physical amenities of a nobleman's country estate, Anne was at first overwhelmed by the wilderness in which she was to begin a new life. Like many other settlers she seems to have had a severe homesickness for England's "green and pleasant land"; in her words, "her heart rose up against" her new environment. But, again like many others, she quickly found solace in her religion and in the belief that she was a participant in divinely decreed events. Later she also found solace in nature, the beauty and orderliness of which confirmed her faith in God, for she admitted that she experienced periods of doubt.

Bradstreet was a devoted wife and mother (of eight children) and an efficient manager of her household. In other words, she faultlessly performed the roles expected of women in her day. During whatever time she could spare from her housewifely duties she wrote poetry, a volume of which, with

8

the title The Tenth Muse, Lately Sprung Up in America, was
published in London in 1650 from a manuscript brought there,
unknown to her, by her brother-in-law. Though the book
was widely read and admired, Bradstreet was displeased that
it had been published without her permission, and she set
about revising its contents and adding other poems to it with
an eye toward a second edition. The poems in The Tenth
Muse are for the most part lengthy didactic pieces with titles
like "The Four Elements," "The Four Monarchies," and "A
Dialogue Between Old England and New." They are compe-
tently written and attest to the superior quality of her education, but they are of little interest to the modern reader.

The second and enlarged edition, titled Several Poems
Compiled with Great Variety of Wit and Learning, which was
published in Boston in 1678, six years after its author's
death, contains poems of a very different order, most of
them gleaned from the poet's papers and some of them probably not intended for publication. These poems record her
private feelings, especially her love for her husband and
children. They are lyrical in tone, sometimes impassioned,
and skillful in their elaboration of metaphor somewhat in the
manner of John Donne and the other English metaphysical
poets. Like the poems that Emily Dickinson wrote two hundred years later they spring from the experiences of a woman whose life is centered in her home and her family. Additional and equally impressive verse by Anne Bradstreet,
and some of her prose, appeared in 1867 in The Works of
Anne Bradstreet in Prose and Verse, edited by John H. Ellis.

In her poetry Bradstreet does not hesitate to convey
feelings about her own ability to write, or women's ability
to rule. She repudiated, to some extent, sexual stereotypes,
undoubtedly a risky statement to make during the Colonial
times in which she lived. The thread of references to illness
and death is not only a probable reflection of her own illnesses but also an indication of the times when many died
young from contagious diseases, infections, and poor sanita-
tion. (The progress the medical profession has made since
that time has been primarily in the area of prevention, not
cure, of disease.)

For fuller critical and biographical studies of Bradstreet, see Josephine K. Piercy, Anne Bradstreet (1965),
and Elizabeth W. White, Anne Bradstreet: The Tenth Muse
(1971). Adrienne Rich's Foreword to The Works of Anne
Bradstreet (1967) is an interesting commentary, as is Charles

Eliot Norton's Introduction to The Poems of Mrs. Anne Bradstreet Together with Her Prose Remains (1897). The selections that follow are from the latter edition.

From "THE PROLOGUE" TO THE TENTH MUSE

I am obnoxious to each carping tongue
Who says my hand a needle better fits.
A poet's pen all scorn I should thus wrong;
For such despite they cast on female wits,
If what I do prove well, it won't advance--
They'll say it's stolen, or else it was by chance.

But sure the antique Greeks were far more mild,
Else of our sex why feigned they those Nine,
And Poesy made Calliope's own child?
So 'mongst the rest they placed the Arts Divine.
But this weak knot they will full soon untie--
The Greeks did naught but play the fools and lie.

Let Greeks be Greeks, and women what they are.
Men have precedency, and still excel.
It is but vain unjustly to wage war:
Men can do best, and women know it well.
Preëminence in all and each is yours--
Yet grant some small acknowledgment of ours.

And oh, ye high flown quills that soar the skies,
And ever with your prey still catch your praise,
If e'er you deign these lowly lines your eyes,
Give thyme or parsley wreath; I ask no bays.
This mean and unrefined ore of mine
Will make your glistering gold but more to shine.

From "IN HONOR OF THAT HIGH AND MIGHTY PRINCESS
QUEEN ELIZABETH OF HAPPY MEMORY," after a lengthy
listing of the Queen's superlative qualities

Yet for our queen is no fit parallel.
She was a phenix queen; so shall she be,
Her ashes not revived, more phenix she.
Her personal perfections who would tell
Must dip his pen in the Heliconian well,
Which I may not; my pride doth but aspire
To read what others write, and so admire.
Now say, have women worth, or have they none?
Or had they some, but with our queen is it gone?
Nay, masculines, you have thus taxed us long,
But she, though dead, will vindicate our wrong.
Let such as say our sex is void of reason
Know 't is a slander now, but once was treason.

"BEFORE THE BIRTH OF ONE OF HER CHILDREN"

All things within this fading world have end.
Adversity doth still our joys attend;
No ties so strong, no friends so dear and sweet,
But with death's parting blow are sure to meet.
The sentence passed is most irrevocable,
A common thing, yet, oh, inevitable.
How soon, my dear, death may my steps attend,
How soon it may be thy lot to lose thy friend,
We both are ignorant; yet love bids me
These farewell lines to recommend to thee,
That when that knot's untied that made us one
I may seem thine who in effect am none.
And if I see not half my days that are due,
What nature would God grant to yours and you.

12

The many faults that well you know I have
Let be interred in my oblivion's grave;
If any worth or virtue were in me,
Let that live freshly in thy memory,
And when thou feelest no grief, as I no harms,
Yet love thy dead, who long lay in thine arms;
And when thy loss shall be repaid with gains
Look to my little babes, my dear remains,
And if thou love thyself, or lovedst me,
These oh protect from stepdam's injury.
And if chance to thine eyes shall bring this verse,
With some sad sighs honor my absent hearse;
And kiss this paper for thy love's dear sake,
Who with salt tears this last farewell did take.

"TO MY DEAR AND LOVING HUSBAND"

If ever two were one, then surely we;
If ever man were loved by wife, then thee;
If ever wife was happy in a man,
Compare with me, ye women, if you can.
I prize thy love more than whole mines of gold,
Or all the riches that the East doth hold.
My love is such that rivers cannot quench,
Nor aught but love from thee give recompense.
Thy love is such I can no way repay;
The heavens reward thee manifold, I pray.
Then while we live in love let 's so persevere
That when we live no more we may live ever.

"A LETTER TO HER HUSBAND, ABSENT UPON PUBLIC EMPLOYMENT"

My head, my heart, mine eyes, my life, --nay, more,

My joy, my magazine of earthly store,--
If two be one, as surely thou and I.
How stayest thou there, whilst I at Ipswich lie?--
So many steps head from the heart to sever;
If but a neck soon should we be together.
I, like the earth this season, mourn in black,
My sun is gone so far in his zodiac,
Whom whilst I enjoyed nor storms nor frosts I
    felt,
His warmth such frigid colds did cause to melt.
My chilled limbs now numbed lie forlorn;
Return, return, sweet Sol, from Capricorn!
In this dead time, alas, what can I more
Than view those fruits which through thy heat I
    bore?--
Which sweet contentment yield me for a space,
True living pictures of their father's face.
O strange effect! now thou art southward gone
I weary grow, the tedious day so long;
But when thou northward to me shalt return
I wish my sun may never set, but burn
Within the Cancer of my glowing breast,
The welcome house of him my dearest guest,
Where ever, ever stay, and go not thence
Till nature's sad decree shall call thee hence.
Flesh of thy flesh, bone of thy bone,
I here, thou there, yet both but one.

"TO HER FATHER: WITH SOME VERSES"

Most truly honored, and as truly dear,
If worth in me or aught I do appear
Who can of right better demand the same
Than may your worthy self, from whom it came?
The principal might yield a greater sum,
Yet, handled ill, amounts but to this crumb.
My stock 's so small I know not how to pay,
My bond remains in force unto this day;
Yet for part payment take this simple mite.
Where nothing 's to be had kings lose their right.
Such is my debt I may not say "Forgive!"

But as I can I'll pay it while I live;
Such is my bond none can discharge but I,
Yet, paying, is not paid until I die.

"IN REFERENCE TO HER CHILDREN, 23 JUNE, 1659"

I had eight birds hatched in one nest;
Four cocks there were, and hens the rest.
I nursed them up with pain and care,
Nor cost nor labor did I spare,
Till at the last they felt their wing,
Mounted the trees, and learned to sing.
Chief of the brood then took his flight
To regions far, and left me quite;
My mournful chirps I after send
Till he return or I do end:
Leave not thy nest, thy dam, and sire;
Fly back and sing amidst this choir.
My second bird did take her flight,
And with her mate flew out of sight;
Southward they both their course did bend,
And seasons twain they there did spend,
Till after, blown by southern gales,
They northward steered with filled sails.
A prettier bird was nowhere seen
Along the beach, among the treen.
I have a third, of color white,
On whom I placed no small delight;
Coupled with mate loving and true,
Hath also bid her dam adieu,
And where Aurora first appears
She now hath perched to spend her years.
One to the academy flew
To chat among that learned crew;
Ambition moves still in his breast
That he might chant above the rest,
Striving for more than to do well--
That nightingales he might excel.
My fifth, whose down is yet scarce gone,
Is 'mongst the shrubs and bushes flown,

And as his wings increase in strength
On higher boughs he 'll perch at length.
My other three still with me nest
Until they 're grown; then, as the rest,
Or here or there they 'll take their flight;
As is ordained, so shall they light.
If birds could weep, then would my tears
Let others know what are my fears
Lest this my brood some harm should catch
And be surprised for want of watch:
Whilst pecking corn, and void of care,
They fall unawares in fowler's snare;
Or whilst on trees they sit and sing,
Some untoward boy at them do fling;
Or whilst allured with bell and glass,
The net be spread, and caught, alas!
Or lest by lime-twigs they be foiled,
Or by some greedy hawks be spoiled.
Oh, would, my young, ye saw my breast,
And knew what thoughts there sadly rest.
Great was my pain when I you bred,
Great was my care when I you fed;
Long did I keep you soft and warm,
And with my wings kept off all harm.
My cares are more, and fears, than ever,
My throbs such now as 'fore were never.
Alas, my birds, you wisdom want;
Of perils you are ignorant--
Ofttimes in grass, on trees, in flight,
Sore accidents on you may light.
Oh, to your safety have an eye;
So happy may you live and die.
Meanwhile my days in tunes I 'll spend
Till my weak lays with me shall end;
In shady woods I 'll sit and sing,
Things that are past to mind I 'll bring--
Once young and pleasant, as are you.
But former toys, --not joys, --adieu!
My age I will not once lament,
But sing my time so near is spent,
And from the top bough take my flight
Into a country beyond sight,
Where old ones instantly grow young,
And there with seraphims set song.
No seasons cold nor storms they see,
But spring lasts to eternity.
When each of you shall in your nest

Among your young ones take your rest,
In chirping language oft them tell
You had a dam that loved you well,
That did what could be done for young,
And nursed you up till you were strong;
And 'fore she once would let you fly
She showed you joy and misery,
Taught what was good, and what was ill,
What would save life, and what would kill.
Thus gone, amongst you I may live,
And dead, yet speak, and counsel give.
Farewell, my birds, farewell, adieu!
I happy am if well with you.

"TO MY DEAR CHILDREN"

This book, by any yet unread,
I leave for you when I am dead,
That, being gone, here you may find
What was your living mother's mind.
Make use of what I leave in love,
And God shall bless you from above.

My Dear Children:

I, knowing by experience that the exhortations of parents take most effect when the speakers leave to speak, and those especially sink deepest which are spoke latest, and being ignorant whether on my death-bed I shall have opportunity to speak to any of you, much less to all, thought it the best, whilst I was able, to compose some short matters (for what else to call them I know not) and bequeath to you, that when I am no more with you yet I may be daily in your remembrance--although that is the least in my aim in what I now do, but that you may gain some spiritual advantage by my experience. I have not studied in this you read to show my skill, but to declare the truth; not to set forth myself, but the glory of God. If I had minded the former, it had been perhaps better pleasing to you; but seeing the last is the best, let it be best pleasing to you.

The method I will observe shall be this: I will begin with God's dealing with me from my childhood to this day. In my young years, about six or seven as I take it, I began to make conscience of my ways, and what I knew was sinful-- as lying, disobedience to parents, etc.--I avoided it. If at any time I was overtaken with the like evils, it was a great trouble. I could not be at rest till by prayer I had confessed it unto God. I was also troubled at the neglect of private duties, though too often tardy that way. I also found much comfort in reading the Scriptures, especially those places I thought most concerned my condition; and as I grew to have more understanding, so the more solace I took in them.

In a long fit of sickness which I had on my bed I often communed with my heart, and made my supplication to the Most High, who set me free from that affliction.

But as I grew up to be about fourteen or fifteen I found my heart more carnal, and, sitting loose from God, vanity and the follies of youth take hold of me.

About sixteen the Lord laid his hand sore upon me and smote me with the small-pox. When I was in my affliction, I besought the Lord, and confessed my pride and vanity, and he was entreated of me and again restored me. But I rendered not to him according to the benefit received.

After a short time I changed my condition and was married, and came into this country, where I found a new world and new manners, at which my heart rose. But after I was convinced it was the way of God, I submitted to it and joined to the church at Boston.

After some time I fell into a lingering sickness like a consumption, together with a lameness, which correction I saw the Lord sent to humble and try me and do me good; and it was not altogether ineffectual.

It pleased God to keep me a long time without a child, which was a great grief to me, and cost me many prayers and tears before I obtained one; and after him gave me many more, of whom I now take the care, that as I have brought you into the world, and with great pains, weakness, cares, and fears brought you to this, I now travail in birth again of you till Christ be formed in you.

Among all my experiences of God's gracious dealings

with me I have constantly observed this, that he hath never
suffered me long to sit loose from him, but by one affliction
or other hath made me look home, and search what was
amiss; so usually thus it hath been with me that I have no
sooner felt my heart out of order but I have expected correction for it, which most commonly hath been upon my own
person in sickness, weakness, pains, sometimes on my soul
in doubts and fears of God's displeasure and my sincerity
towards him. Sometimes he hath smote a child with sickness, sometimes chastened by losses in estate; and these
times, through his great mercy, have been the times of my
greatest getting and advantage--yea, I have found them the
times when the Lord hath manifested the most love to me.
Then have I gone to searching, and have said with David,
"Lord, search me and try me, see what ways of wickedness
are in me, and lead me in the way everlasting." And seldom or never but I have found either some sin I lay under
which God would have reformed, or some duty neglected
which he would have performed. And by his help I have laid
vows and bonds upon my soul to perform his righteous commands.

If at any time you are chastened of God, take it as
thankfully and joyfully as in greatest mercies; for if ye be
his ye shall reap the greatest benefit by it. It hath been
no small support to me in times of darkness when the Almighty hath hid his face from me that yet I have had abundance of sweetness and refreshment after affliction, and more
circumspection in my walking after I have been afflicted. I
have been with God like an untoward child, that no longer
than the rod has been on my back, or at least in sight, but
I have been apt to forget him and myself too. "Before I
was afflicted I went astray, but now I keep thy statutes."

I have had great experience of God's hearing my
prayers and returning comfortable answers to me, either in
granting the thing I prayed for or else in satisfying my mind
without it; and I have been confident it hath been from him,
because I have found my heart through his goodness enlarged
in thankfulness to him.

I have often been perplexed that I have not found that
constant joy in my pilgrimage and refreshing which I supposed most of the servants of God have; although he hath not
left me altogether without the witness of his Holy Spirit, who
hath oft given me his word and set to his seal that it shall
be well with me. I have sometimes tasted of that hidden

manna that the world knows not, and have set up my Ebenez-
er, and have resolved with myself that against such a promise, such tastes of sweetness, the gates of hell shall never
prevail. Yet have I many times sinkings and droopings, and
not enjoyed that felicity that sometimes I have done. But
when I have been in darkness, and seen no light, yet have I
desired to stay myself upon the Lord.

And when I have been in sickness and pain I have
thought if the Lord would but lift up the light of his countenance upon me, although he ground me to powder it would
be but light to me; yea, oft have I thought, were it hell itself, and could there find the love of God toward me, it
would be a heaven. And could I have been in heaven without the love of God, it would have been a hell to me; for,
in truth, it is the absence and presence of God that makes
heaven or hell.

Many times hath Satan troubled me concerning the
verity of the Scriptures; many times by atheism how I could
know whether there was a God. I never saw any miracles
to confirm me, and those which I read of how did I know but
they were feigned? That there is a God my reason would
soon tell me by the wondrous works that I see--the vast
frame of the heaven and the earth, the order of all things,
night and day, summer and winter, spring and autumn, the
daily providing for this great household upon the earth, the
preserving and directing of all to its proper end. The consideration of these things would with amazement certainly resolve me that there is an Eternal Being.

But how should I know he is such a God as I worship
in Trinity, and such a Saviour as I rely upon? Though this
hath thousands of times been suggested to me, yet God hath
helped me over. I have argued thus with myself: That there
is a God I see. If ever this God hath revealed himself, it
must be in his Word, and this must be it or none. Have I
not found that operation by it that no human invention can
work upon the soul? Have not judgments befallen divers who
have scorned and contemned it? Hath it not been preserved
through all ages maugre all the heathen tyrants and all of
the enemies who have opposed it? Is there any story but
that which shows the beginnings of time, and how the world
came to be as we see? Do we not know the prophecies in
it fulfilled which could not have been so long foretold by any
but God himself?

When I have got over this block then have I another put in my way, that, admit this be the true God whom we worship, and that be his Word, yet why may not the popish religion be the right? They have the same God, the same Christ, the same Word; they only interpret it one way, we another. This hath sometimes stuck with me, and more it would but the vain fooleries that are in their religion, together with their lying miracles and cruel persecutions of the saints, which admit were they as they term them, yet not so to be dealt withal. The consideration of these things and many the like would soon turn me to my own religion again.

But some new troubles I have had since the world has been filled with blasphemy and sectaries, and some who have been accounted sincere Christians have been carried away with them, that sometimes I have said, Is there faith upon the earth? and I have not known what to think. But then I have remembered the words of Christ that so it must be, and that, if it were possible, the very elect should be deceived. "Behold," saith our Saviour, "I have told you before." That hath stayed my heart, and I can now say, "Return, O my soul, to thy rest. Upon this rock Christ Jesus will I build my faith; and if I perish, I perish." But I know all the powers of hell shall never prevail against it. I know whom I have trusted, and whom I have believed, and that he is able to keep that I have committed to his charge.

Now to the King immortal, eternal, and invisible, the only wise God, be honor and glory for ever and ever! Amen.

This was written in much sickness and weakness, and is very weakly and imperfectly done; but if you can pick any benefit out of it, it is the mark which I aimed at.

MARY (WHITE) ROWLANDSON

(c.1635-c.1678)

It is thought that Mary Rowlandson was brought from England
to Massachusetts Bay during her childhood. The daughter of
one of the first settlers in the isolated town of Lancaster
about forty miles west of Boston, she married the minister
of that place in 1656 and lived peacefully there until 1675,
when Indians attacked and burnt most of the village. Many
of the inhabitants were killed; but others, Mrs. Rowlandson
among them, were taken captive and forced to accompany the
attackers on an eleven-week trek--during which twenty different
encampments were made--as far west as the Connecticut River
and north into what is now southern Vermont and back again
to a spot near the starting point, where Mrs. Rowlandson
was ransomed to the English for the sum of twenty pounds.

The attack on Lancaster was an episode in King Philip's War, a struggle in which the Native Americans were
permanently subdued in southern New England. The hardships endured by Mrs. Rowlandson, as well as by her cap-
tors, are vividly described in the excerpts from her Narrative that follow. Published after her death, the Narrative
was widely read on both sides of the Atlantic, a classic
among numerous and popular Indian Captivities, as writings
of this sort have come to be known. Its immediate appeal,
of course, is that of any suspenseful story. Rowlandson
represents herself, doubtless truthfully, as being constantly
in danger of being murdered or of starving to death, and one
is not sure until the end whether or not she will actually be
ransomed. The death of her child and the separation of
members of her and other families add pathos to the tale.
Verisimilitude is gained by concrete descriptions of scenes
along the way and of the wretched food the captives and cap-
tors were reduced to eating. A dramatic quality is added
by the author's including snatches of dialogue.

But Rowlandson's--and her publisher's--chief purpose,

ostensibly at least, was not to excite or amuse her readers,
or even to play upon their emotions, unless religious awe be
considered an emotion.   Part of the lengthy title of the book
was: The Sovereignty and Goodness of GOD, Together with
the Faithfulness of His Promises Displayed, Being a Narrative of the Captivity....   As stated in the publisher's Preface
to the second edition (1682; no copy of the first edition now
exists), the "narrative was penned by the gentlewoman herself, to be to her a memorandum of God's dealing with her,
that she might never forget ... all the dayes of her life."
As Mary Rowlandson makes abundantly clear, the Bible--a
copy of which was given to her by an Indian during her cap-
tivity--was her "guide by day, and ... pillow by night." She
regarded her sufferings as willed by God, who nevertheless
provided her, in her Bible, grounds for hope and the spiritual
strength for survival.

Rowlandson, though a frontier woman, was obviously
entirely literate and well educated in religious doctrine.   The
very fact that this forty-year-old woman survived eleven
weeks of a New England winter and spring, with no shelter
other than hastily improvised wigwams and subsisting on a
diet of groundnuts and horses' feet, while traveling, mainly
on foot, close to two hundred miles through the wilderness,
attests to the strength she derived from her faith.   But it
also attests to an almost incredible strength of character and
of body in no way suggestive of the later stereotypes of feminine frailty.   It is interesting to read that in spite of the way
she stereotypes Indians ("ravenous beasts," "black creatures,"
"inhumane") she also comments on their small kindnesses to
her.   Also, at first horrified by the food, which she calls
"filthy trash," she later learns to savor such edibles as bear
and acorns.

Additional information regarding Rowlandson may be
found in Notable American Women.   For a discussion of the
Captivity Narrative as a genre, see R. H. Pearce, "The
Significance of the Captivity Narrative," American Literature,
XIX (1947): 1-20.   The excerpt that follows is taken from
Narrative of the Captivity and Removes of Mrs. Mary Row-
landson, Second Lancaster Edition, 1828.

From THE NARRATIVE OF THE CAPTIVITY AND REMOVES
OF MRS. MARY ROWLANDSON

On the 10th of February, 1675, came the Indians with
great numbers upon Lancaster: their first coming was about
sun-rising; hearing the noise of some guns we looked out; several houses were burning, and the smoke ascending to heaven.
There were five persons taken in one house, the father and mother, and a sucking child they knocked on the head, the other two
they took and carried away alive. There were two others, who
being out of their garrison upon occasion, were set upon, one
was knocked on the head, the other escaped. Another there was
who running along was shot and wounded, and fell down; he begged
of them his life, promising them money, (as they told me) but
they would not hearken to him, but knocked him on the head,
stripped him naked, and split open his bowels. Another seeing
many of the Indians about his barn, ventur'd and went out, but
was quickly shot down. There were three others belonging
to the same garrison who were killed; the Indians getting up
upon the roof of the barn, had advantage to shoot down upon
them over their fortification. Thus these murtherous wretches
went on burning and destroying all before them.

At length they came and beset our house, and quickly
it was the dolefulest day that ever mine eyes saw. The
house stood upon the edge of a hill; some of the Indians got
behind the hill, others into the barn, and others behind any
thing that would shelter them; from all which places they shot
against the house, so that the bullets seemed to fly like hail,
and quickly they wounded one man among us, then another,
and then a third. About two hours (according to my observation in that amazing time) they had been about the house before they prevailed to fire it, (which they did with flax and
hemp which they brought out of the barn, and there being no
defence about the house, only two flankers at two opposite
corners, and one of them not finished) they fired it once,
and one ventured out and quenched it, but they quickly fired
it again, and that took. Now is the dreadful hour come that
I have often heard of (in time of the war, as it was the case
of others) but now mine eyes see it. Some in our house
were fighting for their lives, others wallowing in blood, the

house on fire over our heads, and the bloody heathen ready
to knock us on the head if we stirred out. Now might we
hear mothers and children crying out for themselves and one
another, Lord, what shall we do! Then I took my children
(and one of my sisters her's) to go forth and leave the house:
but as soon as we came to the door, and appear'd, the Indians shot so thick that the bullets rattled against the house
as if one had taken a handful of stones and threw them, so
that we were forced to give back. We had six stout dogs
belonging to our garrison, but none of them would stir,
though at another time if an Indian had come to the door,
they were ready to fly upon him and tear him down. The
Lord hereby would make us the more to acknowledge his
hand, and to see that our help is always in him. But out
we must go, the fire increasing, and coming along behind us
roaring, and the Indians gaping before us with their guns,
spears, and hatchets to devour us. No sooner were we out
of the house, but my brother-in-law (being before wounded
in defending the house, in or near the throat) fell down dead,
whereat the Indians scornfully shouted and hallowed, and were
presently upon him, stripping off his cloaths. The bullets
flying thick, one went through my side, and the same (as
would seem) through the bowels and hand of my poor child
in my arms. One of my elder sister's children (named
William) had then his leg broke, which the Indians perceiv-
ing they knocked him on the head. Thus were we butchered
by those merciless heathens, standing amazed, with the blood
running down to our heels. My eldest sister being yet in the
house, and seeing those woful sights, the infidels halling
mothers one way and children another, and some wallowing
in their blood: and her eldest son telling her that her son
William was dead, and myself was wounded, she said, and
Lord let me die with them: which was no sooner said but
she was struck with a bullet, and fell down dead over the
threshold. I hope she is reaping the fruit of her good la-
bours, being faithful to the service of God in her place. In
her younger years she lay under much trouble upon spiritual
accounts, till it pleased God to make that precious scripture
take hold of her heart, 2 Cor. 12, 9. And he said unto me,
My grace is sufficient for thee. More than twenty years
after, I have heard her tell how sweet and comfortable that
place was to her. But to return: The Indians laid hold of
us pulling me one way, and the children another, and said,
Come, go along with us: I told them they would kill me;
they answered, If I were willing to go along with them, they
would not hurt me.

Oh! the doleful sight that now was to behold at this house! Come, behold the works of the Lord, what desolations he has made in the earth. Of thirty-seven persons who were in this one house, none escaped either present death, or a bitter captivity, save only one, who might say as in Job 1, 15. <u>And I only am escaped alone to tell the news</u>. There were twelve killed, some shot, some stabbed with their spears, some knocked down with their hatchets. When we are in prosperity, Oh the little that we think of such dreadful sights, to see our dear friends and relations lie bleeding out their hearts-blood upon the ground. There was one who was chopt in the head with a hatchet, and stript naked, and yet was crawling up and down. It was a solemn sight to see so many christians lying in their blood, some here and some there, like a company of sheep torn by wolves. All of them stript naked by a company of hell-hounds, roaring, singing, ranting, and insulting, as if they would have torn our very hearts out; yet the Lord, by his almighty power, preserved a number of us from death, for there were twenty-four of us taken alive and carried captive.

I had often before this said, that if the Indians should come, I should chuse rather to be killed by them than taken alive, but when it came to the trial, my mind changed; their glittering weapons so daunted my spirit, that I chose rather to go along with those (as I may say) ravenous bears, than that moment to end my days. And that I may the better declare what happened to me during that grievous captivity, I shall particularly speak of the several Removes we had up and down the wilderness.

The First Remove

Now away we must go with those barbarous creatures, with our bodies wounded and bleeding, and our hearts no less than our bodies. About a mile we went that night, up upon a hill, within sight of the town, where we intended to lodge. There was hard by a vacant house (deserted by the English before, for fear of the Indians;) I asked them whether I might not lodge in the house that night? to which they answered, What, will you love Englishmen still? This was the dolefulest night that ever my eyes saw. Oh the roaring, and singing, and dancing, and yelling of those black creatures in the night, which made the place a lively resemblance of hell: And miserable was the waste that was there made, of horses,

cattle, sheep, swine, calves, lambs, roasting pigs, and
fowls, (which they had plundered in the town) some roasting,
some lying and burning, and some boiling, to feed our merciless enemies; who were joyful enough, though we were disconsolate. To add to the dolefulness of the former day, and
the dismalness of the present night, my thoughts ran upon
my losses and sad, berieved condition. All was gone, my
husband gone, (at least separated from me, he being in the
Bay; and to add to my grief, the Indians told me they would
kill him as he came homeward) my children gone, my relations and friends gone, our house and home, and all our
comforts within door and without, all was gone (except my
life) and I knew not but the next moment that might go too.

There remained nothing to me but one poor, wounded
babe, and it seemed at present worse than death, that it
was in such a pitiful condition, bespeaking compassion, and
I had no refreshing for it, nor suitable things to revive it.
Little do many think, what is the savageness and brutishness
of this barbarous enemy, those even that seem to profess
more than others among them, when the English have fallen
into their hands.

Those seven that were killed at Lancaster the summer before upon a sabbath day, and the one that was afterward killed upon a week day, were slain and mangled in a
barbarous manner, by One-eyed John and Marlborough's
praying Indians, which Capt. Mosely brought to Boston, as
the Indians told me.

The Second Remove

But now (the next morning) I must turn my back upon the
town, and travel with them into the vast and desolate wilderness, I know not whither. It is not my tongue or pen can
express the sorrows of my heart, and bitterness of my spirit,
that I had at this departure: but God was with me in a wonderful manner, carrying me along and bearing up my spirit,
that it did not quite fail. One of the Indians carried my poor
wounded babe upon a horse: it went moaning all along, I
shall die, I shall die. I went on foot after it, with sorrow
that cannot be exprest. At length I took it off the horse,
and carried it in my arms, till my strength failed and I fell
down with it. Then they set me upon a horse with my
wounded child in my lap, and there being no furniture on
the horse's back, as we were going down a steep hill, we

both fell over the horse's head, at which they like inhuman
creatures laughed, and rejoiced to see it, though I thought
we should there have ended our days, overcome with so
many difficulties. But the Lord renewed my strength still,
and carried me along, that I might see more of his power,
yea, so much that I could never have thought of, had I not
experienced it.

After this it quickly began to snow, and when night
came on, they stopt: and now down I must sit in the snow,
by a little fire, and a few boughs behind me, with my sick
child in my lap, and calling much for water, being now,
(through the wound) fallen into a violent fever. My own
wound also growing so stiff, that I could scarce set down
or rise up, yet so it must be, that I must sit all this cold,
winter night, upon the cold snowy ground, with my sick child
in my arms, looking that every hour would be the last of its
life; and having no christian friend near me, either to comfort or help me. Oh I may see the wonderful power of God,
that my spirit did not utterly sink under my affliction; still
the Lord upheld me with his gracious and merciful spirit,
and we were both alive to see the light of the next morning.

The Third Remove

The morning being come they prepared to go on their way,
one of the Indians got upon a horse, and they sat me up behind him, with my poor sick babe in my lap. A very wearisome and tedious day I had of it; what with my own wound,
and my child being so exceeding sick, and in a lamentable
condition with her wound, it may easily be judged what a
poor, feeble condition we were in, there being not the least
crumb of refreshing that came within either of our mouths
from Wednesday night to Saturday night, except only a little
cold water. This day in the afternoon, about an hour by
sun, we came to the place where they intended, viz. an Indian town called Wenimesset, northward of Quabaug. When
we were come, Oh the number of Pagans (now merciless
enemies) that there came about me, that I may say as David,
Psal. 27, 13, I had fainted unless I had believed, &c. The
next day was the sabbath: I then remembered how careless
I had been of God's holy time: how many sabbaths I had lost
and misspent, and how evilly I had walked in God's sight;
which lay so close upon my spirit, that it was easy for me
to see how righteous it was with God to cut off the thread of
my life, and cast me out of his presence forever. Yet the

Lord still shewed mercy to me, and helped me; and as he wounded me with one hand, so he healed me with the other. This day there came to me one Robert Pepper (a man belonging to Roxbury) who was taken at Capt. Beers' fight; and had been now a considerable time with the Indians, and up with them almost as far as Albany, to see King Philip, as he told me, and was now very lately come into these parts. Hearing, I say, that I was in this Indian town, he obtained leave to come and see me. He told me he himself was wounded in the leg, at Capt. Beers' fight; and was not able some time to go, but as they carried him, and that he took oak leaves and laid to his wound, and by the blessing of God, he was able to travel again. Then took I oak leaves and laid to my side, and with the blessing of God, it cured me also: yet before the cure was wrought, I may say as it is in Psal. 38, 5, 6. My wounds stink and are corrupt, I am troubled, I am bowed down greatly, I go mourning all the day long. I sat much alone with my poor wounded child in my lap, which moaned night and day, having nothing to revive the body, or cheer the spirits of her; but instead of that, one Indian would come and tell me one hour, your master will knock your child on the head, and then a second, and then a third, your master will quickly knock your child on the head.

This was the comfort I had from them; miserable comforters were they all. Thus nine days I sat upon my knees, with my babe in my lap, till my flesh was raw again. My child being even ready to depart this sorrowful world, they bid me carry it out to another wigwam: (I suppose because they would not be troubled with such spectacles) whither I went with a very heavy heart, and down I sat with the picture of death in my lap. About two hours in the night, my sweet babe like a lamb departed this life, on Feb. 18, 1675, it being about six years and five months old. It was nine days from the first wounding in this miserable condition, without any refreshing of one nature or another except a little cold water. I cannot but take notice, how at another time I could not bear to be in a room where a dead person was, but now the case is changed; I must and could lie down with my dead babe all the night after. I have thought since of the wonderful goodness of God to me, in preserving me so in the use of my reason and senses, in that distressed time, that I did not use wicked and violent means to end my own miserable life. In the morning when they understood that my child was dead, they sent me home to my master's wigwam. (By my master in this writing, must be understood Quannopin, who was a Saggamore, and married King Philip's wife's sister; not that he first took me, but I was sold to him by a

Narraganset Indian, who took me when I first came out of
the garrison.) I went to take up my dead child in my arms
to carry it with me, but they bid me let it alone. There
was no resisting, but go I must, and leave it. When I had
been awhile at my master's wigwam I took the first opportunity I could get, to go look after my dead child: when I
came I asked them what they had done with it? they told me
it was on the hill; then they went and shewed me where it
was, where I saw the ground was newly digged, and where
they told me they had buried it; there I left that child in the
wilderness, and must commit it and myself also in this wilderness condition, to him who is above all. God having taken
away this dear child, I went to see my daughter Mary, who
was at the same Indian town, at a wigwam not very far off,
though we had little liberty or opportunity to see one another;
she was about ten years old, and taken from the door at
first by a praying Indian, and afterwards sold for a gun.
When I came in sight she would fall a weeping, at which
they were provoked, and would not let me come near her,
but bid me be gone; which was a heart-cutting word to me.
I had one child dead, another in the wilderness, I knew not
where, the third they would not let me come near to; Me
(as he said) have ye bereaved of my children, Joseph is not,
and Simeon is not, and ye will take Benjamin also; all these
things are against me. I could not sit still in this condition,
but kept walking from one place to another. And as I was
going along, my heart was even overwhelmed with the thoughts
of my condition, and that I should have children, and a nation that I knew not ruled over them. Whereupon I earnestly
entreated the Lord that he would consider my low estate, and
shew me a token for good, and if it were his blessed will,
some sign and hope of some relief. And indeed quickly the
Lord answered in some measure my poor prayer: For as I
was going up and down mourning and lamenting my condition,
my son came to me and asked me how I did? I had not seen
him before since the destruction of the town; and I knew not
where he was, till I was informed by himself, that he was
among a smaller parcel of Indians, whose place was about
six miles off, with tears in his eyes he asked me whether
his sister Sarah was dead? and told me he had seen his sister Mary: and prayed me, that I would not be troubled in
reference to himself. The occasion of his coming to see me
at this time was this: there was, as I said, about six miles
from us a small plantation of Indians, where it seems he had
been during his captivity; and at this time, there were some
forces of the Indians gathered out of our company, and some
also from them (amongst whom was my son's master) to go

to assault and burn Medfield; in this time of his master's absence, his dame brought him to see me. I took this to be some gracious answer to my earnest and unfeigned desire. The next day the Indians returned from Medfield; (all the company, for those that belonged to the other smaller company, came through the town that we now were at) but before they came to us, Oh the outrageous roaring and hooping that there was! they began their din about a mile before they came to us. By their noise and hooping they signified how many they had destroyed; which was at that time twenty-three. Those that were with us at home, were gathered together as soon as they heard the hooping, and every time that the other went over their number, these at home gave a shout, that the very earth rang again. And thus they continued till those that had been upon the expedition were come up to the Saggamore's wigwam; and then Oh the hideous insulting and triumphing that there was over some English men's scalps, that they had taken (as their manner is) and brought with them. I cannot but take notice of the wonderful mercy of God to me in those afflictions, in sending me a Bible: one of the Indians that came from Medfield fight, and had brought some plunder, came to me, and asked me if I would have a Bible, he had got one in his basket: I was glad of it, and asked him if he thought the Indians would let me read? he answered yes; so I took the Bible, and in that melancholy time, it came into my mind to read first the 28 chap. of Deuteronomy, which I did, and when I had read it, my dark heart wrought on this manner, that there was no mercy for me, that the blessings were gone, and the curses came in their room, and that I had lost my opportunity. But the Lord helped me still to go on reading, till I came to ch. 30, the seven first verses; where I found there was mercy promised again, if we would return to him, by repentance; and though we were scattered from one end of the earth to the other, yet the Lord would gather us together, and turn all those curses upon our enemies. I do not desire to live to forget this scripture, and what comfort it was to me.

Now the Indians began to talk of removing from this place, some one way and some another. There were now besides myself nine English captives in this place (all of them children except one woman). I got an opportunity to go and take my leave of them, they being to go one way and I another. I asked them whether they were earnest with God for deliverance, they told me they did as they were able, and it was some comfort to me that the Lord stirred up children to

look to him.   The woman, viz.   goodwife Joslin told me she
should never see me again, and that she could find in her
heart to run away by any means for we were near thirty
miles from any English town and she very big with child,
having but one week to reckon; and another child in her arms
two years old, and bad rivers there were to go over, and we
were feeble with our poor and course entertainment.   I had
my Bible with me, I pulled it out, and asked her whether
she would read; we opened the Bible, and lighted on Psal.
27, in which Psalm we especially took notice of that verse,
<u>Wait on the Lord, be of good courage, and he shall strengthen
thine heart, wait I say on the Lord</u>.

The Fourth Remove

And now must I part with the little company I had.   Here I
parted with my daughter Mary (whom I never saw again till
I saw her in Dorchester, returned from captivity) and from
four little cousins and neighbours, some of which I never
saw afterward, the Lord only knows the end of them.   Among
them also was that poor woman before mentioned, who came
to a sad end, as some of the company told me in my travel:
She having much grief upon her spirits about her miserable
condition, being so near her time, she would be often asking
the Indians to let her go home: they not being willing to
that, and yet vexed with her importunity, gathered a great
company together about her, and stript her naked and set
her in the midst of them; and when they had sung and danced
about her (in their hellish manner) as long as they pleased,
they knocked her on the head, and the child in her arms with
her.   When they had done that, they made a fire and put
them both into it, and told the other children that were with
them, that if they attempted to go home they would serve
them in like manner.   The children said she did not shed
one tear, but prayed all the while.   But to turn to my own
journey: We travelled about a half a day or a little more
and came to a desolate place in the wilderness where there
were no wigwams or inhabitants before; we came about the
middle of the afternoon to this place; cold, wet, and snowy,
and hungry, and weary, and no refreshing for man, but the
cold ground to sit on, and our poor Indian cheer.

Heart-aching thoughts here I had about my poor children, who were scattered up and down among the wild beasts
of the forest: My head was light and dissy (either through
hunger or bad lodging, or trouble, or all together) my knees

feeble, my body raw by setting double night and day, that I cannot express to man the affliction that lay upon my spirit, but the Lord helped me at that time to express it to himself. I opened my Bible to read, and the Lord brought that precious scripture to me, Jer. 31, 16. Thus saith the Lord, refrain thy voice from weeping, and thine eyes from tears, for thy work shall be rewarded and they shall come again from the land of the enemy. This was a sweet cordial to me, when I was ready to faint, many and many a time have I sat down and wept sweetly over this scripture. At this place we continued about four days.

The Fifth Remove

The occasion (as I thought) of their removing at this time, was the English army's being near and following them: For they went as if they had gone for their lives, for some considerable way; and then they made a stop, and chose out some of their stoutest men, and sent them back to hold the English army in play whilst the rest escaped; and then like Jehu they marched on furiously, with their old and young: some carried their old, decriped mothers, some carried one, and some another. Four of them carried a great Indian upon a bier; but going through a thick wood with him they were hindered, and could make no haste; whereupon they took him upon their backs, and carried him one at a time, till we came to Bacquag river. Upon Friday a little after noon we came to this river: When all the company was come up, and were gathered together, I thought to count the number of them, but they were so many and being somewhat in motion, it was beyond my skill. In this travel, because of my wound, I was somewhat favoured in my load: I carried only my knitting-work, and two quarts of parched meal: Being very faint, I asked my mistress to give me one spoonful of the meal, but she would not give me a taste. They quickly fell to cutting dry trees, to make rafts to carry them over the river, and soon my turn came to go over. By the advantage of some brush which they had laid upon the raft to sit on, I did not wet my foot (while many of themselves at the other end were mid-leg deep) which cannot but be acknowledged as a favour of God to my weakened body, it being a very cold time. I was not before acquainted with such kind of doings or dangers. When thou passest through the waters I will be with thee, and through the rivers they shall not overflow thee. Isai. 43. 2. A certain number of us got over the river that night, but it was the night after the Sabbath before all the company was got over. On the Saturday they boiled an old horse's leg (which they had got) and so we drank of the broth, as soon as they thought it was ready, and when it was almost all gone they fill'd it up again.

The first week of my being among them, I hardly eat any thing: the second week I found my stomach grow very faint for want of something: and yet it was very hard to get down their filthy trash; but the third week (though I could think how formerly my stomach would turn against this or that, and I could starve and die before I could eat such things, yet) they were pleasant and savoury to my taste. I was at this time knitting a pair of white cotton stockings for my mistress, and I had not yet wrought upon the Sabbath day: When the Sabbath came, they bid me go to work; I told them it was Sabbath day, and desired them to let me rest, and told them I would do as much more work to-morrow; to which they answered me, they would break my face. And here I cannot but take notice of the strange Providence of God in preserving the heathen: They were many hundreds, old and young, some sick, and some lame; many had Papooses at their backs; the greatest number at this time with us were Squaws, and yet they traveled with all they had, bag and baggage, and they got over this river aforesaid; and on Monday they sat their wigwams on fire, and away they went; on that very day came the English army after them to this river, and saw the smoke of their wigwams, and yet this river put a stop to them. God did not give them courage or activity to go over after us; We were not ready for so great a mercy as victory and deliverance; if we had been, God would have found out a way for the English to have passed this river, as well as for the Indians with their Squaws and children, and all their luggage. O that my people had hearkened unto me, and Israel had walked in my ways, I should soon have subdued their enemies, and turned my hand against their adversaries. Psal. 81. 13, 14.

The Sixth Remove

On Monday (as I said) they sat their wigwams on fire, and went away. It was a cold morning, and before us there was a great brook with ice on it; Some waded through it up to the knees and higher, but others went till they came to a beaver dam, and I amongst them, where through the good Providence of God, I did not wet my foot. I went along that day mourning and lamenting (leaving farther my own country, and travelling farther into the vast and howling wilderness) and I understood something of Lot's wife's temptation when she looked back: We came that day to a great swamp, by the side of which we took up our lodging that night. When we came to the brow of the hill that looked toward the swamp, I thought we had been come to a great Indian town (though there were none but our own company) the Indians were as thick as the trees; it seemed as if there had been a thousand hatchets going at once. If one looked before one there was nothing but Indians, and behind one nothing but Indians; and so on either hand; and I myself in the midst, and no christian soul near me, and yet how hath the Lord preserved me in safety! Oh the experience that I have had of the goodness of God to me and mine!

The Seventh Remove

After a restless and hungry night there, we had a wearisome time of it the next day. The swamp by which we lay, was as it were a deep dungeon, and an exceeding high and steep hill before it. Before I got to the top of the hill, I thought my heart and legs and all would have broken, and failed me. What through faintness and soreness of body, it was a grievous day of travel to me. As we went along, I saw a place where English cattle had been, that was a comfort to me, such as it was: Quickly after that we came to an English path, which so took me, that I thought I could there have freely lien down and died. That day, a little after noon, we came to Squaheag, where the Indians quickly spread themselves over the deserted English fields, gleaning what they could find; some pick'd up ears of wheat that were crickled down, some found ears of Indian corn, some found groundnuts, and others sheaves of wheat that were frozen together in the shock, and went to threshing of them out. Myself got two ears of Indian corn, and whilst I did but turn my back, one of them was stole from me which much troubled me. There came an Indian to them at that time, with a basket of horse-liver; I asked him to give me a piece: What, (says he) can you eat horse-liver? I told him I would try, if he would give me a piece, which he did; and I laid it on the coals to roast, but before it was half ready, they got half of it away from me; so that I was forced to take the rest and eat it as it was, with the blood about my mouth, and yet a savory bit it was to me; for to the hungry soul every bitter thing was sweet. A solemn sight methought it was, to see whole fields of wheat and Indian corn forsaken and spoiled, and the re-

mainder of them to be food for our merciless enemies. That
night we had a mess of wheat for our supper.

The Eighth Remove

On the morrow morning we must go over Connecticut river
to meet with King Philip; two canoes full they had carried
over, the next turn myself was to go; but as my foot was
upon the canoe to step in, there was a sudden out-cry among
them, and I must step back; and instead of going over the
river, I must go four or five miles up the river farther
Northward. Some of the Indians ran one way, and some another. The cause of this route was, as I tho't, their espy-
ing some English scouts, who were thereabouts. In this
travel up the river, about noon the company made a stop,
and sat down, some to eat and others to rest them. As I
sat amongst them, musing on things past, my son Joseph
unexpectedly came to me. We asked of each other's welfare, bemoaning our doleful condition, and the change that
had come upon us. We had husband and father, and children and sisters, and friends and relations, and house and
home, and many comforts of this life; but now we might say
as Job, Naked came I out of my mother's womb, and naked
shall I return: The Lord gave, and the Lord hath taken
away, blessed be the name of the Lord. I asked him whether he would read? he told me he earnestly desired it. I
gave him my Bible, and he lighted upon that comfortable
scripture, Psalm 118. 17, 18. I shall not die, but live,
and declare the works of the Lord: The Lord hath chastened
me sore, yet he hath not given me over to death. Look here
mother, (says he) did you read this? And here I may take
occasion to mention one principal ground of my setting forth
these lines, even as the Psalmist says, to declare the works
of the Lord, and his wonderful power in carying us along,
preserving us in the wilderness while under the enemy's
hand, and returning of us in safety again; and his goodness
in bringing to my hand so many comfortable and suitable
scriptures in my distress.

But to return: We travelled on till night, and in the
morning we must go over the river to Philip's crew. When
I was in the canoe, I could not but be amazed at the numerous crew of Pagans that were on the bank on the other side.
When I came ashore, they gathered all about me, I sitting
alone in the midst: I observed they asked one another questions, and laughed, and rejoiced over their gains and vic-

tories. Then my heart began to fail, and I fell a weeping; which was the first time, to my remembrance, that I wept before them; although I had met with so much affliction, and my heart was many times ready to break, yet could I not shed one tear in their sight, but rather had been all this while in a maze, and like one astonished; but now I may say as Psal. 137, 1. By the river of Babylon, there we sat down, yea, we wept, when we remembered Zion. There one of them asked me why I wept? I could hardly tell what to say; yet I answered, they would kill me: No, said he, none will hurt you. Then came one of them, and gave me two spoonfuls of meal (to comfort me) and another gave me half a pint of peas, which was worth more than many bushels at another time. Then I went to see King Philip; he bade me come in, and sit down; and asked me whether I would smoke it? (a usual compliment now a days, among the saints and sinners) but this no ways suited me. For though I had formerly used tobacco, yet I had left it ever since I was first taken. It seems to be a bait the devil lays to make men lose their precious time. I remember with shame, how formerly, when I had taken two or three pipes, I was presently ready for another; such a bewitching thing it is: but I thank God, he has now given me power over it; surely there are many who may be better employed than to sit sucking a stinking tobacco-pipe.

Now the Indians gathered their forces to go against Northampton: Over night one went about yelling and hooting to give notice of the design. Whereupon they went to boiling of ground-nuts, and parching corn (as many as had it) for their provision: and in the morning away they went. During my abode in this place, Philip spake to me to make a shirt for his boy, which I did; for which he gave me a shilling. I offered the money to my mistress, but she bid me keep it, and with it I bought a piece of horse-flesh. Afterward he asked me to make a cap for his boy, for which he invited me to dinner; I went, and he gave me a pancake, about as big as two fingers; it was made of parched wheat, beaten and fried in bear's grease, but I thought I never tasted pleasanter meat in my life. There was a Squaw who spake to me to make a shirt for her Sannup; for which she gave me a piece of beef. Another asked me to knit a pair of stockings, for which she gave me a quart of peas. I boiled my peas and beef together, and invited my master and mistress to dinner; but the proud gossip, because I served them both in one dish, would eat nothing, except one bit that he gave her upon the point of his knife. Hearing that my son was come to this place, I went to see him, and found him lying flat on the ground; I asked him how he could sleep so? he answered me, that he was not asleep, but at prayer; and that he lay so, that they might not observe what he was doing. I pray God he may remember these things now he is returned in safety. At this place (the sun now getting higher) what with the beams and heat of the sun, and smoke of the wigwams, I thought I should have been blinded. I could scarce discern one wigwam from another. There was one Mary Thurston, of Medfield, who seeing how it was with me, lent me a hat to wear; but as soon as I was gone, the Squaw that owned that Mary Thurston, came running after me, and got it away again. Here was a Squaw who gave me a spoonful of meal; I put it in my pocket to keep it safe, yet notwithstanding some body stole it, but put five Indian corns in the room of it; which corns were the greatest provision I had in my travel for one day.

The Indians returning from North-Hampton brought with them some horses, and sheep, and other things which they had taken; I desired them that they would carry me to Albany upon one of those horses, and sell me for powder; for so they had sometimes discoursed. I was utterly helpless of getting home on foot, the way that I came. I could hardly bear to think of the many weary steps I had taken to this place.

SARAH KEMBLE KNIGHT

(1666-1727)

Sarah Kemble Knight, the daughter of a Boston merchant, was not irreligious--that would hardly be possible for a respectable person of her time and place--but she was much less preoccupied with things of the spirit than were Anne Bradstreet, Mary Rowlandson, or Anne Hutchinson. After her father's death, when she was twenty-three, she assumed the management of her family's affairs. While her husband, a ship's captain, was on his voyages, she occupied herself as a teacher of penmanship (Benjamin Franklin is reputed to have been one of her pupils) and as a copyist of legal documents, becoming so knowledgeable in the law that her services and advice were sought in legal matters. It was on legal business for a cousin's widow that in 1704 she traveled on horseback from Boston to New Haven and thence to New York and back to Boston. The journey, often over roads no better than forest tracks, through extensive uninhabited areas, involved fording streams and putting up at primitive taverns, but Madam Knight, as she was called by virtue of her being a schoolteacher, took all in her stride. In fact she seems to have relished every moment of her trip, even its most perilous ones. Curious about all she saw, she recorded her impressions in vivid, flowing, racily colloquial prose with a generous spicing of ironic humor and occasional recourse to light verse.

Sarah Knight's journey was amazing in its day. Her journey in 1704 with male guides who were strangers, through a dangerous wilderness, might be compared to a woman today traveling alone around the world only on local buses. Women alone, especially in such countries as those in the Middle East, are thought to be loose women. In the United States there is the suggestion that an unescorted woman at the movies, in a restaurant, or traveling is a woman available. She is thus frequently defined by men. Most women prefer to be escorted or at least to be with another woman; other-

wise they feel uncomfortable.   Many American women today
would not consider going out or traveling alone.   How much
more remarkable then are the travels of Sarah Knight!   One
cannot but admire her courage (and also enjoy her sense of
humor) about her journey.

    Because the manuscript of Knight's Journal has been
lost, the text of it perforce derives from a volume edited
with an Introduction by the New England poet Theodore Dwight,
published in 1825 and titled The Journals of Madam Knight,
and Rev. Mr. Buckingham from the Original Manuscripts.
In 1920, under the editorship of George P. Winship, the
Knight Journal appeared under the title Private Journal of a
Journey from Boston to New York.   Winship's Introduction
and Dwight's, which Winship reprints, are reliable sources
concerning Knight's career, as is also the article on her in
Notable American Women.   The excerpts that follow are from
Dwight's edition.

From THE PRIVATE JOURNAL KEPT BY MADAM KNIGHT
ON A JOURNEY FROM BOSTON TO NEW YORK IN THE
YEAR 1704

Tuesday, October the third, about 8 in the morning, I with
the Post proceeded forward without observing any thing remarkable; And about two, afternoon, Arrived at the Post's
second stage, where the western Post mett him and exchanged Letters.   Here, having called for something to eat,
the woman bro't in a Twisted thing like a cable, but something whiter; and laying it on the bord, tugg'd for life to
bring it into a capacity to spread; which having with great
pains accomplished, shee serv'd in a dish of Pork and Cab-
age, I suppose the remains of Dinner.   The sause was of a
deep Purple, which I tho't was boil'd in her dye Kettle; the
bread was Indian, and every thing on the Table service
Agreeable to these.   I, being hungry, gott a little down;
but my stomach was soon cloy'd, and what cabbage I swallowed serv'd me for a Cudd the whole day after.

Having here discharged the Ordnary for self and Guide,
(as I understood was the custom,) About Three afternoon went
on with my Third Guide, who Rode very hard; and having
crossed Providence Ferry, we come to a River which they
Generally Ride thro'. But I dare not venture; so the Post
got a Ladd and Cannoo to carry me to tother side, and hee
rid thro' and Led my hors. The Cannoo was very small and
shallow, so that when we were in she seem'd redy to take in
water, which greatly terrified mee, and caused me to be very
circumspect, sitting with my hands fast on each side, my
eyes stedy, not daring so much as to lodg my tongue a hair's
breadth more on one side of my mouth then tother, nor so
much as think on Lott's wife, for a wry thought would have
oversett our wherey: But was soon put out of this pain, by
feeling the Cannoo on shore, which I as soon almost saluted
with my feet; and Rewarding my sculler, again mounted and
made the best of our way forwards. The Rode here was very
even and the day pleasant, it being now near Sunsett. But
the Post told mee we had neer 14 miles to Ride to the next
Stage, (where we were to Lodg.) I askt him of the rest of
the Rode, foreseeing wee must travail in the night. Hee told
mee there was a bad River we were to Ride thro', which
was so very firce a hors could sometimes hardly stem it:
But it was but narrow, and wee should soon be over. I cannot express The concern of mind this relation sett me in; no
thoughts but those of the dang'ros River could entertain my
Imagination, and they were as formidable as varios, still
Tormenting me with blackest Ideas of my Approching fate--
Sometimes seing my self drowning, otherwhiles drowned, and
at the best like a holy Sister Just come out of a Spiritual
Bath in dripping Garments.

Now was the Glorious Luminary, which his swift Cours-
ers arrived at his Stage, leaving poor me with the rest of
this part of the lower world in darkness, with which wee
were soon Surrounded. The only Glimering we now had was
from the spangled Skies, Whose Imperfect Reflections rendered every Object formidable. Each lifeless Trunk, with
its shatter'd Limbs, appear'd an Armed Enymie; and every
little stump like a Ravenous devourer. Nor could I so much
as discern my Guide, when at any distance, which added to
the terror.

Thus, absolutely lost in Thought, and dying with the
very thoughts of drowning, I come up with the post, who I
did not see till even with his Hors: he told mee he stopt
for mee; and wee Rode on Very deliberatly a few paces, when

we entred a Thickett of Trees and Shrubbs, and I perceived
by the Hors's going, we were on the descent of a Hill, which,
as wee come neerer the bottom, 'twas totaly dark with the
Trees that surrounded it. But I knew by the Going of the
Hors wee had entred the water, which my Guide told mee
was the hazzardos River he had told me off; and hee, Riding
up close to my Side, Bid me not fear--we should be over
Imediatly. I now ralyed all the Courage I was mistriss of,
Knowing that I must either Venture my fate of drowning, or
be left like the Children in the wood. So, as the Post bid
me, I gave Reins to my Nagg; and sitting as Stedy as Just
before in the Cannoo, in a few minutes got safe to the other
side, which hee told mee was the Narragansett country.

Here We found great difficulty in Travailing, the way
being very narrow, and on each side the Trees and bushes
gave us very unpleasent welcomes with their Branches and
bow's, which wee could not avoid, it being so exceeding dark.
My Guide, as before so now, putt on harder than I, with my
weary bones, could follow; so left mee and the way beehind
him. Now Returned my distressed apprehensions of the place
where I was: the dolesome woods, my Company next to none,
Going I knew not whither, and encompased with Terrifying
darkness; The least of which was enough to startle a more
Masculine courage. Added to which the Reflections, as in
the afternoon of the day that my Call was very Questionable,
which till then I had not so Prudently as I ought considered.
Now, coming to the foot of a hill, I found great difficulty in
ascending; But being got to the Top, was there amply recom-
penced with the friendly Appearance of the Kind Conductress
of the night, Just then Advancing above the Horisontall Line.
The Raptures which the Sight of that fair Planett produced
in mee, caus'd mee, for the Moment, to forgett my present
wearyness and past toils; and Inspir'd me for most of the
remaining way with very divirting tho'ts, some of which,
with the other Occurances of the day, I reserved to note
down when I should come to my Stage. My tho'ts on the
sight of the moon were to this purpose:

Fair Cynthia, all the Homage that I may
Unto a Creature, unto thee I pay;
In Lonesome woods to meet so kind a guide,
To Mee 's more worth than all the world beside.
Some Joy I felt just now, when safe got or'e
Yon Surly River to this Rugged shore,
Deeming Rough welcomes from these clownish Trees,
Better than Lodgings with Nereidees.

Yet swelling fears surprise; all darkapp ears--
Nothing but Light can disipate those fears.
My fainting vitals can't lend strength to say,
But softly whisper, O I wish 'twere day.
The murmer hardly warm'd the Armbient air,
E're thy Bright Aspect rescues from dispair;
Makes the old Hagg her sable mantle loose,
And a Bright Joy do's through my Soul diffuse.
The Boistero's Trees now Lend a Passage Free,
And pleasent prospects thou giv'st light to see.

From hence wee kept on, with more ease than before:
the way being smooth and even, the night warm and serene,
and the Tall and thick Trees at a distance, especially when
the moon glar'd light through the branches, fill'd my Imagination with the pleasent delusion of a Sumpteous citty, fill'd
with famous Buildings and churches, with their spring stee-
ples, Balconies, Galleries and I know not what: Granduers
which I had heard of, and which the stories of foreign countries had given me the Idea of.

Here stood a Lofty church--there is a steeple,
And there the Grand Parade--O see the people!
That Famouse Castle there, were I but nigh,
To see the mote and Bridg and walls so high--
They'r very fine! sais my deluded eye.

Being thus agreably entertain'd without a thou't of any thing
but thoughts themselves, I on a suden was Rous'd from these
pleasing Imaginations, by the Post's sounding his horn, which
assured mee hee was arrived at the Stage, where we were
to Lodg: and that musick was then most musickall and agreeable to mee.

Being come to mr. Havens', I was very civilly Received,
and courteously entertained, in a clean comfortable House;
and the Good woman was very active in helping off my Riding
clothes, and then ask't what I would eat. I told her I had
some Chocolett, if shee would prepare it; which with the help
of some Milk, and a little clean brass Kettle, she soon ef-
fected to my satisfaction. I then betook me to my Apartment,
which was a little Room parted from the Kitchen by a single
bord partition; where, after I had noted the Occurrances of
the past day, I went to bed, which, tho' pretty hard, Yet
neet and handsome. But I could get no sleep, because of
the Clamor of some of the Town tope-ers in next Room, Who
were entred into a strong debate concerning the Signifycation

of the name of their Country, (viz.) Narraganset. One said
it was named so by the Indians, because there grew a Brier
there, of a prodigious Highth and bigness, the like hardly
ever known, called by the Indians Narragansett; And quotes
an Indian of so Barberous a name for his Author, that I
could not write it. His Antagonist Replyed no--It was from
a Spring it had its name, which hee well knew where it was,
which was extreem cold in summer, and as Hott as could be
imagined in the winter, which was much resorted too by the
natives, and by them called Narragansett, (Hott and Cold,)
and that was the originall of their places name--with a thousand Impertinances not worth notice, which He utter'd with
such a Roreing voice and Thundering blows with the fist of
wickedness on the Table, that it peirced my very head. I
heartily fretted, and wish't 'um tongue tyed; but with as little succes as a freind of mine once, who was (as shee said)
kept a whole night awake, on a Jorny, by a country Left.
and a Sergent, Insigne and a Deacon, contriving how to bring
a triangle into a Square. They kept calling for tother Gill,
which while they were swallowing, was some Intermission;
But presently, like Oyle to fire, encreased the flame. I
set my Candle on a Chest by the bed side, and setting up,
fell to my old way of composing my Resentments, in the
following manner:

I ask thy Aid, O Potent Rum!
To Charm these wrangling Topers Dum.
Thou hast their Giddy Brains possest--
The man confounded with the Beast--
And I, poor I, can get no rest.
Intoxicate them with thy fumes:
O still their Tongues till morning comes!

And I know not but my wishes took effect; for the dispute
soon ended with 'tother Dram; and so Good night!

Wedensday, October 4th. About four in the morning,
we set out for Kingston (for so was the Town called) with a
french Docter in our company. Hee and the Post put on very
furiously, so that I could not keep up with them, only as now
and then they'd stop till they see mee. This Rode was poorly
furnished with accommodations for Travellers, so that we
were forced to ride 22 miles by the post's account, but neerer thirty by mine, before wee could bait so much as our
Horses, which I exceedingly complained of. But the post
encourag'd mee, by saying wee should be well accommodated
anon at mr. Devills, a few miles further. But I questioned

whether we ought to go to the Devil to be helpt out of affliction.   However, like the rest of Deluded souls that post to
the Infernal denn, Wee made all posible speed to this Devil's
Habitation; where alliting, in full assurance of good accommodation, wee were going in.   But meeting his two daughters,
as I suposed twins, they so neerly resembled each other,
both in features and habit, and look't as old as the Divel
himselfe, and quite as Ugly, We desired entertainm't, but
could hardly get a word out of 'um, till with our Importunity,
telling them our necesity, &c. they call'd the old Sophister,
who was as sparing of his words as his daughters had bin,
and no, or none, was the reply's hee made us to our demands.   Hee differed only in this from the old fellow in
to'ther Country: hee let us depart.   However, I thought it
proper to warn poor Travailers to endeavour to Avoid falling
into circumstances like ours, which at our next Stage I sat
down and did as followeth:

> May all that dread the cruel feind of night
> Keep on, and not at this curs't Mansion light.
> 'Tis Hell; 'tis Hell! and Devills here do dwell:
> Here dwells the Devill--surely this's Hell.
> Nothing but Wants: a drop to cool yo'r Tongue
> Cant be procur'd these cruel Feinds among.
> Plenty of horrid Grins and looks sevear,
> Hunger and thirst, But pitty's bannish'd here--
> The Right hand keep, if Hell on Earth you fear!

Thus leaving this habitation of cruelty, we went forward; and
arriving at an Ordinary about two mile further, found toller-
able accommodation.   But our Hostes, being a pretty full
mouth'd old creature, entertain'd our fellow travailer, the
french Docter, with Inumirable complaints of her bodily infirmities; and whispered to him so lou'd, that all the House
had as full a hearing as hee: which was very divirting to
the company, (of which there was a great many,) as one
might see by their sneering.   But poor weary I slipt out to
enter my mind in my Jornal, and left my Great Landly with
her Talkative Guests to themselves.

MERCY OTIS WARREN

(1728-1814)

Mercy Otis was born in 1728 at Barnstable on Cape Cod.
Her father, in addition to farming, was a lawyer and a county judge. Her brother was James Otis, author of The Rights
of the British Colonies Asserted and Proved (1764), an important contribution to the polemics preceding the American
Revolution. In 1754 she married James Warren, who also
became active in the cause of independence. Henceforth,
with the exception of ten post-Revolutionary years, when she
resided at former Governor Hutchinson's house in Milton,
she lived on the Warren farm at Plymouth, Massachusetts.

Mercy Warren fervently shared her husband's and
brother's political convictions. Endowed with seemingly in-
exhaustible energy, she found time, while raising a family
and supervising a farm during her husband's long absences,
to carry on a voluminous correspondence and to write satirical poems and dramas on the events and politics of the times.
Parts of two of her poems--one occasioned by the Boston Tea
Party and the other by the need, as she saw it, to curtail
commerce with Great Britain--are included in this volume.
Her poetical gift, as is obvious, was not great, but no one
can fault her for lack of zeal. As a letter-writer she was
much more talented. In her correspondence she wrote on
political, personal, literary, and other matters. Not as out-
spoken on the status and rights of women as her close friend
and frequent correspondent Abigail Adams, she nevertheless
did have thoughts on these subjects, and excerpts from some
of the letters in which she expresses these thoughts will be
found in the following pages.

Warren's major work was her three-volume History
of the Rise, Progress and Termination of the American Revolution (1805). Drawing from her involvement in events and
from her acquaintance with major figures in the Revolution,
she wrote with patriotic ardor and a keen eye for character

delineation. Biased, of course, but usually factually accurate, her book was offensive to some, especially to her old
friend John Adams, whom she represented, not untruthfully,
as having once entertained the idea of establishing a monarchy
to rule the newly independent nation. This and other comments in the History sparked a bitter controversy between
the author and the ex-President, which after a long exchange
of aggrieved and angry letters was finally resolved by the
intervention of friends.

The excerpts from Warren's verse and letters that
follow are presented as introduced and edited by Alice Brown
in her biography Mercy Warren, published in 1896 by Charles
Scribner's Sons as a volume in a series titled "Women of
Colonial and Revolutionary Times." Alice Brown, a story
by whom appears in this volume, is a New England author
of very considerable merit, and her end-of-the-century comments on Warren's views concerning women are significant
in their own right. In addition to Brown's biography the
reader is referred to Katherine Anthony, First Lady of the
Revolution: The Life of Mercy Otis Warren (1958).

Alice Brown introduces Mercy Warren's two poems, inspired
by the events of 1774, with the following quotation from a
letter to Warren dated December 5, 1774, from her friend
Abigail Adams, wife of John Adams:

> "... The tea that bainful weed is arrived. Great
> and I hope effectual opposition has been made to
> the landing of it--To the publick papers I must re-
> fer you for particulars--you will there find that the
> proceedings of our citizens have been united spirited
> and firm--The flame is kindled and like lightning it
> catches from soul to soul."

The poems as presented in Alice Brown's book and
with her comments follow:

> Mrs. Warren's poem is headed "The Squabble of the
> Sea Nymphs: or the Sacrifice of the Tuscararoes."

Bright Phoebus drove his rapid car amain,
And plung'd his steeds beyond the western plain,
Behind a golden skirted cloud to rest.
Ere ebon night had spread her sable vest,
And drawn her curtain o'er the fragrant vale,
Or Cynthia's shadows dress'd the lonely dale,
The heroes of the Tuscararo tribe,
Who scorn'd alike a fetter or a bribe,
In order rang'd and waited freedom's nod,
To make an offering to the wat'ry god.

Grey Neptune rose, and from his sea green bed,
He wav'd his trident o'er his oozy head;
He stretch'd, from shore to shore, his regal wand,
And bade the river deities attend;
Triton's hoarse clarion summon'd them by name,
And from old ocean call'd each wat'ry dame.

In council met to regulate the state,
Among their godships rose a warm debate,
What luscious draught they next should substitute,
That might the palates of celestials suit,
As Nectar's stream no more meandering rolls,
The food ambrosial of their social bowls
Profusely spent;--nor, can Scamander's shore,
Yield the fair sea nymphs one short banquet more.

The Titans all with one accord arous'd,
To travel round Columbia's coast propos'd;
To rob and plunder every neighb'ring vine,
(Regardless of Nemisis' sacred shrine;)
Nor leave untouch'd the peasant's little store,
Or think of right, while demi gods have power.

But nymphs and goddesses [Brown continues] fell into
squabbling over the brand of drink to be preferred.

'Till fair Salacia perch'd upon the rocks,
The rival goddess wav'd her yellow locks,
Proclaim'd, hysonia shall assuage their grief,
With choice souchong, and the imperial leaf.

The champions of the Tuscararan race,
(Who neither hold, nor even wish a place,
While faction reigns, and tyranny presides,

And base oppression o'er the virtues rides;
While venal measures dance in silken sails,
And avarice o'er earth and sea prevails;
While luxury creates such mighty feuds,
E'en in the bosoms of the demi gods;)
Lent their strong arm in pity to the fair,
To aid the bright Salacia's generous care;
Pour'd a profusion of delicious teas,
Which, wafted by a soft favonian breeze,
Supply'd the wat'ry deities, in spite
Of all the rage of jealous Amphytrite.

The fair Salacia, victory, victory, sings,
In spite of heroes, demi gods, or kings;
She bids defiance to the servile train,
The pimps and sycophants of George's reign.

The crying question of the day becomes, "What can
we do without?" And Mrs. Warren appears with her
pertinent occasional poem: "To the Hon. J. Winthrop,
Esq. Who, on the American Determination, in 1774,
to suspend all Commerce with Britain, (except for the
real Necessaries of life) requested a poetical List of
the Articles the Ladies might comprise under that
Head."
It is in her customary vein of satire. She inquires:--

But what's the anguish of whole towns in tears,
Or trembling cities groaning out their fears?
The state may totter on proud ruin's brink,
The sword be brandish'd or the bark may sink;
Yet shall Clarissa check her wanton pride,
And lay her female ornaments aside?
Quit all the shining pomp, the gay parade,
The costly trappings that adorn the maid?
What! all the aid of foreign looms refuse!
(As beds of tulips strip'd of richest hues,
Or the sweet bloom that 's nip'd by sudden frost,
Clarissa reigns no more a favorite toast.)
For what is virtue, or the winning grace,
Of soft good humour, playing round the face;
Or what those modest antiquated charms,
That lur'd a Brutus to a Portia's arms;
Or all the hidden beauties of the mind,
Compar'd with gauze, and tassels well combin'd?

. . . .
But does Helvidius, vigilant and wise,
Call for a schedule, that may all comprise?
'T is so contracted, that a Spartan sage,
Will sure applaud th' economizing age.

But if ye doubt, an inventory clear,
Of all she needs, Lamira offers here;
Nor does she fear a rigid Cato's frown,
When she lays by the rich embroider'd gown,
And modestly compounds for just enough--
Perhaps, some dozens of more flighty stuff;
With lawns and lustrings--blond, and mecklin laces,
Fringes and jewels, fans and tweezer cases;
Gay cloaks and hats, of every shape and size,
Scarfs, cardinals, and ribbons of all dyes;
With ruffles stamp'd, and aprons of tambour,
Tippets and handkerchiefs, at least three score;
With finest muslins that fair India boasts,
And the choice herbage from Chinesan coasts;
(But while the fragrant hyson leaf regales,
Who'll wear the homespun produce of the vales?
For if 't would save the nation from the curse
Of standing troops; or, name a plague still worse,
Few can this choice delicious draught give up,
Though all Medea's poisons fill the cup.)
Add feathers, furs, rich sattins, and ducapes,
And head dresses in pyramidial shapes;
Side boards of plate, and porcelain profuse,
With fifty dittos that the ladies use.

. . . .
But though your wives in fripperies are dress'd,
And public virtue is the minion's jest,
America has many a worthy name,
Who shall, hereafter, grace the rolls of fame.
Her good Cornelias, and her Arrias fair,
Who, death, in its most hideous forms, can dare,
Rather than live vain fickle fortune's sport,
Amidst the panders of a tyrant's court;
With a long list of gen'rous, worthy men,
Who spurn the yoke, and servitude disdain;
Who nobly struggle in a vicious age,
To stem the torrent of despotic rage;
Who leagu'd, in solemn covenant unite,
And by the manes of good Hampden plight,
That while the surges lash Britannia's shore,

Or wild Ni'gara's cataracts shall roar,
And Heaven looks down, and sanctifies the deed,
They 'll fight for freedom, and for virtue bleed.

Alice Brown presents certain excerpts from Mercy Warren's
letters, as follows:

> Mrs. Warren treads delicately the ground occupied by
> the modern anti-suffragist (when the latter is a woman
> of intelligence). She considers herself the equal,
> mental and moral, of the more fortunate sex; but she
> concludes that, for purposes of social organization and
> government, a technical headship is necessary. Such
> ascendency need not of necessity find its root in the
> nature of things. It merely happens that the well-
> being of society, according to the Divine dispensation,
> demands it. She very concisely defines her "platform"
> to one of the young ladies who so often sought her for
> counsel and advice:--

"... You seem hurt by the general aspersions so often
thrown on the Understanding of ours by the Illiberal Part of
the other Sex.--I think I feel no partiality on the Female Side
but what arises from a love to Justice, & freely acknowledge
we too often give occasion (by an Eager Pursuit of Trifles)
for Reflections of this Nature.--Yet a discerning & generous
Mind should look to the origin of the Error, and when that is
done, I believe it will be found that the Deficiency lies not
so much in the Inferior Contexture of Female Intellects as in
the different Education bestow'd on the Sexes, for when the
Cultivation of the Mind is neglected in Either, we see Ignorance, Stupidity, & Ferocity of Manners equally Conspicuous
in both.

"It is my Opinion that that Part of the human Species
who think Nature (as well as the infinitely wise & Supreme
Author thereof) has given them the Superiority over the other,
mistake their own Happiness when they neglect the Culture of
Reason in their Daughters while they take all possible Methods
of improving it in their sons.

"The Pride you feel on hearing Reflections indiscrimi-
nately Cast on the Sex, is laudable if any is so.--I take it,
it is a kind of Conscious Dignity that ought rather to be cher-

ish'd, for while we own the Appointed Subordination (perhaps
for the sake of Order in Families) let us by no Means Acknowledge such an Inferiority as would Check the Ardour of
our Endeavours to equal in all Accomplishments the most
masculine Heights, that when these temporary Distinctions
subside we may be equally qualified to taste the full Draughts
of Knowledge & Happiness prepared for the Upright of every
Nation & Sex; when Virtue alone will be the Test of Rank,
& the grand Economy for an Eternal Duration will be properly
Adjusted."

There speaks the feminine wisdom of the ages:
"My dear, it may be necessary for you to seem inferior; but you need not be so.   Let them have their
little game, since it may have been so willed.   It
won't hurt you; it will amuse them."
Of this same subtlety of worldly wisdom, though of
another complexion, is the sage advice written to her
son Henry's young wife soon after marriage: "Many
of our thoughtless sex as soon as the connubial knot
is tied neglect continual attention (which is necessary
without discovering the exertion) to keep the sacred
flame of love alive."
Note the significance of the italicized words!   Mrs.
Warren had learned that the woman who would reign
must be mistress of an exquisite tact.
She is not to be deluded by conventional judgments,
the snap-shots of criticism.   In writing Mrs. Adams,
she refers to their common curiosity regarding certain political letters, adding:--

"[It is] the one quality which the other sex so generously Consign over to us.   Though for no other Reason but
because they have the opportunity of indulging their inquisi-
tive Humour to the utmost in the great school of the World,
while we are confined to the Narrower Circle of Domestic
Care.   But we have yet one Advantage peculiar to ourselves.
If the Mental Faculties of the Female are not improved it
may be Concealed in the obscure retreats of the Bedchamber
or the kitchen which she is not Necessitated to Leave."

But alas!   when she speaks from the insecure mo-
rass of nervous panic her conclusions are less assured.   Thus does she write in the early days of
the war, after much talk of political apprehensions:--

"As our weak & timid sex is only the echo of the other, & like some pliant peace of Clock work the springs of our souls move slow or more Rapidly: just as hope, fear or courage gives motion to the conducting wires that govern all our movements, so I build much on the high key that at present seems to Animate the American patriots."

ABIGAIL ADAMS

Abigail Adams, the wife of President John Adams, was born in 1744 at Weymouth, Massachusetts, where her father was minister of the Congregational Church. During much of her childhood she lived with her maternal grandparents, the John Quincys, at Mt. Wollaston (now Quincy), just south of Boston. After her marriage in 1764 she resided on the Adams farm, also in Quincy, except during four years spent with her diplomat husband in France and England and, later, during the years in Philadelphia and in Washington while John Adams was Vice-President and President. Abigail and John Adams were apparently a devoted couple, and the numerous letters exchanged between them during his many lengthy absences from home constitute a correspondence distinguished for its literary quality and its historical importance. The two saw eye-to-eye on most political matters, both being ardent advocates of the Federalist Party. Abigail is in fact reputed to have exerted a strong influence on her husband's policies.

Abigail, of course, wrote letters to others than her husband, notably to her close friend Mercy Warren, who also was deeply concerned with political matters and who, like Abigail, proved herself an efficient manager of the family farm during her husband's absences. Abigail's convictions, however, were firmer than her friend's in regard to women's rights; nor as the letters that follow suggest, did she seem to be in agreement with her husband on this subject. But no matter what topic she wrote on, she seldom abandoned the wit and lightness of touch that make her letters a literary treat. She is two generations ahead of her time in speaking of the lack of power of women in relation to men, when she likens the position of women to the other groups at that time who also had less power--i.e., to "children," "apprentices," "Indians," "Negroes." Her talk of "fomenting a Rebellion" foreshadows Elizabeth Cady Stanton's and Susan B. Anthony's protests in the next century.

The letters that follow have been taken from the following sources: letter of 7 May 1776, from Charles Francis Adams, ed., Letters of Mrs. Adams, the Wife of John Adams (1848); letters of 31 March, 14 April, and 14 August 1776, from Charles Francis Adams, ed., Familiar Letters of John Adams and His Wife Abigail Adams, During the Revolution (1876); letter of 27 April 1776, from Alice Brown, Mercy Warren (1896). In 1975 Harvard University Press published an interesting volume, The Book of Abigail and John: Selected Letters of the Adams Family, 1762-1784, ed. L. H. Butterfield et al. A good recent biography is Charles W. Akers, Abigail Adams: An American Woman (1980).

TO JOHN ADAMS

Braintree, 31 March, 1776

I wish you would ever write me a letter half as long as I write you, and tell me, if you may, where your fleet are gone; what sort of defense Virginia can make against our common enemy; whether it is so situated as to make an able defense. Are not the gentry lords, and the common people vassals? Are they not like the uncivilized vassals Britain represents us to be? I hope their riflemen, who have shown themselves very savage and even blood-thirsty, are not a specimen of the generality of the people. I am willing to allow the colony great merit for having produced a Washington; but they have been shamefully duped by a Dunmore.

I have sometimes been ready to think that the passion for liberty cannot be equally strong in the breasts of those who have been accustomed to deprive their fellow-creatures of theirs. Of this I am certain, that it is not founded upon that generous and Christian principle of doing to others as we would that others should do unto us.

Do not you want to see Boston? I am fearful of the small-pox, or I should have been in before this time. I got

Mr. Crane to go to our house and see what state it was in.
I find it has been occupied by one of the doctors of a regi-
ment; very dirty, but no other damage has been done to it.
The few things which were left in it are all gone.   I look
upon it as a new acquisition of property--a property which
one month ago I did not value at a single shilling, and would
with pleasure have seen it in flames.

The town in general is left in a better state than we
expected; more owing to a precipitate flight than any regard
to the inhabitants; though some individuals discovered a sense
of honor and justice, and have left the rent of the houses in
which they were, for the owners, and the furniture unhurt,
or, if damaged, sufficient to make it good.   Others have
committed abominable ravages.   The mansion-house of your
President is safe, and the furniture unhurt; while the house
and furniture of the Solicitor General have fallen a prey to
their own merciless party.   Surely the very fiends feel a
reverential awe for virtue and patriotism, whilst they detest
the parricide and traitor.

I feel very differently at the approach of spring from
what I did a month ago.   We knew not then whether we could
plant or sow with safety, whether where we had tilled we
could reap the fruits of our own industry, whether we could
rest in our own cottages or whether we should be driven
from the seacoast to seek shelter in the wilderness; but now
we feel a temporary peace, and the poor fugitives are returning to their deserted habitations.

Though we felicitate ourselves, we sympathize with
those who are trembling lest the lot of Boston should be
theirs.   But they cannot be in similar circumstances unless
pusillanimity and cowardice should take possession of them.
They have time and warning given them to see the evil and
shun it.

I long to hear that you have declared an independency.
And, by the way, in the new code of laws which I suppose
it will be necessary for you to make, I desire you would remember the ladies and be more generous and favorable to
them than your ancestors.   Do not put such unlimited power
into the hands of the husbands.   Remember, all men would
be tyrants if they could.   If particular care and attention is
not paid to the ladies, we are determined to foment a rebellion, and will not hold ourselves bound by any laws in which
we have no voice or representation.

That your sex are naturally tyrannical is a truth so thoroughly established as to admit of no dispute; but such of you as wish to be happy willingly give up the harsh title of master for the more tender and endearing one of friend. Why, then, not put it out of the power of the vicious and the lawless to use us with cruelty and indignity with impunity? Men of sense in all ages abhor those customs which treat us only as the vassals of your sex; regard us then as beings placed by Providence under your protection, and in imitation of the Supreme Being make use of that power only for our happiness. Adieu

In a letter written April 14, 1776, John Adams made the following comment to his wife regarding her request in behalf of "the ladies":

"As to your extraordinary code of laws, I cannot but laugh. We have been told that our struggle has loosened the bonds of government everywhere; that children and apprentices were disobedient; that schools and colleges were grown turbulent; that Indians slighted their guardians, and negroes grew insolent to their masters. But your letter was the first intimation that another tribe, more numerous and powerful than all the rest, were grown discontented. This is rather too coarse a compliment, but you are so saucy, I won't blot it out. Depend upon it, we know better than to repeal our masculine systems. Although they are in full force, you know they are little more than theory. We dare not exert our power in its full latitude. We are obliged to go fair and softly, and, in practice, you know we are the subjects. We have only the name of masters, and rather than give up this, which would completely subject us to the despotism of the petticoat, I hope General Washington and all our brave heroes would fight; I am sure every good politician would plot, as long as he would against despotism, empire, monarchy, aristocracy, oligarchy, or ochlocracy. A fine story, indeed! I begin to think the ministry as deep as they are wicked. After stirring up Tories, land-jobbers, trimmers, bigots, Canadians, Indians, negroes, Hanoverians, Hessians, Russians, Irish Roman Catholics, Scotch renegadoes, at last they have stimulated the ------ to demand new privileges and threaten to rebel."

In a letter of April 27, 1776, Abigail Adams wrote

to Mercy Warren as follows regarding the exchange
with her husband.

TO MERCY WARREN

He [Mr. Adams] is very sausy to me, in return for a List
of Female Grievances which I transmitted to him.   I think I
will get you to join me in a petition to Congress.   I thought
it was very probable our Wise Statesmen would erect a New
Government & form a New Code of Laws, I ventured to
speak a Word in behalf of our Sex who are rather hardly
Dealt with by the Laws of England which gives such unlimited
power to the Husband to use his wife Ill.   I requested that
our Legislators would consider our case and as all Men of
Delicacy & Sentiment are averse to exercising the power
they possess, yet as there is a Natural propensity in Human
Nature to domination I thought the Most Generous plan was
to put it out of the power of the Arbitrary & tyranick to injure us with impunity by establishing some Laws in our Favour upon just & Liberal principals.

I believe I even threatened fomenting a Rebellion in
case we were not considerd and assured him we would not
hold ourselves bound by any Laws in which we had neither
a voice nor representation.

In return he tells me he cannot but Laugh at my Ex-
tradonary Code of Laws that he had heard their struggle had
loosned the bonds of Government, that children & apprentices
were disobedient, that Schools and Colledges were grown turbulent, that Indians slighted their Guardians and Negroes
grew insolent to their Masters.   But my letter was the first
intimation that another Tribe more Numerous & powerfull
than all the rest were grown discontented.   This is rather
too coarse a compliment, he adds, but that I am so sausy
he wont blot it out.

So I have helped the Sex abundantly, but I will tell
him I have only been making trial of the disinterestedness of
his Virtue & when weighd in the balance have found it wanting.

It would be bad policy to grant us greater power say they since under all the disadvantages we labour we have the ascendancy over their hearts

"And charm by accepting, by submitting sway."

TO JOHN ADAMS

Braintree, 7 May, 1776

How many are the solitary hours I spend, ruminating upon the past, and anticipating the future, whilst you, overwhelmed with the cares of state, have but a few moments you can devote to any individual. All domestic pleasures and enjoyments are absorbed in the great and important duty you owe your country, "for our country is, as it were, a secondary god, and the first and greatest parent. It is to be preferred to parents, wives, children, friends, and all things, the gods only excepted; for, if our country perishes, it is as impossible to save an individual, as to preserve one of the fingers of a mortified hand." Thus do I suppress every wish, and silence every murmur, acquiescing in a painful separation from the companion of my youth, and the friend of my heart.

I believe 't is near ten days since I wrote you a line. I have not felt in a humor to entertain you. If I had taken up my pen perhaps some unbecoming invective might have fallen from it. The eyes of our rulers have been closed, and a lethargy has seized almost every member. I fear a fatal security has taken possession of them. Whilst the building is in flames, they tremble at the expense of water to quench it. In short, two months have elapsed since the evacuation of Boston, and very little has been done in that time to secure it, or the harbour, from future invasion. The people are all in a flame, and no one among us, that I have heard of, even mentions expense. They think, universally, that there has been an amazing neglect somewhere. Many have turned out as volunteers to work upon Noddle's Island, and many more would go upon Nantasket, if the business was once set on foot. "'T is a maxim of state, that power and liberty are like heat and moisture. Where they

are well mixed, every thing prospers; where they are single,
they are destructive."

A government of more stability is much wanted in this
colony, and they are ready to receive it from the hands of
the Congress. And since I have begun with maxims of state,
I will add another, namely, that a people may let a king fall,
yet still remain a people; but, if a king let his people slip
from him, he is no longer a king. And as this is most certainly our case, why not proclaim to the world, in decisive
terms, your own importance?

Shall we not be despised by foreign powers, for hesi-
tating so long at a word?

I cannot say, that I think you are very generous to
the ladies; for, whilst you are proclaiming peace and good-
will to men, emancipating all nations, you insist upon retain-
ing an absolute power over wives. But you must remember,
that arbitrary power is like most other things which are very
hard, very liable to be broken; and, notwithstanding all your
wise laws and maxims, we have it in our power, not only to
free ourselves, but to subdue our masters, and, without violence, throw both your natural and legal authority at our
feet;--

"Charm by accepting, by submitting sway,
Yet have our humor most when we obey."

I thank you for several letters which I have received
since I wrote last; they alleviate a tedious absence, and I
long earnestly for a Saturday evening, and experience a similar pleasure to that which I used to find in the return of my
friend upon that day after a week's absence. The idea of a
year dissolves all my philosophy.

Our little ones, whom you so often recommend to my
care and instruction, shall not be deficient in virtue or prob-
ity, if the precepts of a mother have their desired effect; but
they would be doubly enforced, could they be indulged with
the example of a father alternately before them. I often point
them to their sire,

"engaged in a corrupted state,
Wrestling with vice and faction."

9 May

I designed to have finished the sheet, but, an opportunity offering, I close, only just informing you that, May the 7th, our privateers took two prizes in the bay, in fair sight of the man-of-war; one, a brig from Ireland; the other from Fayal, loaded with wine, brandy, &c.; the other with beef, &c. The wind was east, and a flood tide, so that the tenders could not get out, though they tried several times; the lighthouse fired signal guns, but all would not do. They took them in triumph, and carried them into Lynn.

Pray be kind enough to remember me at all times, and write, as often as you possibly can, to your

Portia
[Abigail frequently signed her letters "Portia."]

TO JOHN ADAMS

---

14 August, 1776

Your letter of August 3 came by this day's post. I find it very convenient to be so handy. I can receive a letter at night, sit down and reply to it, and send it off in the morning.

You remark upon the deficiency of education in your countrymen. It never, I believe, was in a worse state, at least for many years. The college is not in the state one could wish. The scholars complain that their professor in philosophy is taken off by public business, to their great detriment. In this town I never saw so great a neglect of education. The poorer sort of children are wholly neglected, and left to range the streets, without schools, without business, given up to all evil. The town is not, as formerly, divided into wards. There is either too much business left upon the hands of a few, or too little care to do it. We daily see the necessity of a regular government.

You speak of our worthy brother. I often lament it, that a man so peculiarly formed for the education of youth, and so well qualified as he is in many branches of literature, excelling in philosophy and the mathematics, should not be employed in some public station.   I know not the person who would make half so good a successor to Dr. Winthrop.   He has a peculiar, easy manner of communicating his ideas to youth; and the goodness of his heart and the purity of his morals, without an affected austerity, must have a happy effect upon the minds of pupils.

If you complain of neglect of education in sons, what shall I say with regard to daughters, who every day experience the want of it?   With regard to the education of my own children, I find myself soon out of my depth, destitute and deficient in every part of education.

I most sincerely wish that some more liberal plan might be laid and executed for the benefit of the rising generation, and that our new Constitution may be distinguished for encouraging learning and virtue.   If we mean to have heroes, statesmen, and philosophers, we should have learned women.   The world perhaps would laugh at me and accuse me of vanity, but you, I know, have a mind too enlarged and liberal to disregard the sentiment.   If much depends, as is allowed, upon the early education of youth, and the first principles which are instilled take the deepest root, great benefit must arise from literary accomplishments in women.

Excuse me.   My pen has run away with me.   I have no thoughts of coming to Philadelphia.   The length of time I have and shall be detained here would have prevented me, even if you had no thoughts of returning till December; but I live in daily expectation of seeing you here.   Your health, I think, requires your immediate return.   I expected Mr. G------ would have set off before now, but he perhaps finds it very hard to leave his mistress.   I won't say harder than some do to leave their wives.   Mr. Gerry stood very high in my esteem.   What is meat for one is not for another. No accounting for fancy.   She is a queer dame and leads people wild dances.

But hush!   Post, don't betray your trust and lose my letter.

Portia

HANNAH MATHER CROCKER

Born in Boston in 1752, Hannah Mather Crocker was the
fourth daughter of a clergyman and a direct descendant of
the famous Puritan divines Increase and Cotton Mather. On
her mother's side she was descended from Anne Hutchinson.
Thomas Hutchinson, the next-to-last Royal Governor of Massachusetts, was her uncle. Her education seems to have
been quite informal, but she doubtless benefited from her
scholarly father's extensive library. In 1779 she married
Joseph Crocker, a Harvard graduate and a captain in the
Revolutionary Army who after the war became a Boston shop-
keeper. In the years before her marriage she had made a
study of Freemasonry in order to reassure her woman friends
that Masonic meetings were not primarily the occasions for
nocturnal debauchery on the part of the members. An out-
growth of this study was her establishing in 1778 a "woman's
lodge," which she described as being devoted to "improving
the mind; that by strength and wisdom, we might beautifully
adorn the female character...." (See Notable American Women, 1:406). Her marriage and the subsequent birth of ten
children put an end to this activity; but in 1810, a widow of
thirteen years, she wrote and published A Series of Letters
on Freemasonry, again defending the Masons and advocating
that women form self-improvement societies like her former
"woman's lodge." In 1816 she published The School of Reform, or Seaman's Safe Pilot to the Cape of Good Hope, the
ambitious purpose of which was to induce sailors to abandon
drink and immorality.

Her most significant work, virtually ignored in her
lifetime, was Observations on the Real Rights of Women,
published by subscription in 1818. Her claim for equality
of the sexes is, predictably, based on her ancestral religion,
according to which she found that God shows no preference
because of sex in His distribution of grace. In this view she
was supported by the woman to whom she dedicated her book,

62

the English evangelist Hannah More. In the writings of Mary
Wollstonecraft she found support for her recommendation for
providing women with an education that would enable them,
if necessary, to support themselves and for her advocacy of
marriage as an equal partnership in all respects, including
financial matters. In her insistence that in the eyes of God
women are equal to men, she shares the spirit, if not the
aggressiveness, of her forebear Anne Hutchinson. The excerpts that follow indicate the tenor of her thought.

For additional information concerning Crocker's life
and work, the reader is referred to Notable American Women.

From OBSERVATIONS ON THE REAL RIGHTS OF WOMEN

CHAP. I

Of the creation and fall of our first parents

The foundation stone of the present work must be laid in the
first creation of the human race. When the great Jehovah
had created the earth, and all things therein, he created man;
male and female created he them, in his own image, so far
as he endowed him with intellectual powers and faculties, and
gave him an immortal and rational soul, and powers of mind
capable of reasoning on the nature of things. And the Lord
God said, it is not good for man to be alone; I will make him
an help meet, for him: And the Lord God caused a deep
sleep to fall upon Adam, and he slept: and he took one of
his ribs, and closed up the flesh instead thereof. And the
rib, which the Lord God had taken from man, made he a
woman: and brought her unto the man, and Adam said, this
is now bone of my bone, and flesh of my flesh; she shall be
called woman, because she was taken out of man; as she
partakes of my original nature, she shall therefore partake
of my name; therefore shall a man leave his father and his
mother, and shall cleave unto his wife, and they shall be one
flesh: See Gen. ii. 24.

It seems, says an able commentator, to have been the Creator's design to have inculcated the lesson of perfect love and union, by forming the woman out of the man's body, and from a part of it so near the heart, as well as to make woman of a more refined and delicate nature, by thus causing the original clay to pass, as it were, twice through his refining hand. Now it is consistent to say, if they are become one flesh, there should be but one and the same spirit operating equally upon them both, for their mutual happiness. Adam, having given her a name, and placed himself as her guardian, became in some measure, responsible for her conduct, as the rightful protector of her innocence. It should be recollected, as a small palliative for Eve, that the command, respecting the tree of knowledge and forbidden fruit, was before the woman was made: see Gen. ii. 16 and 17. And the Lord God commanded the man, saying, of every tree of the garden thou mayest freely eat; but of the tree of knowledge, of good and evil thou shalt not eat, for in the day thou eatest thereof, thou shalt surely die. She must therefore have received her information from Adam, if she knew of any command; as she probably had heard of it, by her answer to the serpent. Perhaps Adam communicated it to her as the injunction of their Maker, but possibly with such mildness and indifference, that she was not fully impressed with the importance of the command.

It seems, that, in an unfortunate hour, these then pure and happy beings, were separated. Oh, fatal hour! Oh, inconsiderate Adam! How couldst thou leave the friend of thy affection to wander in the garden, unaided by the support and strength of thy arm, and the pleasure of thy conversation. Didst thou for one moment feel the supreme dignity and full consequence of being placed lord of the lower creation? Didst thou walk forth to survey the animals created for thy use, and subjected to thy dominion? No, no; we say pride had not then polluted the human heart. Thou wast not then puffed up with the idea of knowing good and evil; but thou might have had tenderness enough for thy "rib, that was taken from thy side," to have kept near enough to her to protect her innocence from the wiles of the tempter. Nothing can justify Eve's imprudence in parlying with the serpent at all; and she is condemnable for holding any converse, or supposing knowledge was ever desirable, that must be obtained in any clandestine or dishonorable manner. No one can approve of the asperity of Adam's answer to his maker, when called on to answer how he knew that he was naked. He answered evidently with a very indignant air: The woman thou gavest to be with me, gave me of the fruit of the tree, and I did eat. It does not appear, from his own account, that Adam withstood the temptation with more fortitude than Eve did; for she presented the fruit, and he received it without hesitation; but it is plain she did not yield immediately, though the most subtle agent of the devil told her that her eyes should be opened, and that she should be like a god. When indeed she saw that the tree was good for food, and that it was pleasant to the eyes, and a tree to be desired to make one wise, she took of the fruit thereof, and did eat. It appears her desire was to obtain knowledge, which might be laudable, though her reason was indeed deceived.

And reason is quickly deceived, says the eloquent Saurin, when the senses have been seduced. It was already yielding to the temptation, to hearken so long to the tempter.

By the joint transgression of our first parents, sin, misery and death were introduced into this present world: They appear equally culpable; yet God, who is ever wise and just in his dealings, passed the most severe sentence on the woman, as she was told her sorrows should be multiplied. And a still harder fate attended her. She was reduced, from a state of honorable equality, to the mortifying state of subjection: Thy desire shall be to thy husband, and he shall rule over thee. Heaven never intended she should be ruled with a rod of iron; but drawn by the cords of the man, in the bonds of love. It is however evident, Adam was placed over her as her lord and master, for a certain period, and by the express will of his maker, and was taught to appreciate his own judgment, as every creature was brought to him to give them names; and whatsoever names he gave them, they were called: And he gave his rib the name of woman, and displayed some judgment in the reason given for calling her woman: For she is bone of my bone, and flesh of my flesh, and therefore she shall be my equal. She shall have equal right to think, reason and act for herself, with my advice corroborating. He should therefore have resisted the temptation with manly fortitude, and, not only by precept, but by example, strengthened her resolution to resist the evil spirit: but he fell a prey to his own credulity, and sunk his posterity in depravity.

However strange their conduct may appear to the human understanding, we fully believe, in the great scale of divine providence, it was perfectly just they should be left to commit sin and folly, to convince the human race of their insufficiency, when left to act for themselves; and, from their example, shew to their posterity, the propriety of placing their dependence on Him, who alone is able to keep us from falling.

There is a very beautiful description of our primeval parent's first interview, in Miss Akin's epistles on women. We give the extract in her own style:

"See where the world's new master roams along,
Vainly intelligent, and idly strong;
Marks his long listless steps and turpid air,
His brow of densest gloom, and fix'd infantile stare.
No mother's voice has touch'd that slumb'ring ear,
Nor glist'ning eye beguiled him with a tear.
Love nurs'd not him with sweet endearing wiles,
Nor woman taught the sympathy of smiles.
Ah! hapless world, that such a wretch obeys,
Ah! joyless Adam, though a world he sways.
But see they meet, they gaze, the new born pair,
Mark now the youth, and now the wond'ring fair.
Sure a new soul that moping idiot warms,
Dilates his statue, and his mein informs.
A brighter crimson tints his gloomy cheeks,
His broad eye kindles, and his glances speaks."

From this description, there appears to commence a sympathy of nature, which perhaps might operate on Adam's sensibility, and cause him insensibly to partake of the forbidden fruit that proved their fatal fall, and her deepest humiliation; as she is placed under subjection to the man: And the command was put into full force under the old Jewish dispensation, as they bought and sold their wives and daughters, and made trafficks of them as they did their cattle. But, blessed be God, the bonds are dissolved, the snare is broken, and woman has escaped by the blessing of the gospel.

CHAP. II

Woman is restored to her original rights of equality under the christian dispensation

Here, indeed, is the love of God manifested to the disobedient children of men. Though by the fall of our first parents misery and death was the consequence; yet the promise is made good to man, that the seed of the woman should bruise the serpent's head, and that in her seed, all mankind should be restored to peace and happiness. And at the appointed time Jehovah was pleased to over-shadow the espoused wife of Joseph: and there was more than a common presence of the divine eradiator attending at his birth. The wise men or astrologers of the east, had calculated a new star that would appear about that time, and it forboded some great event to take place. Agreeably to their calculation, at the very time they were gazing for the stranger, behold it did appear agreeable to their expectation, and by the bright and effulgent light of this new and till now unknown star, the wise men of the east were directed till the star reflected on the menial place of the birth of our Saviour. And here was the degraded woman found; exalted to the highest honour of embracing in her maternal arms the Son of God himself in human nature. What an interesting scene it must have been to the wise men that had been looking for some great event to take place! What a scene it must have been to the man of sensibility! The amiable, the devout Mary, apparently degraded, is now exalted to the highest honour among men; and life and immortality are brought to light, by the divine influence of the gospel, under the dispensation of grace. She, who was condemned to servitude, is now, by the blessing of the dispensation, restored to her original privileges: As the woman was first in the transgression, and, in some measure, the cause of their fall, she is now, by divine goodness, made the instrument of bringing life and future happiness to mankind.

The prophecy is accomplished, that in her seed all nations shall be blessed: Herein she is exalted, and fully restored to her original dignity, by being the mother of our blessed Lord and Saviour Jesus Christ, according to his human nature. This, surely, must place her equal with man, under the christian system. Since the christian era she is no longer commanded to be the slave to man, and he is no longer commanded to rule over her.

The offers of divine grace are equally tendered to both male and female; and all have equal right to accept the blessing; and if any judgment can be formed from the visible church, there is reason to conclude that women embrace the privileges of the gospel, with as much, or more energy, than men. If we trace throughout the known world, it will be found that there are more open professors of religion amongst women, than there are amongst men. And they have an undoubted right to this distinction, as their powers of mind are not inferiour, and their sensibilities are certainly greater, or as keen. There must be a moral and physical distinction of sexes, from the organization of the human frame, as well as from their different modes of life and education, as from their different appropriate duties; and women for the most part are not called to make the same exertions in life; yet there are frequent instances of women, when called in providence to the trial, have made as great exertions as men; and have stemmed the torrent of human misery, with equal fortitude to any man, under like circumstances. They can claim no superiority of opinion, only an equal right of judgment with the bolder sex. They are not called to plough on masculine grounds, from the moral distinction there is in nature.

It must be the appropriate duty and privilege of females, to convince by reason and persuasion. It must be their peculiar province to sooth the turbulent passions of men, when almost sinking in the sea of care, without even an anchor of hope to support them. Under such circumstances women should display their talents by taking the helm, and steer them safe to the haven of rest and peace, and that should be their own happy mansion, where they may always retire and find a safe asylum from the rigid cares of business. It is woman's peculiar right to keep calm and serene under every circumstance in life, as it is undoubtedly her appropriate duty, to sooth and alleviate the anxious cares of man, and her friendly and sympathetic breast should be found the best solace for him, as she has an equal right to partake with him the cares, as well as the pleasures of life.

It was evidently the design of heaven, by the mode of our first formation, that they should walk side by side, as mutual supports in all times of trial. There can be no doubt, that, in most cases, their judgment may be equal with the other sex; perhaps even on the subject of law, politics or religion, they may form good judgment, but it would be morally improper, and physically very incorrect, for the female character to claim the statesman's birth, or ascend the rostrum to gain the loud applause of men, although their powers of mind may be equal to the task.

We find among men, that their powers of mind are not equal in all cases; if the wise author of nature has been graciously pleased to endow all men with the same powers of mind, they do not all improve them to the same advantage; or from some imperfection in the organization of the human frame, the powers or faculties cannot operate on all alike. Some minds are so enfeebled that they are rendered incapable of judging right from wrong; therefore it appears necessary, from the very order of nature, that there should be a distinction in society, and that those whose minds are more expanded should be looked up to, as guides, to the general mass of the citizens. Females have equal right with the male citizen, to claim the protection, friendship and the approbation of such a class of men. As she is now restored to her original right by the blessing of the christian system, no longer is she the slave, but the friend of man. From the local circumstances, and the domestic cares in which most females are involved, it cannot be expected they should make so great improvement in science and literature, as those whose whole life has been devoted to their studies. It must not be expected that the reputable mechanic will rival the man of letters and science, neither would it well suit the female frame or character, to boast of her knowledge in mechanism, or her skill in the manly art of slaughtering fellow-men. It is woman's appropriate duty and peculiar privilege to cultivate the olive branches around her table. It is for her to implant in the juvenile breast the first seed of virtue, the love of God, and their country, with all the other virtues that shall prepare them to shine as statesmen, soldiers, philosophers and christians. Some of our first worthies have boasted that they imbibed their heroic principles with their mother's milk; and by precept and example were first taught the love of virtue, religion, and their country. Surely they should have a right to share with them the laurel, but not the right of conquest; for that must be man's prerogative, and woman is to rejoice in his conquest. There may be a few groveling minds who think woman should not aspire to any further knowledge than to obtain enough of the cymical [chemical] art to enable them to compound a good pudding, pie, or cake, for her lord and master to discompound. Others, of a still weaker class, may say, it is enough for woman scientifically to arrange the spinning-wheel and distaff, and exercise her extensive capacity in knitting and sewing, since the fall and restoration of woman these employments have been the appropriate duties of the female sex. The art of dress, which in some measure produced the art of industry, did not commence till sin, folly and shame, introduced the first invention of dress, which ought to check the modest female from every species of wantonness and extravagance in dress; cultivate the mind, and trifling in dress will soon appear in its true colours.

To those who appear unfriendly to female literature let me say, in behalf of the sex, they claim no right to infringe on any domestic economy; but those ladies, who continue in a state of celibacy, and find pleasure in literary researches, have a right to indulge the propensity, and solace themselves with the feast of reason and knowledge; also those ladies who in youth have laid up a treasure of literary and scientific information, have a right to improve in further literary researches, after they have faithfully discharged their domestic duties. With maternal affections, when her olive branches have spread forth to form new circles in society, the maternal mind has become satiated with the common concerns of life, and the real christian wishes for peace and retirement, for contemplation; and this is the most convenient season for to take a retrospect of past scenes, and this is a fully ripe season to read, write, meditate and compose, if the body and mind are not enfeebled by infirmities. The well informed mind, if still in full vigour, is now fully ripe for composing; and females of that class must have a right to unbend their minds in well digested thoughts for the improvement of the rising generation; and if they can by well digested sentiments, implant in the youthful breast, by precept and their example, the seeds of virtue and religion, it will fully compensate, for a long life of toil and study. The furrows of age shall be cheered with the expectation of a rich harvest of mental improvement and satisfaction; and where religion sways, the whole deportment will be calm, serene and placid, and the infirmities natural to the decline of life, will be alleviated in the bright prospect of immortality, to which both sexes are equally entitled to aspire.

Women have an equal right, with the other sex, to form societies for promoting religious, charitable and benevolent purposes. Every association formed for benevolence, must have a tendency to make man mild, and sociable to man; an institution formed for historical and literary researches, would have a happy effect on the mind and manners of the youth of both sexes. As the circulating libraries are often resorted to after novels by both sexes for want of judgment to select works of more merit, the study of history would strengthen their memory, and improve the mind, whereas novels have a tendency to vitiate the mind and morals of the youth of each sex before they are ripe for more valuable acquisitions. Much abstruse study or metaphysical reasoning seldom agrees with the natural vivacity or the slender frame of many females, therefore the moral and physical distinction of the sex must be allowed; if the powers

of the mind are fully equal, they must still estimate the
rights of men, and own it their prerogative exclusively to
contend for public honours and preferment, either in
church or state, and females may console themselves and
feel happy, that by the moral distinction of the sexes they
are called to move in a sphere of life remote from those
masculine contentions, although they hold equal right with
them of studying every branch of science, even jurispru-
dence.

But it would be morally wrong, and physically im-
prudent, for any woman to attempt pleading at the bar of
justice, as no law can give her the right of deviating from
the strictest rules of rectitude and decorum. No servile
dependence on men can be recommended under the christian
system, for that abolished the law of slavery, and left only
a claim on their friendship; as the author of their nature
originally intended, they should be the protectors of female
innocence, and not the fatal destroyers of their peace and
happiness. They claim no right at the gambling table, and
to the moral sensibility of females how disgusting must be
the horse-race, the bull-bate, and the cock-fight. These
are barbarous scenes, ill suited to the delicacy of females.

It must be woman's prerogative to shine in the domestic circle, and her appropriate duty to teach and regulate the opening mind of her little flock, and teach their
juvenile ideas how to shoot forth into well improved sentiments. It is most undoubtedly the duty and privilege of woman to regulate her garrison with such good order and propriety, that the generalissimo of her affection, shall never
have reason to seek other quarters for well disciplined and
regulated troops, and there must not a murmur or beat be
heard throughout the garrison, except that of the heart vi-
brating with mutual affection, reciprocally soft. The rights
of woman displayed on such a plan, might perhaps draw the
other sex from the nocturnal ramble to the more endearing
scenes of domestic peace and harmony. The woman, who
can gain such a victory, as to secure the undivided affection
of her generalissimo, must have the exclusive right to shine
unrivalled in her garrison. There is no distinction of sexes
in heaven, which may be found agreeable to scripture in our
blessed Master's answer to the Sadducees when they inter-
rogated him respecting the woman who had been the wife of
seven brethren, Matthew xxii. 29, 30. Jesus answered and
said unto them, ye do err, not knowing the scriptures, nor

the power of God. For in the resurrection they neither marry nor are given in marriage, but are as the angels of God in heaven. . . .

SARAH WENTWORTH APTHORP MORTON

(1759-1846)

Sarah Wentworth Apthorp Morton was born in Boston in 1759.
Her father, James Apthorp, was a prosperous merchant; her
mother was descended from a leading New Hampshire family,
the Wentworths. Sarah was brought up in Boston and nearby
Quincy (then a part of Braintree). At the age of twenty-one
she married a Boston lawyer, Perez Morton. During her
married years she lived first in Boston and then in Dorchester, bore five children, produced a steady output of poems (several of book length), and established herself as a
leader in Boston literary circles. Her marriage in its early
years was rocked, but not wrecked, by a love affair between
her husband and her sister, the sister ultimately committing
suicide. This scandal was used by William Hill Brown, an
acquaintance of the Mortons, as the basis for his didactic
novel, The Power of Sympathy (1789), usually credited with
being the first American novel and long thought to be from
the pen of Sarah Morton herself.

Morton's poetry is unread and perhaps unreadable to-
day. Her only book of continuing interest is My Mind and
Its Thoughts (1823), from which the selections in this volume
have been excerpted. The book's title exactly describes its
contents: a miscellany of personal observations and brief
familiar essays reflecting her thoughts during a full and
sometimes tragic life. She died in 1846 in her old home
in Quincy, where she had moved after her husband's death
nine years earlier.

Sarah Morton states that men in her time had a better
life than women. They had authority, dignity, and pleasures.
Women suffered, sacrificed, and bore sorrows. However,
instead of exploring these apparent inequities in life's roles,
she goes on to say that women are not physically, mentally,
or morally able to do what men can, and thus rationalizes
their lesser status in life. She then defines women by their

73

74

relationships to men rather than as individual beings. Women,
she states, basically civilize men; they are companions, confidants, comforters, and "guardians of his happiness." One
could say that her value was in opening up valid areas of
thinking; however, she pursued none to a logical conclusion
or in any depth.

For further information on Morton, see Emily Pendle-
ton and Milton Ellis, Philenia: The Life and Works of Sarah
Wentworth Morton (1931).

From MY MIND AND ITS THOUGHTS

Rights and Wrongs
Essay VI

How prone is the daring mind to assert its individual rights,
how seldom does it recur to its personal duties. As if the
mere abstract power implied the necessity, admitted the fitness, gave permission, or, in fact, brought apology for de-
viation of any kind.

Since to every individual right, there is morally an-
nexed a relative duty; if the wife or daughter of a prosperous
or industrious man have the right of subsistence from his in-
come, or through his exertions, there is equally due the re-
turns of attention, assistance and obedience. Even as political protection claims allegiance, support implies dependence,
and benefits call for every possible remuneration.

Mary Wolstoncroft [sic], by her pernicious precepts,
and still more pernicious practice, has, in proclaiming "the
rights of woman," involved the sex in more real wrongs, and
been the occasion of greater restraints upon their intellectual
character, than the whole host of masculine revilers; since,
if those who are most capable of comprehending the perfection
of moral beauty, turn aside, in preference, to the deformity
of vice, if the clear light of knowledge prove to the female

vision, a mere ignis fatuus, leading on and plunging down to
deep depravity and hopeless perdition; it were better, infinitely better, to remain amid the darkness of folly, or in the
vacuity of ignorance.

Yet if one presumptuous woman, possessed of mind,
and cultivating its attainments, has vainly rejected the good,
in weak preference of evil, not only by personal error, but
by profligate opinion, wandering from the straight path, with
endeavours to seduce the innocent, and mislead the unwary;
let her remain the land-mark and not the model of her kind;
while the correct and capable translator of Epictetus, the
pious and enlightened Barbauld, the instructing and delighting
Edgeworth, the profound, the eloquent, the admired Lucy
Aikin, with the many, and nearly innumerable female writers,
whose genius, virtues, and feminine graces, having improved
and embellished the sex, and the species, still remain exam-
plars worthy of applause, and meriting imitation.

Let these, and such as these, be seen effectually con-
vincing, and eventually converting, the disclaimer and the
skeptic; by their own incontrovertible evidence, be it admitted,
that cultivated talents, and literary endowment, may, in mel-
iorating the condition of the individual, instruct the mind,
improve the heart and protect the morals, even of the least
powerful portion of the human family.

Mary Wolstoncroft, affecting to appear a hot-headed
Republican, resorted to revolutionary France, and in the
levity of her restless and unsubdued spirit, among jacobin
compatriots, learned to distort and to distract; like those
Architects of ruin, was ambitious to overthrow, and destroy;
but how did the daring experiment end? Even by a life of
mental extravagance, and counteracted passions, an attempted
suicide, and a disastrous fate. In fine, misery, ignominy
and destitution.

In throwing aside the regulations, and disdaining the
consolations of christianity, the morals and the destiny of
this woman would have dishonored the principles, and disgraced the profession of a pagan.

Most surely, neither the physical, the mental, nor the
moral constitution of woman, admit of her leading armies,
or directing navies. To hold the helm of command either
upon the ocean or the soil; she cannot acquire the hardy
nerve of the surgeon, nor the bold voice of the public ora-

tor; debate does not become her, and her authority is never to be maintained by coercion. Yet her station is high and important; her influence and her duties, lasting and mighty; the enchantment of beauty, the delight of kind and healing conciliations, the world of literature, the fine arts, the eloquent superiority of conversation, with the homage of admiration, respect and attachment, are supremely her own. Also the first ideas of filial infancy, the early impressions of maturing youth, and the late consolations of departing age, are her peculiar attributes.

What is man, deprived of honourable affectionate woman? A brutal sensualist, or a gloomy misanthrope, whom individuals do not respect, and the best portion of society derides and deserts.

Neither has it been thought that political opinion, the sciences, nor any of those themes, which interest the feelings, and occupy the understanding of her companion man, are so far out of her department as to be regarded by woman with indifference, provided violence and supercilious demeanour be not permitted to carry their disgrace to her person.

When high endowments and decided talents are united with mild manners and modesty of deportment, they will please in either sex; and for woman, when the despotic reign of beauty has faded away, the influence of such talents, and such manners, will remain powerful and attractive, ever honoured, and always admired.

If the coarse conduct, plain persons, and neglectful habits of some literary women, are decidedly repulsive, those defects, and not the additional accomplishment of understanding, are the cause of that repulsion; for the mind of woman is degraded only, when, forfeiting her real rank and forgetting its influence, she endeavours or affects to steal upon the bold occupations, the active professions, the exclusive dictatorship of man.

To conclude; the high station which woman sustains in the Christian world, is surely due to the benign influence of the Christian religion. What is woman in Barbarian, Pagan and Mahomedan countries? What was she in the polished region of enchanting Greece, or in the glorious empire of triumphant Rome? With the exception of ten or twelve solitary instances, a slave or a victim.

Amid the civilized blessings of Christianity, she is the companion, the confidant, the adviser and the consoler of man--the guide and guardian of his happiness, the comforter of his afflictions, upon whose attractions his eye dwells, and his hope rests, from the first dawn of awakened reason, to the last shade of declining memory: and from that ever sacred source we are taught that the true rights and the real happiness of woman, are only to be protected and enlarged, by her conforming to its divine precepts of forbearance and reliance, remembering and regarding the reasonable limitation of her power, as the honourable extent of her duties.

Woman
Essay XIV

The influence of Woman in society, is most generally apportioned to her personal charms, and if accomplishments of mind, and elegance of manner be united to these, the fair mortal, exalted to a divinity, receives worship and adoration, in praises, and prayers, and sacrifices.

Yet so fallacious are the very best promises of life, that this brightness of beauty seems, in shining, but to expose, or mislead; hence the most lovely are, even when unerring, usually among the most unfortunate of women; either as the victims of married, or of solitary existence.

Where beauty is, and love is not, envy comes, and fastidious criticism follows. Talents are termed pretence, or accused of ostentation. If modestly conversable, she is deemed conceited. If timidly silent--stupid. The graciousness of true delicacy is held as affectation; reserve imputed to pride, and the heavenly smile of native attraction, given to coquetry: while the langour of disgust and distress, resulting from baffled hopes, and counteracted affections, is considered a false display of interest, and assuming refinement.

Such are the evil passions of the great world, there, Beauty finds but few friends, and accomplishment many foes; and yet, contradictory as it may seem, the attraction of young and innocent loveliness cannot ultimately be resisted. The magnet of her influence not only impels the strong and polished steel of masculine mind, but like the pure and precious composition of amber, attracts and collects the more worthless and volatile substances of the earth.

At the same time, and under every circumstance, for her, envy always lives, and never disappears; the enchantment of her influence can neither disarm the fury, nor avert its detractions, nor command her own destiny to rise beyond the reach of any earthly misfortune.

If of youthful and accomplished Beauty, such are the fortunes and the fate; neither is it thought that happiness will come with faded bloom, and bringing the oblivion of wrongs; since, when no longer young, like dethroned monarchs, born to arbitrary power, it is as difficult for the abdicated beauty to forego authority, and to feel submission, as it is for the loyal and obedient lover, living on retrospection, to bestow the homage of his passionate regard on the mere dream of long extinguished glory.

But safety, and serenity, may, at this period be her own, if not rejected for the vain hope of yet reaping the exhausted field of conquest: where wounds, defeat, and consequently disgrace, are the only remaining harvest.

In fine, let the sensible amiable woman, who pleases without the sorcery of personal charms, and who can interest by manners, mind and morals, reflect, that if her empire be less supreme than that of unfortunate beauty, it has more of peace, and is of greater duration, less of bitterness and inevitable disaster. Since to her, the world is kind; it grants to her affections the reward of fidelity--it allows to her misfortunes the loyalty of respect--it concedes to her virtues the tribute of approbation.

Marriage
Essay XV

Man looks for honour and for happiness, and with these in view, he marries. That disappointment may not cross his path, let him reason on effects, and in his wanderings and through his seekings, be not unmindful of consistency and coincidence.

She who has proved an observant daughter, and been an obliging sister, cannot fail of becoming a true and amiable wife; as, having held sacred the native charities, she will not slight those which society has instituted.

Having studied and learned, to confer with willingness,

and to comply with readiness, she will equally understand
where to command with instruction, and how to preside with
decorum; and in respecting the mild duties of domestic subordination, display the dignified gentleness of real authority.

Has she practiced and preferred the simplicity of elegant neatness, as beyond the lustre of costly decoration?
she will, in her household, prove more regardful of econom-
ical propriety, than of ostentatious display.

While in her heart religion is a sentiment, affianced
to the sanctity of morals, she will give meekness and mod-
eration to mark its course, and to prescribe its limits:
while that attentive usefulness, which in all things regards
the relative and the social, remains the best hand-maid of
rectitude and propriety.

Has she honoured her first home, in feeling that her
kindest duty and her first good principles originated there?
surely she will never permit that duty and those principles
to wander from her better and more permanent establishment.

The woman who has known, and does in all truth, follow the precept of such opinions, and is happily selected by
the husband of her love, and obtains in that husband, a guardian, and guide, of kind and capable superiority; a friend,
trusting and assiduous, an affection, undeviating and unsus-
pecting; let him not doubt that his will be the home of honour, and of happiness: since among the events of human
life, nothing is more unusual than the dereliction of a strictly
educated woman, who has realized in the object of her preference, goodness, confidence, fidelity and protection.

For a woman thus taught, and thus habituated, is tender and grateful; she feels, and she sympathizes; she re-
flects and she benefits--her desire to merit estimation, and
her hope to obtain respect; for she well knows that in the
moral observances there is worth and reputation; but her
heart also aspires to the blessings of honour and of happiness; from the possession of which, if she have delicacy,
she dare not, and if she have understanding, she does not
wander.

Yet should the donation of that honour which regards,
and the possession of that happiness which rewards, be denied to her virtues, when her pure and sensible heart awak-
ens to hope, and animates to reciprocation; is it harrowed

by disappointment, and distressed by dissimilarity? is it defrauded of that protection, and refused that fidelity, which she sought, in which she trusted, and would gratefully and eternally have cherished; does she find herself pitied by the affectionate, and possibly admired by the presumptuous; at once pursued and repulsed--pure in conduct, perhaps beautiful in person--yet left to coldness, neglect and desertion-- what remedy remains?

Even that of her own approving conscience! with the high estimation of the good, who can understand her feelings and her fate; and the tender and applauding sentiment of the benevolent, who are willing to sympathize with every sufferer.

The million--blending the penalties of misfortune with those of misconduct, may, in their ignorance, mistake the true meaning of such a mind, and seeing her surrounded by attractions and followed by injuries, even think it possible that the sacredness of principle would not rise above the united influence of both; as if the Almighty had not endowed the guileless with strength apportioned to their trials.

Yet these--even the million--will learn to know, and in knowing, to venerate, where veneration is legitimately due.

HARRIOT KEZIA HUNT

(1805-1875)

Harriot Kezia Hunt was born in Boston in 1805, the daughter
of Joab and Kezia (Wentworth) Hunt. Both parents were of
old New England stock. Her father was a shipbuilder, a
navigator, and, in a small way, a ship-owner. Her mother
was deeply involved in philanthropic works. Religion was
taken seriously in the Hunt family. The husband was originally a Congregationalist and the wife a devout Episcopalian,
but after their marriage both were converted to Universalism,
which taught the un-Calvinistic doctrine that God's intention
is to save all souls rather than only a chosen few. Harriot
Hunt later abandoned Universalism in favor of the mysticism
of the Swedenborgian New Church.

Harriot and her younger sister, Sarah, were educated
in private schools in Boston. For a time Harriot conducted
a school of her own, but later, coming under the influence
of an English couple, Dr. and Mrs. Mott, who had set up in
Boston as practicing physicians, she became a fervent student
of medicine. Her sister joined her in these studies, and
eventually the two began the practice of medicine themselves--
the first American women to do so. Their practice, which
was frowned upon by the medical profession, was mainly
among women and children, and of course they were excluded
from hospitals. Later Sarah married and withdrew from
medical practice, but Harriot continued to build up a reputation based on her many cures where other physicians had
failed. Her methods were unconventional, relying mainly on
bodily and dietary hygiene rather than on dosages of medicines as prescribed with abandon by most doctors of the day.
Moreover, she was convinced that many illnesses, especially
among women, were traceable to emotional and spiritual
problems and could be cured or alleviated by sympathetic
counseling. The restrictions on and deprivations of women--
education inadequate as preparation for the exigencies of life,
lack of training for remunerative work, exclusion from most

81

of the professions, and the like--she considered to be con-
tributory to many of the ailments of her patients. Thus she
was a vehement advocate for broader rights and liberties for
women. She herself had of course been ineligible for admission to medical school, having received her training under
the tutelage of the Motts. She had once applied for permission to attend lectures on medicine at Harvard, but her request had been denied. When later she was granted permission, the senior class, already incensed by the admission of
three blacks to the school, objected so vigorously that she
decided not to attend. Eventually she received an honorary
M. D. degree from the Female Medical College of Philadelphia.

Harriot Hunt lectured widely on physiology and in 1843
founded a Ladies' Physiology Society. She believed that women would benefit from an understanding of the functioning
of their bodies--a knowledge that most male doctors failed
to impart to them. She also involved herself in other reform movements, among them temperance and abolition.
Yearly after 1852, on paying her taxes in Boston, she
submitted the letter of protest included below. In 1856 she
published an autobiographical volume, Glances and Glimpses;
or Fifty Years Social, Including Twenty Years Professional
Life.

In her philosophy of medicine Hunt puts forth many
ideas that have become common in recent medical thinking
in this country. Formerly it was the practice to keep the
patient ignorant of his or her condition when the doctor
thought it advisable. Within the past decade a law was
passed giving patients the right to see their records.
Hunt's idea about sharing information with the patient we
now know is based upon the sound belief that "not knowing" provokes more anxiety and fear than explanation and
discussion of an illness. Her holistic approach demands
that we should know our body and be responsible for our
health and that patients as well as doctors play a part
in curing illness. She stresses the importance of the influence of the mind on the body. These last two concepts are
not always discussed in detail in medical-school curricula
even today.

From GLANCES AND GLIMPSES

From Chapter XI

Years came laden with duties and uses, and they went away.
What burden did they take with them? This is often the
searching question the soul asks. In healthy mental conditions we realize the value of duties performed and uses accomplished. The reader who has followed me thus far,
must perceive that these calendar cycles of time had a
great mission for us sisters. They gave us deep, earnest,
interior experiences. They brought to our view all activities of mind and body individually and collectively; and each
demanded our utmost clearness of perception, and all different standpoints of observation. Diseases of the mind--
nervous affections in their diverse forms and endless vari-
ety--overaction on one hand, and inaction on the other--both
preparing their several victims for insane asylums--pre-
sented themselves for medical treatment. I regret that I
did not faithfully note each case on paper. Various were
the conditions of those who called upon us. The refined and
elegant owner of thousands, the inheritor of wealth, the quiet
vest-maker, who, for years, had day after day wrought
stitch by stitch in her work, came with her experience; the
poor orphan girl, boarding out respectably, and living a life
of painful self-denial that she might do so--for she was a
sempstress with no superfluity of wages--came also. A
kind word to such has filled their eyes with tears, and a
kind pressure of the hand strengthened their souls as well
as ours--for their trust in us taught us to trust in our Heavenly Father. Yes:--many children, and girls, and women
found their way to us that they might obtain from woman an
interest in the diseases which often grew out of their hardships. It was startling to read these chapters of real life,
so often written in the language of sorrow and pain. How
frequently I have heard that woman's sphere is at home,
and, remembering the many women among my patients whose
poverty denied them a home, felt the cruelty of this mockery
of the poor! On the other hand, I met with many women
who had homes filled with every luxury, and cared not for
the treasure; for while labor is considered mean and servile,

your woman of the world will think a home troublesome, annoying, and perplexing. Young girls came to me for relief; the secret of their maladies was in their overtaxed brains, for their education was to be finished at eighteen years--and these poor deluded children--as well as their mothers, really thought going to school was education, and leaving it for the market was life! When I traced diseases to causes like these, I never feared to use the utmost boldness of speech; for I certainly felt that volcanic eruptions of condemnation were safe remedial agents, when love had melted the lava. The awful and utter perversions of life which I constantly witnessed, would have chilled my ardent nature, had I not known that ignorance of physical laws was the cause of them all. I wondered and wondered again why physicians had not enlightened the families they attended, and awakened their attention to this great subject. I often found myself soliloquizing in this way:--Why Dr. ------ has been the attending physician in that family for nearly a quarter of a century, and its members do not know the first hygienic rule! I took this for a hint, and many people I attended can bear testimony to their being their own physicians after my visits, except in cases of emergency. The slight and contempt with which some doctors spoke of us to their patients when they found them opening their eyes, deepened by conviction of their unfaithfulness. Wherever I had aroused a family to thought on these matters, I heard that the attending physician, with few exceptions, had said something to this effect--"It is not fitting for women to know about themselves; it makes them nervous!" My sisters, what a comment on woman! About a score of righteous physicians in this city saved the profession. Judge for yourselves if this be true. I remember a conversation I had with a lady patient who was telling me of the quarrel she had had with her family physician, who utterly opposed any recognition of women in the profession. Said she to me, "He was so obstinate! He said 'it would make women nervous to know about themselves.'" "Are they not nervous enough through ignorance?"--I asked him; "but it won't do for them to be physicians." I interrupted her by asking his name. She told me. "Now," said I, "I have a message for this doctor--will you give it to him?" "Yes," she answered. "Very well," I continued; "now for the message:--I know that his last year's bill, to a certain family in this city, was three quarters less than it has been for years. I know also that some of that family consulted me; and I know that I have not received the large amount of this difference. Now tell him Harriot K. Hunt had but a small bill in comparison with his, to present to

that family; but that she was permitted to arouse its members to their daily violation of physical laws, by which their
repeated sicknesses were first created and then developed.
Say still further to your medical friend, that I am very happy to share his displeasure with George Combe and others;
and tell him that it was the knowledge I gave his patients,
and which they acted upon, and not the money they paid me
for attendance, that has lessened his bill!" Experiences of
this nature--some sad--some amusing--met me constantly.
In the journeys I was in the habit of taking, --so many of my
own speculations received confirmation, and were lifted to
the dignity of facts, that I marvelled.   Country, as well as
city, practice gave me a broader view of this need of woman
in the medical life--the positive want of her, and the havoc
of health without her.   Not that I was a physician and bent
every thing down to my idea; but that my idea was bent down
by every thing.   Before me was the broad field of the diseases of women; and certainly men had had no one there to
interfere or compete with them in giving relief; why, then,
was every thing in this state, if their practice had been
right?   There had been no professional interference on the
part of woman!   I want the reader's attention here.   How
did matters stand when woman first came into the profession?

     In a few years the medical profession will be equally
shared between men and women; public opinion is fast tending to bring this about.   Now we would forestall a question
which will then unavoidably arise.   Is the health of woman
improved by this innovation--normality is not, but feeble suffering women are.   But look at the mothers of the present,
and the children who are to become mothers, and ask--What
have we a right to expect, when the majority of male physicians are letting their female patients remain in ignorance of
the physiological laws, whose observance can alone keep them
in health and enable them to transmit it to their children?--
on those physicians, therefore, rests all the responsibility of
the diseases of the future.   The faithful female physician of
that day, must not be expected to cure maladies transmitted
from the present, which the male physicians of the present
will have rendered incurable, by having neglected to prevent.
The patient calls in her doctor for advice; he gives her treatment.   She asks for bread, and gets a stone.   She wants a
homeopathic globule of permanent prevention; he waits till
tendencies ripen to disease, and then gives her an allopathic
dose of temporary cure.

I do not wish to have it understood that I include all physicians in these strictures. There are exceptions in this city who are all that can be desired. Country physicians I only know through their patients--very true mirrors of them! Some I found to be noble and faithful men who had awakened thought; counselled the well; healed the sick; instructed the convalescent in the laws of their maladies to enable them to avoid relapses; and inspired their patients with religious trust. Such physicians are blessed by Him who was the Great Physician. They are an honor to the profession, and, in their respective towns, are recognized as such;--though I was not by them, for if I had had cholera, hydrophobia, smallpox, or any malignant disease, I could not have been more avoided than I was; and I can say that the clergymen generally, did me the honor of placing me in the same professional quarantine as scrupulously as the doctors!

I have said that the quality of homes are labelled on children for the teacher to read. In like manner the quality of physicians is labelled on patients. The continual proof I had of this fact, impressed me with a lasting sense of the deep responsibility attached to the medical life. Weak, discouraging, depressing physicians, were seen in weak, discouraged, depressed patients. I shall, hereafter, throw out some random hours I had with patients, for it is my purpose to awaken public thought to the positive need of women entering the profession. It is not my intention to treat of diseases; for my diagnosis and prognosis would be rather novel, and the character of this book is expressed in its title of Glances and Glimpses. The present state of the medical world is discouraging to the philanthropist; and if this work induces my readers to recall their own observations, or catechize their own experiences on this subject, it will have a salutary effect.

The myriad mysteries of sin are laid bare to the medical practitioner--they are the fruitful causes of suffering. Ah! what need has that practitioner to be a woman, when the patient is a woman wearied, saddened, and broken-hearted with sicknesses, mental and physical! What need is there of the feminine element, when the sins and sorrows of a woman are to be disclosed for the first time--when frenzied memories require soothing--the causes of suffering to be kindly opened and explained, and the remedy to be carefully pointed out! Diseases of women have been treated by us which few male practitioners could have treated, not only because they were beyond the reach of mere medication, and had no nomenclature in the list of maladies, but because the male practitioner could not have drawn their diagnosis, without that confession from the patient which could not be given in most cases with delicacy except to a woman. Here were women whose spiritual sufferings have at length poisoned their physical organizations;--perhaps women who had loved with all the strength and fervor of their natures, and whose love had changed to agony at the revelation of the infidelity of the object of their affections: These causes often produce physical disease, must not the "balm for distempered minds" be among the medicaments for such diseases? Will the women who suffer from them, confide their corroding sorrows to any but those of their own sex, if even to them? I have known love betrayed by a worldling, and the sufferer, sinking in a decline, has come to a woman, who dared say to her, that property had attracted to her side a selfish, heartless man, who had deserted her because her father, then reputed wealthy, had become poor; and thus rescue her from a hopeless malady by arousing her womanhood and awakening her self-respect. Such, are often the diseases the physician is called upon to treat, and such must be the ministrations to a mind diseased. Dosing is of no avail. The medicine, and the diagnosis, are both above the region of physics, in the domain of metaphysics. I do not deny that there are some,--male physicians in whom the feminine element is beautifully developed,--who through faith in something higher than medication, are fully competent to treat such maladies. Nor do I deny that there are a few male physicians who are the confidants of their female patients. But they are few. No male practitioner can demand it as his right, that a woman shall make him her father-confessor; nor is it his office to probe wounds in a nature with which his is not sexually identified. Women of refinement and purity will generally reserve their confidence for those of their own sex. There must be always oneness between the doctor and the patient. The prevailing idea as before remarked is, that the doctor is to cure the disease. It is not so. The doctor and the patient together, are to cure or mitigate the disease. They must be coworkers. In order to be so, there must be the fullest--the most cordial sympathy and frankness between them. It is rarely that this can be so between a male physician and a female patient. Therefore, the female physician, is the physician for the female patient.

This is but a hint, but it may be of service not only to those who are gathering facts and arguments to prove the necessity of medical women, but to all women who are enter-

ing the profession. Let them remember that medication is
second and not first. Let them study to be physicians of the
soul. Let them remember that the souls of patients grow
strong through struggles with mental tendencies and conditions. Bodies are worn with pain that spirits may be puri-
fied. Holy unions within--reconciliations of jarring elements
in the mind--have often broken up external maladies. Diseases are often the result of departures from duty, or law.
It is for the physician to win the patient back to normality--
to duty--as the first and most powerful means of cure. Medication alone is not to be relied on. In one half the cases
medicine is not needed, or is worse than useless. Obedience to spiritual and physical laws--hygeine of the body, and
hygeine of the spirit--is the surest warrant for health and
happiness. It is only the quacks of the profession, emulous
of the quacks ostracized by the faculty, who put their trust
in dosing. The true physician knows better. Let the woman
who has newly entered the medical life remember, that she
must inspire her patients with hope and courage from her
own experience, and thus allay their fears and strengthen
their hopes. She must live so true to physical laws herself,
that her example may enforce confidence in them. She must
always show the warmest--the most affectionate--sympathy
with them. There are those to whom she must only mani-
fest it silently, a pressure of the hand, a look of tenderness
speaks more than language. Perhaps they may be those
whose maladies are issuant from the soul--whose diseases
are the result of some spiritual anguish. They must be approached with the sympathetic love that melts the ice of their
reserve to tears. Such tears are the flowings off of the
frost-bound freshet of sorrow. They presage the subversion
of morbid feelings, and promise a mental state in which the
patient can accept the trials as a wholesome discipline.
These are the opportunities for which the female physician
must watch. The hour of tenderness with the patient, is the
hour for reason with the physician. She has then an opportunity to teach her patient the value of her existence; these
seasons are the golden opportunities in a medical life. Physicians are more or less successful in proportion as they in-
tuitively discern and judiciously use these opportunities.

Heart experiences, whose evidences are broken down
constitutions, are all around us. They take the forms of
fevers, spinal affections, neuralgia, and such like;--accord-
ing to hereditary organization, or temperamental condition.
Their causes are distinct from them. Nostrums are in vain
unless these are recognized, and without their recognition

there cannot be a clear diagnosis. Yet, from male physicians the causes of the diseases of women, as well as the extent of those diseases, are often concealed! Hospitals! if you could speak how you would startle us! When public sentiment grows true on this subject, woman will be allowed to come into those institutions as physicians, and, with the nurse, open books that are sealed. Let the thoughtful and intelligent reader just think of our sex in hospitals without a female practitioner!

I have said before that I was much troubled with my medical reading. It did not seem to meet my cases. Sometimes I found myself querying. Why are my cases so different from those recorded in the books? Why cannot the books determine symptomatic conditions by the eye, the tongue, the pulse? True they did determine symptoms by the state of tongues and pulses; but I soon ceased to place reliance on these indications, finding that transient circumstances, fleeting emotions--a thought, a fear, an angry feeling--could alter them. I was often puzzled, and wished more women were in the profession that we might compare notes and talk the matter over. My desire on the subject became intense, for the more thoughtfully, quietly, and carefully I examined my cases, the more was the conclusion forced upon me, that the false position of our sex had much to do with their diseases; and that as both sexes were suffering, both sexes must come to the rescue:--masculine women and feminine men, if you like that order;--I do not; but I like to see men and women helping men and women.

From Chapter XX

To Frederick U. Tracy, Treasurer, and the Assessors, and other authorities of the City of Boston, and the citizens generally.

Harriot K. Hunt, physician, a native and permanent resident of the City of Boston, and for many years a tax payer therein, in making payment of her city taxes for the coming year, begs leave to protest against the injustice and inequality of levying taxes upon women, and at the same time refusing them any voice or vote in the imposition and expenditure of the same. The only classes of male persons, required to pay taxes, and not at the same time allowed the privilege of voting, are aliens and minors. The objection in the case of aliens, is, their supposed want of interest in our institutions and knowledge of them. The objection in case of minors is, the want of sufficient understanding. These objections certainly cannot apply to women, natives of the city, all whose property and interests are here, and who have accumulated by their own sagacity and industry, the very property on which they are taxed. But this is not all; the alien by going through the forms of naturalization, the minor on coming of age, obtain the right of voting, and so long as they continue to pay a mere poll-tax of a dollar and a half, they may continue to exercise it, though so ignorant as not to be able to sign their names, or read the very votes they put into the ballot boxes. Even drunkards, felons, idiots, or lunatics of men, may still enjoy that right of voting, to which no woman, however large the amount of taxes she pays, however respectable her character, or useful her life, can ever attain. Wherein, your remonstrant would inquire, is the justice, equality, or wisdom of this? That the rights and interests of the female part of community are sometimes forgotten or disregarded in consequence of their deprivation of political rights, is strikingly evinced, as appears to your remonstrant, in the organization and administration of the city public schools. Though there are open in this State and neighborhood, a great multitude of colleges and professional schools, for the education of boys and young men, yet the city has very properly provided two high schools of its own, one Latin, the other English, at which the male graduates of the grammar schools may pursue their education still further at the public expense, and why is not a like provision made for the girls? Why is the public provision for their education stopped short, just as they have attained the age best fitted for progress, and the preliminary knowledge necessary to facilitate it, thus giving the advantage of superior culture to sex, not to mind? The fact that our colleges and professional schools are closed against females, of which your remonstrant has had personal and painful experience, having been in the year 1847, after twelve years of medical practice in Boston, refused permission to attend the lectures of Harvard Medical College, that fact would seem to furnish an additional reason, why the city should provide at its own expense, those means of superior education, which, by supplying our girls with occupation and objects of interest, would not only save them from lives of frivolity and emptiness, but which might open the way to many useful and lucrative pursuits, and so raise them above that degrading dependence, so fruitful a source of female misery.

Reserving a more full exposition of the subject to future occasions, your remonstrant in paying her tax for the current year, begs leave to protest against the injustice and inequalities above pointed out.

This is respectfully submitted,

Harriot K. Hunt, 32 Green street

Boston, Oct. 18, 1852

The protest was copied in many American, as well as some English papers--it elicited inquiry, and many facts were brought to light illustrating the injustice of taxation without representation.   This question is now to be decided.   We take our stand on the Declaration of Independence, an immovable platform.   Liberty inspires us, and justice presents her scales.   Woman slavery has yet to be discussed in connection with African slavery.   No marvel our Southern compatriots look doubtingly on our boasted love of freedom and equality, when the women of New England are deprived of a right, granted recklessly to every foreigner....

(SARAH) MARGARET FULLER

Sarah Margaret Fuller (she later dropped the Sarah) was born in 1810 in Cambridgeport, now part of Cambridge, Massachusetts. Her father, Timothy Fuller, a lawyer, subjected her at a very early age to a rigorous course of study, including history, several languages, English literature, Biblical scholarship, and mathematics. In 1824 and 1825 she attended a girls' boarding school at Groton, Massachusetts, an agonizing experience that is described semifictionally in her story "Mariana," published posthumously in Life Without and Life Within (1874). On her return home she continued her studies under her father's exacting supervision. Among her accomplishments was a mastery of the German language and literature, which found fruition later in a lengthy and perceptive essay on Goethe (Dial, July 1841) and in a translation of Eckermann's Conversations with Goethe (1839). No favorite son could have been given better intellectual and educational training by a father. Her writing on the status of women indicates his success, in that she is clear-thinking and logical. That Margaret Fuller's views are so similar to current writing indicates how little has changed in the past hundred and twenty years.

When Fuller was twenty-three, her father moved his family to a farm in Groton, thus depriving her of association with Harvard friends in Cambridge and making inaccessible to her the Harvard library, to which she was the first woman to be admitted as a reader. Upon the death of her father two years later Margaret perforce took on the support of the family. After several years of school-teaching, one of them at Bronson Alcott's experimental school in Boston, she began to conduct conversations for women on intellectual and spiritual subjects. In the meanwhile she had become acquainted with Emerson and other Transcendentalists and had been welcomed as one of the few female members of the Transcendental Club. From 1840 to 1842 she coedited with Emerson (though she did most of the work) the Dial, in which much of her writing, including "The Great Lawsuit" (July

1843), was published.   A trip West with friends in 1843 resulted in her writing A Summer on the Lakes, a book seldom
read today.   In 1844 she completed her greatest work, Woman in the Nineteenth Century.   In the same year she was
appointed literary editor of the New York Tribune, the first
woman in the United States to be employed as a full-time
journalist.   In 1846, after publishing a volume entitled Papers on Literature and Art, she began a tour of Europe, during which she made the acquaintance of such luminaries as
Thomas Carlyle, Mazzini, and, of great importance to her,
George Sand (Madame Dudevant), whom she admired for her
liberated way of life as well as for her literary talent.   Interested by Mazzini in the cause of Italian independence, she
took up residence in Rome in 1847.   Here she became the
lover of the Marquis Giovanni Angelo Ossoli, a fighter for
Italian freedom.   A son was born to the couple, who were
eventually married.   After the collapse of the insurgent forces
in Rome the Ossolis moved to Florence, where after some
months they took passage for New York.   On July 19, 1850,
all three died in a shipwreck off Fire Island, within a few
miles of New York Harbor.

   The Mariana she describes in her story has obviously
an individual character and personality, and is a free and independent spirit.   Too nonconforming for her time, Mariana
suffered from a lack of understanding and came to a sad end.
But undoubtedly she was an interesting person who did not
fit the usual female role of the day.

   Much has been written about Fuller.   Of especial interest and usefulness are Arthur W. Brown, Margaret Fuller
(1964), Madeleine B. Stern, The Life of Margaret Fuller
(1942), and Paula Blanchard, Margaret Fuller: From Transcendentalism to Revolution (1978).

From LIFE WITHOUT AND LIFE WITHIN

Mariana

Among those whom I met in a recent visit at Chicago was

Mrs. Z., the aunt of an old schoolmate, to whom I impatiently hastened, to demand news of Mariana. The answer startled me. Mariana, so full of life, was dead. That form, the most rich in energy and coloring of any I had ever seen, had faded from the earth. The circle of youthful associations had given way in the part that seemed the strongest. What I now learned of the story of this life, and what was by myself remembered, may be bound together in this slight sketch.

At the boarding school to which I was too early sent, a fond, a proud, and timid child, I saw among the ranks of the gay and graceful, bright or earnest girls, only one who interested my fancy or touched my young heart; and this was Mariana. She was, on the father's side, of Spanish Creole blood, but had been sent to the Atlantic coast, to receive a school education under the care of her aunt, Mrs. Z.

This lady had kept her mostly at home with herself, and Mariana had gone from her house to a day school; but the aunt being absent for a time in Europe, she had now been unfortunately committed for some time to the mercies of a boarding school.

A strange bird she proved there--a lonely one, that could not make for itself a summer. At first, her schoolmates were captivated with her ways, her love of wild dances and sudden song, her freaks of passion and of wit. She was always new, always surprising, and, for a time, charming.

But, after a while, they tired of her. She could never be depended on to join in their plans, yet she expected them to follow out hers with their whole strength. She was very loving, even infatuated in her own affections, and exacted from those who had professed any love for her, the devotion she was willing to bestow.

Yet there was a vein of haughty caprice in her character; a love of solitude, which made her at times wish to retire entirely; and at these times she would expect to be thoroughly understood, and let alone, yet to be welcomed back when she returned. She did not thwart others in their humors, but she never doubted of great indulgence from them.

Some singular ways she had, which, when new, charmed, but, after acquaintance, displeased her companions. She had by nature the same habit and power of excitement that is de-

scribed in the spinning dervishes of the East. Like them,
she would spin until all around her were giddy, while her
own brain, instead of being disturbed, was excited to great
action. Pausing, she would declaim verse of others or her
own; perform many parts, with strange catch-words and burdens that seemed to act with mystical power on her own fancy, sometimes stimulating her to convulse the hearer with
laughter, sometimes to melt him to tears. When her power
began to languish, she would spin again till fired to recom-
mence her singular drama, into which she wove figures from
the scenes of her earlier childhood, her companions, and the
dignitaries she sometimes saw, with fantasies unknown to
life, unknown to heaven or earth.

This excitement, as may be supposed, was not good
for her. It oftenest came on in the evening, and spoiled her
sleep. She would wake in the night, and cheat her restless-
ness by inventions that teased, while they sometimes diverted
her companions.

She was also a sleep-walker; and this one trait of her
case did somewhat alarm her guardians, who, otherwise,
showed the same profound stupidity, as to this peculiar being, usual in the overseers of the young. They consulted a
physician, who said she would outgrow it, and prescribed a
milk diet.

Meantime, the fever of this ardent and too early stimulated nature was constantly increased by the restraints and
narrow routine of the boarding school. She was always de-
vising means to break in upon it. She had a taste, which
would have seemed ludicrous to her mates, if they had not
felt some awe of her, from a touch of genius and power,
that never left her, for costume and fancy dresses; always
some sash twisted about her, some drapery, something odd
in the arrangement of her hair and dress; so that the me-
thodical preceptress dared not let her go out without a careful scrutiny and remodelling, whose soberizing effects generally disappeared the moment she was in the free air.

At last, a vent for her was found in private theatri-
cals. Play followed play, and in these and the rehearsals
she found entertainment congenial with her. The principal
parts, as a matter of course, fell to her lot; most of the
good suggestions and arrangements came from her, and for
a time she ruled masterly and shone triumphant.

During these performances the girls had heightened
their natural bloom with artificial red; this was delightful to
them--it was something so out of the way. But Mariana,
after the plays were over, kept her carmine saucer on the
dressing table, and put on her blushes regularly as the morning.

When stared and jeered at, she at first said she did
it because she thought it made her look prettier; but, after
a while, she became quite petulant about it--would make no
reply to any joke, but merely kept on doing it.

This irritated the girls, as all eccentricity does the
world in general, more than vice or malignity.   They talked
it over among themselves, till they got wrought up to a desire of punishing, once for all, this sometimes amusing, but
so often provoking nonconformist.

Having obtained the leave of the mistress, they laid,
with great glee, a plan one evening, which was to be carried
into execution next day at dinner.

Among Mariana's irregularities was a great aversion
to the meal-time ceremonial.   So long, so tiresome she
found it, to be seated at a certain moment, to wait while
each one was served at so large a table, and one where
there was scarcely any conversation; from day to day it became more heavy to her to sit there, or go there at all.
Often as possible she excused herself on the ever-convenient
plea of headache, and was hardly ever ready when the dinner
bell rang.

To-day it found her on the balcony, lost in gazing on
the beautiful prospect.   I have heard her say, afterwards,
she had rarely in her life been so happy--and she was one
with whom happiness was a still rapture.   It was one of the
most blessed summer days; the shadows of great white clouds
empurpled the distant hills for a few moments only to leave
them more golden; the tall grass of the wide fields waved in
the softest breeze.   Pure blue were the heavens, and the
same hue of pure contentment was in the heart of Mariana.

Suddenly on her bright mood jarred the dinner bell.
At first rose her usual thought, I will not, cannot go; and
then the must, which daily life can always enforce, even
upon the butterflies and birds, came, and she walked reluc-
tantly to her room.   She merely changed her dress, and
never thought of adding the artificial rose to her cheek.

When she took her seat in the dining hall, and was asked if she would be helped, raising her eyes, she saw the person who asked her was deeply rouged, with a bright, glaring spot, perfectly round, in either cheek. She looked at the next--the same apparition! She then slowly passed her eyes down the whole line, and saw the same, with a suppressed smile distorting every countenance. Catching the design at once, she deliberately looked along her own side of the table, at every schoolmate in turn; every one had joined in the trick. The teachers strove to be grave, but she saw they enjoyed the joke. The servants could not suppress a titter.

When Warren Hastings stood at the bar of Westminster Hall; when the Methodist preacher walked through a line of men, each of whom greeted him with a brickbat or a rotten egg,--they had some preparation for the crisis, and it might not be very difficult to meet it with an impassive brow. Our little girl was quite unprepared to find herself in the midst of a world which despised her, and triumphed in her disgrace.

She had ruled like a queen in the midst of her companions; she had shed her animation through their lives, and loaded them with prodigal favors, nor once suspected that a powerful favorite might not be loved. Now, she felt that she had been but a dangerous plaything in the hands of those whose hearts she never had doubted.

Yet the occasion found her equal to it; for Mariana had the kind of spirit, which, in a better cause, had made the Roman matron truly say of her death wound, "It is not painful, Poetus." She did not blench--she did not change countenance. She swallowed her dinner with apparent composure. She made remarks to those near her as if she had no eyes.

The wrath of the foe of course rose higher, and the moment they were freed from the restraints of the dining room, they all ran off, gayly calling, and sarcastically laughing, with backward glances, at Mariana, left alone.

She went alone to her room, locked the door, and threw herself on the floor in strong convulsions. These had sometimes threatened her life, as a child, but of later years she had outgrown them. School hours came, and she was not there. A little girl, sent to her door, could get no answer. The teachers became alarmed, and broke it open.

Bitter was their penitence and that of her companions at the
state in which they found her. For some hours terrible anxiety was felt; but at last, Nature, exhausted, relieved herself by a deep slumber.

From this Mariana rose an altered being. She made
no reply to the expressions of sorrow from her companions,
none to the grave and kind, but undiscerning comments of
her teacher. She did not name the source of her anguish,
and its poisoned dart sunk deeply in. It was this thought
which stung her so. --"What, not one, not a single one, in
the hour of trial, to take my part! not one who refused to
take part against me!" Past words of love, and caresses
little heeded at the time, rose to her memory, and gave
fuel to her distempered thoughts. Beyond the sense of universal perfidy, of burning resentment, she could not get.
And Mariana, born for love, now hated all the world.

The change, however, which these feelings made in
her conduct and appearance bore no such construction to the
careless observer. Her gay freaks were quite gone, her
wildness, her invention. Her dress was uniform, her manner much subdued. Her chief interest seemed now to lie in
her studies and in music. Her companions she never sought;
but they, partly from uneasy, remorseful feelings, partly
that they really liked her much better now that she did not
oppress and puzzle them, sought her continually. And here
the black shadow comes upon her life--the only stain upon
the history of Mariana.

They talked to her as girls, having few topics, naturally do of one another. And the demon rose within her,
and spontaneously, without design, generally without words
of positive falsehood, she became a genius of discord among
them. She fanned those flames of envy and jealousy which
a wise, true word from a third person will often quench forever; by a glance, or a seemingly light reply, she planted
the seeds of dissension, till there was scarce a peaceful affection or sincere intimacy in the circle where she lived,
and could not but rule, for she was one whose nature was
to that of the others as fire to clay.

It was at this time that I came to the school, and
first saw Mariana. Me she charmed at once, for I was a
sentimental child, who, in my early ill health, had been indulged in reading novels till I had no eyes for the common
greens and browns of life. The heroine of one of these,

"the Bandit's Bride," I immediately saw in Mariana. Surely
the Bandit's Bride had just such hair, and such strange,
lively ways, and such a sudden flash of the eye. The Bandit's Bride, too, was born to be "misunderstood" by all but
her lover. But Mariana, I was determined, should be more
fortunate; for, until her lover appeared, I myself would be
the wise and delicate being who could understand her.

It was not, however, easy to approach her for this
purpose. Did I offer to run and fetch her handkerchief, she
was obliged to go to her room, and would rather do it herself. She did not like to have people turn over for her the
leaves of the music book as she played. Did I approach my
stool to her feet, she moved away, as if to give me room.
The bunch of wild flowers which I timidly laid beside her
plate was left there.

After some weeks my desire to attract her notice
really preyed upon me, and one day, meeting her alone in
the entry, I fell upon my knees, and kissing her hand, cried,
"O Mariana, do let me love you, and try to love me a little."
But my idol snatched away her hand, and, laughing more
wildly than the Bandit's Bride was ever described to have
done, ran into her room. After that day her manner to me
was not only cold, but repulsive; I felt myself scorned, and
became very unhappy.

Perhaps four months had passed thus, when, one afternoon, it became obvious that something more than common was brewing. Dismay and mystery were written in
many faces of the older girls; much whispering was going
on in corners.

In the evening, after prayers, the principal bade us
stay; and, in a grave, sad voice, summoned forth Mariana
to answer charges to be made against her.

Mariana came forward, and leaned against the chim-
neypiece. Eight of the older girls came forward, and preferred against her charges--alas! too well founded--of cal-
umny and falsehood.

My heart sank within me, as one after the other
brought up their proofs, and I saw they were too strong to
be resisted. I could not bear the thought of this second disgrace of my shining favorite. The first had been whispered
to me, though the girls did not like to talk about it. I must

confess, such is the charm of strength to softer natures, that neither of these crises could deprive Mariana of hers in my eyes.

At first, she defended herself with self-possession and eloquence. But when she found she could no more resist the truth, she suddenly threw herself down, dashing her head, with all her force, against the iron hearth, on which a fire was burning, and was taken up senseless.

The affright of those present was great. Now that they had perhaps killed her, they reflected it would have been as well if they had taken warning from the former occasion, and approached very carefully a nature so capable of any extreme. After a while she revived, with a faint groan, amid the sobs of her companions. I was on my knees by the bed, and held her cold hand. One of those most aggrieved took it from me to beg her pardon, and say it was impossible not to love her. She made no reply.

Neither that night, nor for several days, could a word be obtained from her, nor would she touch food; but, when it was presented to her, or any one drew near for any cause, she merely turned away her head, and gave no sign. The teacher saw that some terrible nervous affection had fallen upon her--that she grew more and more feverish. She knew not what to do.

Meanwhile, a new revolution had taken place in the mind of the passionate but nobly-tempered child. All these months nothing but the sense of injury had rankled in her heart. She had gone on in one mood, doing what the demon prompted, without scruple and without fear.

But at the moment of detection, the tide ebbed, and the bottom of her soul lay revealed to her eye. How black, how stained and sad! Strange, strange that she had not seen before the baseness and cruelty of falsehood, the loveliness of truth. Now, amid the wreck, uprose the moral nature which never before had attained the ascendant. "But," she thought, "too late sin is revealed to me in all its deformity, and sin-defiled, I will not, cannot live. The mainspring of life is broken."

And thus passed slowly by her hours in that black despair of which only youth is capable. In older years men suffer more dull pain, as each sorrow that comes drops its

leaden weight into the past, and, similar features of character bringing similar results, draws up the heavy burden
buried in those depths. But only youth has energy, with
fixed, unwinking gaze, to contemplate grief, to hold it in
the arms and to the heart, like a child which makes it
wretched, yet is indubitably its own.

The lady who took charge of this sad child had never
well understood her before, but had always looked on her
with great tenderness. And now love seemed--when all
around were in greatest distress, fearing to call in medical
aid, fearing to do without it--to teach her where the only
balm was to be found that could have healed this wounded
spirit.

One night she came in, bringing a calming draught.
Mariana was sitting, as usual, her hair loose, her dress
the same robe they had put on her at first, her eyes fixed
vacantly upon the whited wall. To the proffers and entreat-
ies of her nurse she made no reply.

The lady burst into tears, but Mariana did not seem
even to observe it.

The lady then said, "O my child, do not despair; do
not think that one great fault can mar a whole life. Let me
trust you, let me tell you the griefs of my sad life. I will
tell to you, Mariana, what I never expected to impart to any
one. "

And so she told her tale: it was one of pain, of
shame, borne, not for herself, but for one near and dear
as herself. Mariana knew the lady--knew the pride and reserve of her nature. She had often admired to see how the
cheek, lovely, but no longer young, mantled with the deepest blush of youth, and the blue eyes were cast down at any
little emotion: she had understood the proud sensibility of
the character. She fixed her eyes on those now raised to
hers, bright with fast-falling tears. She heard the story to
the end, and then, without saying a word, stretched out her
hand for the cup.

She returned to life, but it was as one who has passed
through the valley of death. The heart of stone was quite
broken in her, the fiery life fallen from flame to coal. When
her strength was a little restored, she had all her companions
summoned, and said to them, "I deserved to die, but a gen-

erous trust has called me back to life. I will be worthy of
it, nor ever betray the truth, or resent injury more. Can
you forgive the past?"

And they not only forgave, but, with love and earnest
tears, clasped in their arms the returning sister. They vied
with one another in offices of humble love to the humbled
one; and let it be recorded as an instance of the pure honor
of which young hearts are capable, that these facts, known
to forty persons, never, so far as I know, transpired beyond
those walls.

It was not long after this that Mariana was summoned
home. She went thither a wonderfully instructed being, though
in ways that those who had sent her forth to learn little
dreamed of.

Never was forgotten the vow of the returning prodigal.
Mariana could not resent, could not play false. The terrible
crisis which she so early passed through probably prevented
the world from hearing much of her. A wild fire was tamed
in that hour of penitence at the boarding school such as has
oftentimes wrapped court and camp in its destructive glow.

But great were the perils she had yet to undergo, for
she was one of those barks which easily get beyond soundings,
and ride not lightly on the plunging billow.

Her return to her native climate seconded the effects
of inward revolutions. The cool airs of the north had exas-
perated nerves too susceptible for their tension. Those of
the south restored her to a more soft and indolent state.
Energy gave place to feeling--turbulence to intensity of character.

At this time, love was the natural guest; and he came
to her under a form that might have deluded one less ready
for delusion.

Sylvain was a person well proportioned to her lot in
years, family, and fortune. His personal beauty was not
great, but of a noble description. Repose marked his slow
gesture, and the steady gaze of his large brown eye; but it
was a repose that would give way to a blaze of energy, when
the occasion called. In his stature, expression, and heavy
coloring, he might not unfitly be represented by the great
magnolias that inhabit the forests of that climate. His voice,

like every thing about him, was rich and soft, rather than
sweet or delicate.

Mariana no sooner knew him than she loved; and her
love, lovely as she was, soon excited his. But O, it is a
curse to woman to love first, or most! In so doing she re-
verses the natural relations; and her heart can never, never
be satisfied with what ensues.

Mariana loved first, and loved most, for she had
most force and variety to love with. Sylvain seemed, at
first, to take her to himself, as the deep southern night
might some fair star; but it proved not so.

Mariana was a very intellectual being, and she needed
companionship. This she could only have with Sylvain, in
the paths of passion and action. Thoughts he had none, and
little delicacy of sentiment. The gifts she loved to prepare
of such for him he took with a sweet but indolent smile; he
held them lightly, and soon they fell from his grasp. He
loved to have her near him, to feel the glow and fragrance
of her nature, but cared not to explore the little secret paths
whence that fragrance was collected.

Mariana knew not this for a long time. Loving so
much, she imagined all the rest; and, where she felt a blank,
always hoped that further communion would fill it up. When
she found this could never be,--that there was absolutely a
whole province of her being to which nothing in his answered,
--she was too deeply in love to leave him. Often, after
passing hours together beneath the southern moon, when,
amid the sweet intoxication of mutual love, she still felt the
desolation of solitude, and a repression of her finer powers,
she had asked herself, Can I give him up? But the heart
always passionately answered, No! I may be wretched with
him, but I cannot live without him.

And the last miserable feeling of these conflicts was,
that if the lover--soon to be the bosom friend--could have
dreamed of these conflicts, he would have laughed, or else
been angry, even enough to give her up.

Ah, weakness of the strong! of those strong only
where strength is weakness! Like others, she had the decisions of life to make before she had light by which to make
them. Let none condemn her. Those who have not erred
as fatally should thank the guardian angel who gave them

more time to prepare for judgment, but blame no children
who thought at arm's length to find the moon. Mariana, with
a heart capable of highest Eros, gave it to one who knew
love only as a flower or plaything, and bound her heartstrings
to one who parted his as lightly as the ripe fruit leaves the
bough. The sequel could not fail. Many console themselves
for the one great mistake with their children, with the world.
This was not possible to Mariana. A few months of domestic life she still was almost happy. But Sylvain then grew
tired. He wanted business and the world: of these she had
no knowledge, for them no faculties. He wanted in her the
head of his house; she to make her heart his home. No
compromise was possible between natures of such unequal
poise, and which had met only on one or two points. Through
all its stages she

    "felt
  The agonizing sense
Of seeing love from passion melt
  Into indifference;
The fearful shame, that, day by day,
  Burns onward, still to burn,
To have thrown her precious heart away,
  And met this black return, "

till death at last closed the scene. Not that she died of one
downright blow on the heart. That is not the way such cases
proceed. I cannot detail all the symptoms, for I was not
there to watch them, and aunt Z., who described them, was
neither so faithful an observer or narrator as I have shown
myself in the school-day passages; but, generally, they were
as follows.

    Sylvain wanted to go into the world, or let it into his
house. Mariana consented; but, with an unsatisfied heart,
and no lightness of character, she played her part ill there.
The sort of talent and facility she had displayed in early days
were not the least like what is called out in the social world
by the desire to please and to shine. Her excitement had
been muse-like--that of the improvisatrice, whose kindling
fancy seeks to create an atmosphere round it, and makes the
chain through which to set free its electric sparks. That
had been a time of wild and exuberant life. After her character became more tender and concentrated, strong affection
or a pure enthusiasm might still have called out beautiful
talents in her. But in the first she was utterly disappointed.
The second was not roused within her mind. She did not ex-

pand into various life, and remained unequal; sometimes too passive, sometimes too ardent, and not sufficiently occupied with what occupied those around her to come on the same level with them and embellish their hours.

Thus she lost ground daily with her husband, who, comparing her with the careless shining dames of society, wondered why he had found her so charming in solitude.

At intervals, when they were left alone, Mariana wanted to open her heart, to tell the thoughts of her mind. She was so conscious of secret riches within herself, that sometimes it seemed, could she but reveal a glimpse of them to the eye of Sylvain, he would be attracted near her again, and take a path where they could walk hand in hand. Sylvain, in these intervals, wanted an indolent repose.   His home was his castle.   He wanted no scenes too exciting there.   Light jousts and plays were well enough, but no grave encounters.   He liked to lounge, to sing, to read, to sleep.   In fine, Sylvain became the kind but preoccupied husband, Mariana the solitary and wretched wife.   He was off, continually, with his male companions, on excursions or affairs of pleasure.   At home Mariana found that neither her books nor music would console her.

She was of too strong a nature to yield without a struggle to so dull a fiend as despair.   She looked into other hearts, seeking whether she could there find such home as an orphan asylum may afford.   This she did rather because the chance came to her, and it seemed unfit not to seize the proffered plank, than in hope; for she was not one to double her stakes, but rather with Cassandra power to discern early the sure course of the game.   And Cassandra whispered that she was one of those

"Whom men love not, but yet regret;"

and so it proved.   Just as in her childish days, though in a different form, it happened betwixt her and these companions. She could not be content to receive them quietly, but was stimulated to throw herself too much into the tie, into the hour, till she filled it too full for them.   Like Fortunio, who sought to do homage to his friends by building a fire of cinnamon, not knowing that its perfume would be too strong for their endurance, so did Mariana.   What she wanted to tell they did not wish to hear; a little had pleased, so much overpowered, and they preferred the free air of the street, even, to the cinnamon perfume of her palace.

However, this did not signify; had they staid, it would not have availed her. It was a nobler road, a higher aim, she needed now; this did not become clear to her.

She lost her appetite, she fell sick, had fever. Sylvain was alarmed, nursed her tenderly; she grew better. Then his care ceased; he saw not the mind's disease, but left her to rise into health, and recover the tone of her spirits, as she might. More solitary than ever, she tried to raise herself; but she knew not yet enough. The weight laid upon her young life was a little too heavy for it. One long day she passed alone, and the thoughts and presages came too thick for her strength. She knew not what to do with them, relapsed into fever, and died.

Notwithstanding this weakness, I must ever think of her as a fine sample of womanhood, born to shed light and life on some palace home. Had she known more of God and the universe, she would not have given way where so many have conquered. But peace be with her; she now, perhaps, has entered into a larger freedom, which is knowledge. With her died a great interest in life to me. Since her I have never seen a Bandit's Bride. She, indeed, turned out to be only a merchant's. Sylvain is married again to a fair and laughing girl, who will not die, probably, till their marriage grows a "golden marriage."

Aunt Z. had with her some papers of Mariana's, which faintly shadow forth the thoughts that engaged her in the last days. One of these seems to have been written when some faint gleam had been thrown across the path only to make its darkness more visible. It seems to have been suggested by remembrance of the beautiful ballad, Helen of Kirconnel Lee, which once she loved to recite, and in tones that would not have sent a chill to the heart from which it came.

"Death
Opens her sweet white arms, and whispers, Peace;
Come, say thy sorrows in this bosom! This
Will never close against thee, and my heart,
Though cold, cannot be colder much than man's."

Disappointment

"I wish I were where Helen lies."

A lover in the times of old,
Thus vents his grief in lonely sighs,
And hot tears from a bosom cold.

But, mourner for thy martyred love,
    Couldst thou but know what hearts must feel,
Where no sweet recollections move,
    Whose tears a desert fount reveal!

When "in thy arms bird Helen fell,"
    She died, sad man, she died for thee;
Nor could the films of death dispel
    Her loving eye's sweet radiancy.

Thou wert beloved, and she had loved,
    Till death alone the whole could tell;
Death every shade of doubt removed,
    And steeped the star in its cold well.

On some fond breast the parting soul
    Relies--earth has no more to give;
Who wholly loves has known the whole;
    The wholly loved doth truly live.

But some, sad outcasts from this prize,
    Do wither to a lonely grave;
All hearts their hidden love despise,
    And leave them to the whelming wave.

They heart to heart have never pressed,
    Nor hands in holy pledge have given,
By father's love were ne'er caressed,
    Nor in a mother's eye saw heaven.

A flowerless and fruitless tree,
    A dried-up stream, a mateless bird,
They live, yet never living be,
    They die, their music all unheard.

I wish I were where Helen lies,
    For there I could not be alone;
But now, when this dull body dies,
    The spirit still will make its moan.

Love passed me by, nor touched my brow;
    Life would not yield one perfect boon;
And all too late it calls me now--
    O, all too late, and all too soon.

If thou couldst the dark riddle read
    Which leaves this dart within my breast,
Then might I think thou lov'st indeed,
    Then were the whole to thee confest.

Father, they will not take me home;
    To the poor child no heart is free;
In sleet and snow all night I roam;
    Father, was this decreed by thee?

I will not try another door,
    To seek what I have never found;
Now, till the very last is o'er,
    Upon the earth I'll wander round.

I will not hear the treacherous call
    That bids me stay and rest a while,
For I have found that, one and all,
    They seek me for a prey and spoil.

They are not bad; I know it well;
    I know they know not what they do;
They are the tools of the dread spell
    Which the lost lover must pursue.

In temples sometimes she may rest,
    In lonely groves, away from men,
There bend the head, by heats distressed,
    Nor be by blows awoke again.

Nature is kind, and God is kind;
    And, if she had not had a heart,
Only that great discerning mind,
    She might have acted well her part.

But O this thirst, that nought can fill,
    Save those unfounden waters free!
The angel of my life must still
    And soothe me in eternity!

It marks the defect in the position of woman that one
like Mariana should have found reason to write thus. To a
man of equal power, equal sincerity, no more!--many re-
sources would have presented themselves. He would not have
needed to seek, he would have been called by life, and not
permitted to be quite wrecked through the affections only.

But such women as Mariana are often lost, unless they meet some man of sufficiently great soul to prize them.

Van Artevelde's Elena, though in her individual nature unlike my Mariana, is like her in a mind whose large impulses are disproportioned to the persons and occasions she meets, and which carry her beyond those reserves which mark the appointed lot of woman. But, when she met Van Artevelde, he was too great not to revere her rare nature, without regard to the stains and errors of its past history; great enough to receive her entirely, and make a new life for her; man enough to be a lover! But as such men come not so often as once an age, their presence should not be absolutely needed to sustain life.

From "THE GREAT LAWSUIT. MAN VERSUS MEN. WOMAN VERSUS WOMEN," Dial, IV, 1 (July 1843)

It is not surprising that it should be the Anti-Slavery party that pleads for woman, when we consider merely that she does not hold property on equal terms with men; so that, if a husband dies without a will, the wife, instead of stepping at once into his place as head of the family, inherits only a part of his fortune, as if she were a child, or ward only, not an equal partner.

We will not speak of the innumerable instances, in which profligate or idle men live upon the earnings of industrious wives; or if the wives leave them and take with them the children, to perform the double duty of mother and father, follow from place to place, and threaten to rob them of the children, if deprived of the rights of a husband, as they call them, planting themselves in their poor lodgings, frightening them into paying tribute by taking from them the children, running into debt at the expense of these otherwise so overtasked helots. Though such instances abound, the public opinion of his own sex is against the man, and when cases of extreme tyranny are made known, there is private action in the wife's favor. But if woman be, indeed, the weaker party, she ought to have legal protection, which would make such oppression impossible.

And knowing that there exists, in the world of men, a tone of feeling towards women as towards slaves, such as is expressed in the common phrase, "Tell that to women and children;" that the infinite soul can only work through them in already ascertained limits; that the prerogative of reason, man's highest portion, is allotted to them in a much lower degree; that it is better for them to be engaged in active labor, which is to be furnished and directed by those better able to think, &c. &c.; we need not go further, for who can review the experience of last week, without recalling words which imply, whether in jest or earnest, these views, and views like these? Knowing this, can we wonder that many reformers think that measures are not likely to be taken in behalf of women, unless their wishes could be publicly represented by women?

That can never be necessary, cry the other side. All men are privately influenced by women; each has his wife, sister, or female friends, and is too much biassed by these relations to fail of representing their interests. And if this is not enough, let them propose and enforce their wishes with the pen. The beauty of home would be destroyed, the delicacy of the sex be violated, the dignity of halls of legislation destroyed, by an attempt to introduce them there. Such duties are inconsistent with those of a mother; and then we have ludicrous pictures of ladies in hysterics at the polls, and senate chambers filled with cradles.

But if, in reply, we admit as truth that woman seems destined by nature rather to the inner circle, we must add that the arrangements of civilized life have not been as yet such as to secure it to her. Her circle, if the duller, is not the quieter. If kept from excitement, she is not from drudgery. Not only the Indian carries the burdens of the camp, but the favorites of Louis the Fourteenth accompany him in his journeys, and the washerwoman stands at her tub and carries home her work at all seasons, and in all states of health.

As to the use of the pen, there was quite as much opposition to woman's possessing herself of that help to free-agency as there is now to her seizing on the rostrum or the desk; and she is likely to draw, from a permission to plead her cause that way, opposite inferences to what might be wished by those who now grant it.

As to the possibility of her filling, with grace and dignity, any such position, we should think those who had seen the great actresses, and heard the Quaker preachers of modern times, would not doubt, that woman can express publicly the fulness of thought and emotion, without losing any of the peculiar beauty of her sex.

As to her home, she is not likely to leave it more than she now does for balls, theatres, meetings for promoting missions, revival meetings, and others to which she flies, in hope of an animation for her existence, commensurate with what she sees enjoyed by men. Governors of Ladies' Fairs are no less engrossed by such a charge, than the Governor of the State by his; presidents of Washingtonian societies, no less away from home than presidents of conventions. If men look straitly to it, they will find that, unless their own lives are domestic, those of the women will not be. The female Greek, of our day, is as much in the street as the male, to cry, What news? We doubt not it was the same in Athens of old. The women, shut out from the market-place, made up for it at the religious festivals. For human beings are not so constituted, that they can live without expansion; and if they do not get it one way, must another, or perish.

And, as to men's representing women fairly, at present, while we hear from men who owe to their wives not only all that is comfortable and graceful, but all that is wise in the arrangement of their lives, the frequent remark, "You cannot reason with a woman," when from those of delicacy, nobleness, and poetic culture, the contemptuous phrase, "Women and children," and that in no light sally of the hour, but in works intended to give a permanent statement of the best experiences, when not one man in the million, shall I say, no, not in the hundred million, can rise above the view that woman was made for man, when such traits as these are daily forced upon the attention, can we feel that man will always do justice to the interests of woman? Can we think that he takes a sufficiently discerning and religious view of her office and destiny, ever to do her justice, except when prompted by sentiment; accidentally or transiently, that is, for his sentiment will vary according to the relations in which he is placed. The lover, the poet, the artist, are likely to view her nobly. The father and the philosopher have some chance of liberality; the man of the world, the legislator for expediency, none.

Under these circumstances, without attaching importance in themselves to the changes demanded by the champions of woman, we hail them as signs of the times. We would have every arbitrary barrier thrown down. We would have every path laid open to woman as freely as to man. Were this done, and a slight temporary fermentation allowed to subside, we believe that the Divine would ascend into nature to a height unknown in the history of past ages, and nature, thus instructed, would regulate the spheres not only so as to avoid collision, but to bring forth ravishing harmony.

Yet then, and only then, will human beings be ripe for this, when inward and outward freedom for woman, as much as for man, shall be acknowledged as a right, not yielded as a concession. As the friend of the negro assumes that one man cannot, by right, hold another in bondage, should the friend of woman assume that man cannot, by right, lay even well-meant restrictions on woman. If the negro be a soul, if the woman be a soul, apparelled in flesh, to one master only are they accountable. There is but one law for all souls, and, if there is to be an interpreter of it, he comes not as man, or son of man, but as Son of God.

Were thought and feeling once so far elevated that man should esteem himself the brother and friend, but nowise the lord and tutor of woman, were he really bound with her in equal worship, arrangements as to function and employment would be of no consequence. What woman needs is not as a woman to act or rule, but as a nature to grow, as an intellect to discern, as a soul to live freely, and unimpeded to unfold such powers as were given her when we left our common home. If fewer talents were given her, yet, if allowed the free and full employment of these, so that she may render back to the giver his own with usury, she will not complain, nay, I dare to say she will bless and rejoice in her earthly birth-place, her earthly lot.

Let us consider what obstructions impede this good era, and what signs give reason to hope that it draws near.

I was talking on this subject with Miranda, a woman, who, if any in the world, might speak without heat or bitterness of the position of her sex. Her father was a man who cherished no sentimental reverence for woman, but a firm belief in the equality of the sexes. She was his eldest child, and came to him at an age when he needed a companion. From the time she could speak and go alone, he addressed her not as a plaything, but as a living mind. Among the few verses he ever wrote were a copy addressed to this child, when the first locks were cut from her head, and the reverence expressed on this occasion for that cherished head he never belied.   It was to him the temple of immortal intellect. He respected his child, however, too much to be an indulgent parent.   He called on her for clear judgment, for courage, for honor and fidelity, in short for such virtues as he knew. In so far as he possessed the keys to the wonders of this universe, he allowed free use of them to her, and by the incentive of a high expectation he forbade, as far as possible, that she should let the privilege lie idle.

Thus this child was early led to feel herself a child of the spirit.   She took her place easily, not only in the world of organized being, but in the world of mind.   A dignified sense of self-dependence was given as all her portion, and she found it a sure anchor.   Herself securely anchored, her relations with others were established with equal security. She was fortunate, in a total absence of those charms which might have drawn to her bewildering flatteries, and of a strong electric nature, which repelled those who did not belong to her, and attracted those who did.   With men and women her relations were noble; affectionate without passion, intellectual without coldness.   The world was free to her, and she lived freely in it.   Outward adversity came, and inward conflict, but that faith and self-respect had early been awakened, which must always lead at last to an outward serenity, and an inward peace.

Of Miranda I had always thought as an example, that the restraints upon the sex were insuperable only to those who think them so, or who noisily strive to break them. She had taken a course of her own, and no man stood in her way.   Many of her acts had been unusual, but excited no uproar.   Few helped, but none checked her; and the many men, who knew her mind and her life, showed to her confidence as to a brother, gentleness as to a sister.   And not only refined, but very coarse men approved one in whom they saw resolution and clearness of design.   Her mind was often the leading one, always effective.

When I talked with her upon these matters, and had said very much what I have written, she smilingly replied, And yet we must admit that I have been fortunate, and this should not be.   My good father's early trust gave the first bias, and the rest followed of course.   It is true that I have had less outward aid, in after years, than most women, but that is of little consequence.   Religion was early awakened in my soul, a sense that what the soul is capable to ask it must attain, and that, though I might be aided by others, I must depend on myself as the only constant friend. This self-dependence, which was honored in me, is deprecated as a fault in most women. They are taught to learn their rule from without, not to unfold it from within.

This is the fault of man, who is still vain, and wishes to be more important to woman than by right he should be.

Men have not shown this disposition towards you, I said.

No, because the position I early was enabled to take, was one of self-reliance. And were all women as sure of their wants as I was, the result would be the same. The difficulty is to get them to the point where they shall natural-ly develop self-respect, the question how it is to be done.

Once I thought that men would help on this state of things more than I do now. I saw so many of them wretched in the connections they had formed in weakness and vanity. They seemed so glad to esteem women whenever they could!

But early I perceived that men never, in any extreme of despair, wished to be women. Where they admired any woman they were inclined to speak of her as above her sex. Silently I observed this, and feared it argued a rooted skep-ticism, which for ages had been fastening on the heart, and which only an age of miracles could eradicate.

Ever I have been treated with great sincerity; and I look upon it as a most signal instance of this, that an inti-mate friend of the other sex said in a fervent moment, that I deserved in some star to be a man. Another used as high-est praise, in speaking of a character in literature, the words "a manly woman."

It is well known that of every strong woman they say she has a masculine mind.

This by no means argues a willing want of generosity towards woman. Man is as generous towards her, as he knows how to be.

Wherever she has herself arisen in national or private history, and nobly shone forth in any ideal of excellence, men

have received her, not only willingly, but with triumph.
Their encomiums indeed are always in some sense mortifying, they show too much surprise.

In every-day life the feelings of the many are stained
with vanity. Each wishes to be lord in a little world, to be
superior at least over one; and he does not feel strong enough
to retain a life-long ascendant over a strong nature. Only a
Brutus would rejoice in a Portia. Only Theseus could conquer before he wed the Amazonian Queen. Hercules wished
rather to rest from his labors with Dejanira, and received
the poisoned robe, as a fit guerdon. The tale should be interpreted to all those who seek repose with the weak.

But not only is man vain and fond of power, but the
same want of development, which thus affects him morally
in the intellect, prevents his discerning the destiny of woman.
The boy wants no woman, but only a girl to play ball with
him, and mark his pocket handkerchief.

Thus in Schiller's Dignity of Woman, beautiful as the
poem is, there is no "grave and perfect man," but only a
great boy to be softened and restrained by the influence of
girls. Poets, the elder brothers of their race, have usually
seen further; but what can you expect of every-day men, if
Schiller was not more prophetic as to what women must be?
Even with Richter one foremost thought about a wife was that
she would "cook him something good."

The sexes should not only correspond to and appreciate one another, but prophesy to one another. In individual
instances this happens. Two persons love in one another the
future good which they aid one another to unfold. This is
very imperfectly done as yet in the general life. Man has
gone but little way, now he is waiting to see whether woman
can keep step with him, but instead of calling out like a good
brother; You can do it if you only think so, or impersonally;
Any one can do what he tries to do, he often discourages
with school-boy brag; Girls can't do that, girls can't play ball.
But let any one defy their taunts, break through, and be
brave and secure, they rend the air with shouts.

No! man is not willingly ungenerous. He wants faith
and love, because he is not yet himself an elevated being.
He cries with sneering skepticism; Give us a sign. But if
the sign appears, his eyes glisten, and he offers not merely
approval, but homage.

The severe nation which taught that the happiness of the race was forfeited through the fault of a woman, and showed its thought of what sort of regard man owed her, by making him accuse her on the first question to his God, who gave her to the patriarch as a handmaid, and, by the Mosaical law, bound her to allegiance like a serf, even they greeted, with solemn rapture, all great and holy women as heroines, prophetesses, nay judges in Israel; and, if they made Eve listen to the serpent, gave Mary to the Holy Spirit. In other nations it has been the same down to our day. To the woman, who could conquer, a triumph was awarded. And not only those whose strength was recommended to the heart by association with goodness and beauty, but those who were bad, if they were steadfast and strong, had their claims allowed. In any age a Semiramis, an Elizabeth of England, a Catharine of Russia makes her place good, whether in a large or small circle.

How has a little wit, a little genius, always been celebrated in a woman! What an intellectual triumph was that of the lonely Aspasia, and how heartily acknowledged! She, indeed, met a Pericles. But what annalist, the rudest of men, the most plebeian of husbands, will spare from his page one of the few anecdotes of Roman women?--Sappho, Eloisa! The names are of thread-bare celebrity. The man habitually most narrow towards women will be flushed, as by the worst assault on Christianity, if you say it has made no improvement in her condition. Indeed, those most opposed to new acts in her favor are jealous of the reputation of those which have been done....

HARRIET BEECHER STOWE

(1811-1896)

Harriet Beecher Stowe was born in Litchfield, Connecticut, where her father, Lyman Beecher, was minister of the Congregational Church. After the death of her mother, Roxana (Foote) Beecher, when Harriet was four years old, her upbringing was in the hands of her father and her sister Catharine, ten years her senior. After elementary education in Litchfield she attended a "female seminary" newly founded by Catharine in Hartford. In 1832 Lyman Beecher moved with his family to Cincinnati to take the position of president of Lane Theological Seminary. There four years later Harriet married Calvin Stowe, a member of her father's faculty. She had already had some success as a writer, and after her marriage, in time salvaged from housekeeping and childbearing, she continued to write, publishing in 1843 a collection titled The Mayflower; or, Sketches of Scenes and Characters Among the Descendants of the Puritans. The story included in the present anthology, "The Yankee Girl," first appeared in a gift book, The Token and Atlantic Souvenir for 1842.

In 1850, Calvin Stowe having been appointed to the Bowdoin College faculty, the family moved to Brunswick, Maine. Here Harriet wrote Uncle Tom's Cabin, the book that made her world-famous as well as financially independent. From then until ten years before her death in 1896 she turned out a steady flow of books, the most notable and enduring being a number of loosely constructed novels depicting New England rural and small-town life, among them The Pearl of Orr's Island (1862) and Oldtown Folks (1869). As a Beecher she was intensely concerned with religion, and in her youth had had agonizing doubts about the validity of her own conversion. In later life she abandoned the rigid Calvinism of her father and regularly attended services of the Episcopal Church, whose doctrines conformed more closely to her own growing belief in a God of love rather than of wrath.

A good biography of Stowe is Robert Forrest Wilson, Crusader in Crinoline: The Life of Harriet Beecher Stowe (1941). Perceptive critical studies of her work are Charles H. Foster, The Rungless Ladder: Harriet Beecher Stowe and New England Puritanism (1954), and John R. Adams, Harriet Beecher Stowe (1963).

"THE YANKEE GIRL"

Every land has its own "beau ideal" of woman, and its own ladies have been bepraised in certain good set terms, with which everybody the least read in polite literature is perfectly acquainted. Who has not heard of the noble bearing, the beauty and domestic virtue of the dames of England? Of the sprightliness, grace and fascination of the ladies of France? How have the light footstep of Spain, the melting eye of Italy been said and sung. And to this florist's feast of nations, may not the plain old farmer, New England, come spade in hand, and bring the flower of his own land? Let the English lady be enthroned as the lily, --the French, the ever bright and varying tulip, --the Spanish and Italian, the full moss rose: the richest and most voluptuous of flowers. The Yankee girl is the rose laurel, whose blossoms no garden flower ever excelled in rosy delicacy and gracefulness of form, but whose root asks neither garden-bed nor gardener's care, but will take for itself strong hold where there is a handful of earth in the cleft of a rock, whose polished leaf shakes green and cheerful over the snows of the keenest winter. In her you shall find the union of womanly delicacy and refinement with manly energy and decision, womanly ingenuity and versatility in contrivance, with manly promptness and efficiency in execution.

While some ladies found their claim to interest on a delicate ignorance and inability as to all the practical parts of life, the only fear of the New England girl is that there should be anything that woman ever did, which she cannot do, and has not done a little better than ever it was done before.

Born of frugal parents, who, with any other habits would be
poor, she learns early to make energy and ingenuity supply
the place of wealth. Born in a land where all are equal, no
princess could surpass her in the feeling of self-respect.
Born where the universal impulse of all is to rise, there is
nothing in the way of knowledge and accomplishment, which
she does not hope some day to acquire, and even without
any advantages of culture, womanly tact, quickness of mind,
and lady-like self-possession, add the charm of grace to her
beauty. Now if you wish to find this lady of our fancy you
must not look for her in our cities, where all the young
ladies speak French, play on the piano, and are taught to
be as much like one another as their bonnets. If you wish to
investigate the flowers of a country, you do not look for them
under the shade of damask curtains, in the windows of drawing rooms, but seek them, as they grow free and individual
at the roots of old mossy trees, and in the clefts of over-
hanging ledges of rocks, or forming eye-lashes to the thousand bright eyes of merry brooks. So if you would see this
Yankee girl as she is, take a flight up with us,--up--up--not
to the skies, but to the north of New Hampshire. Alight with
us now in this cosy little nook, where the retiring mountains
have left space for cultivation, and hard hands have been
found to improve it. There, on the green breasted turf, have
been dropped some dozen or so of dwellings, a meeting house,
and a school house, all in very nondescript and unutterable
styles of architecture. There, in that village which never
was roused by the rattle and tramp of the mail coach, whose
only road has a green ribband of turf in the middle, with a
little turfy line on each side, you will perhaps find what I
speak of. How still and sabbath-like seems the place to-day
--does anybody live here? There is nobody to be seen in
the streets--nothing stirring but the leaves of the dense heavy
sugar maples, that shade the old brown houses, and the blue
flies and humble bees which are buzzing about, with great
pretension to business, in the clover fields. But stay! there
are signs of life; else why the rows of shining milk pans,--
and hark! by the loud drawl from the open windows of yonder
school house, you perceive there is a rising generation in the
land. Come with us, where a large, motherly, old-fashioned
house seems to have sat down to cool itself on that velvet
slope of turf, while the broad masses of the maples and the
superb arches of the elms, form an array of foliage about it,
truly regal. That house is the palace royal of one of the
sovereign people of New Hampshire, to wit, Jonathan Parsons. Jonathan is a great man, and rich in the land, a wise
man, and a man of valor, moreover. He is great, politically,

for he keeps the post office. He is rich too, for he is the undisputed possessor of all that he wants. He is wise, for he knows a little more than anybody about him, and as to his valor, it is self-evident from the fact that he has been promoted with unparalleled rapidity to be Captain, Colonel, and finally General Parsons. Accordingly he is commonly recognized by his martial title, "the General." He is a hale, upright, cheerful man of fifty or thereabouts, with a bluff, ruddy face, and a voice as cheerful and ringing as a sleigh-bell. He turns his hand to more kinds of business than any one in the village, and, what is uncommon, thrives in all. He keeps the post office, and therewith also a small assort-ment of groceries, thread, tape, darning needles, tin pans, and axe-heads, and the usual miscellaneous stock of a coun-try store. He has a thriving farm, --possesses legal knowl-edge enough to draw deeds and contracts, and conduct all the simple law business of his neighbourhood, and besides this, he attends, in a general way, not only to the government of the United States, but of all the countries in the world; for Jonathan takes a weekly newspaper from Boston, and makes up his mind once as to all matters and things the world around, and his convictions, doubts and opinions on these points, are duly expounded to his townsmen, while he is weighing out sugar or tea, or delivering letters in the course of the week. It is a pity that the President of the United States or the crowned heads of Europe never send to Jona-than for his opinion, --for they would always find it snugly made up and ready for instant delivery. We have only to say in addition, that besides the patriarchal wealth of flocks and herds, Jonathan has a patriarchal complement of sons and daughters, among whom we shall only mention the eldest, whom we introduce by the ever verdant name of Mary. The village had called her mother a beauty before her, and Mary has borne that name ever since she shook the golden curls of careless childhood. Yet it is not the impression of mere physical beauty that she produces upon you: there is both in-telligence and energy in the deep violet of her eye, and de-cision as well as sweetness in the outline of her beautiful mouth. Her form, naturally slender, is developed by con-stant and healthful exercise, and displays in every motion the elastic grace of her own mountain sweet-brier. And, more than all this, there is a certain cool, easy air, a free-dom and nobility of manner, a good taste in speaking and acting, that give to her, though untaught in the ways of the world, that charm beyond beauty, which is woman's most graceful gift. For this instinctive sense of what really is due to one's self and others--this perception of times, places

and proprieties, which forms the highest attraction of the
lady, though it may be wrought out by laborious drilling, and
the tutelage of etiquette, is often the free gift of nature,
poured on the fair head of some one who has never trod a
carpet, seen a piano, or taken one step in the labyrinth of
artificial life.

Mary's amount of accomplishments, so called, was
small, --including not a word of French, and no more music
than was comprised in the sweetest of natural voices, taught
in the common evening singing school of the village. But as
a daughter and sister and housewife, her accomplishments
were innumerable. Enter the cool, quiet house, not a room
of which boasts a carpet, but whose snowy floors need no
such concealment. The chief of all that is done in the house,
in providing, making, mending, cleaning, and keeping in order, is by the single hands of Mary and her mother. We
know this may lead the minds of some of our readers to very
prosaic particulars. We have heard a deal of heroines playing on the harp and so forth, but who ever heard of a heroine washing or ironing? The most that has ever been accomplished in these respects, was by the lovely Charlotte of
Goethe, whom he introduces to us cutting bread and butter
for her little brothers and sisters. We can assure all our
fair readers who are inclined to be fastidious on the point,
however, that had they lived under the roof of Jonathan Parsons, they could scarcely have been scandalized by any dis-
agreeable particulars. Even at the wash bench, our heroine,
in her neat, close fitting calico, never looked so little like
a lady as some fair ones we have seen in curl papers and
morning gowns, before they were made up for company; and
moreover, much that seems so laborious would be over with
and out of sight, long before they are in the habit of having
their eyes open in the morning. Many days they would find
our heroine in possession of leisure to draw, read, write,
sew or work muslin, quite equal to their own. They would
see that by ingenuity and that quick observation in which pretty women are seldom lacking, she could fashion her attire so
as not to be far from the rules of good usage; and that, though
her knowledge from books was limited, her mind was active
and full of thought, and as ready to flash at the entrance of
knowledge, as a diamond at the entrance of light.

You are not to suppose that a lady of such accomplishments, natural and acquired, a lady of rank and station,
moreover, passed to her seventeenth year unwooed. So far
from it, there was scarcely a personable article in the way

of a beau, who had not first or last tried a hand in this matter. There were two dilapidated old bachelors, one disconsolate widower, half a dozen school masters, one doctor and one lawyer, already numbered among the killed and wounded, and still Miss Mary carried her head with that civil, modest, "what-do-I-care-for-you" air, that indicated that her heart remained entirely untouched--and all the wonder was, whom would she marry?

It came to pass, one bright summer afternoon, that as two young gentlemen, strangers in the village, were riding by the house of Jonathan Parsons, the sudden explosion of a gun caused the horse of one of them to start, and throw his rider, who, falling against a post in front of the door, was very seriously injured. The consequence of all this was, that the two very good looking young gentlemen were detained at the house for some two or three weeks. They were from Canada, and had come down into New Hampshire on a summer shooting and exploring expedition. The younger of them was the young Earl of Beresford, and the gentleman with him, a Mr. Vincent, his travelling companion, to whom happened the unlucky accident. He was so seriously hurt as to be confined entirely to his bed, and my young lord being thus suddenly thrown out of business, and into a dismally calm, roomy, clean, uninteresting old house, with no amusement but to tend a sick friend, and no reading but Scott's Family Bible and the Almanac, thought himself in very deplorable circumstances, until he caught a glimpse of the elegant form and face of Mary, which suddenly roused him from his apathy. Now when one is treading carpeted floors, lounging on damask sofas, and smelling cologne water, a pretty girl is very much a matter of course, unless her beauty be of a peculiarly rare and striking character. But where there are no curtains, no pictures, no carpets, and nothing more luxurious than a very high backed, perpendicular rocking chair, a pretty girl becomes an angel forthwith, and such was the case at present. The young earl really thought, all things considered, that he would do our fair Yankee the honor to institute a flirtation with her--so at least said his manner, when he made his first advances. He was repulsed, however, with a cool and determined indifference, which seemed to him quite unaccountable. We could have told the young gentleman the reason. It was not that Mary had not a woman's love of admiration, when honestly and sincerely offered, but there was something in the gallantry of Beresford altogether too taking-for-granted and condescending. She could perceive from his travelling equipments, his general air and manner, that he had alighted among them from quite another orb of society than any of which she had ever conceived, and there was a something indefinite even in his politeness, that told her that he looked down both on her and her parents as beings of a vastly inferior order, --and the thought roused all the woman's pride within her. No princess of the blood could have been more stately, self-possessed and politely determined to keep one at a distance, than our village beauty.

The Earl of Beresford was a mere man of fashion, with no more than a barely comfortable degree of reflection and feeling. Entirely incapable of estimating the real worth of Mary's character, and valuing her merely by the rules of conventional life, he was still struck, by the quiet determination of her manner, into something like respect. Our gentleman, however, had been thoroughly accustomed to have his own way, and as is usual with such persons, the thing he could not attain assumed in his eyes a sovereign value. He, moreover, piqued himself particularly on his success with women, and was not disposed to yield his laurels in an obscure country village. Consequently, the more Mary receded, the more eagerly he advanced, --the less she seemed disposed to value his attentions, the more obsequious they became, till at length my young lord grew so excited, that he determined on the magnanimous expedient of declaring his name and rank and making love in regular form, rather than lose the game.

"Vincent!--" said Beresford to his friend, one evening, after walking up and down the room several times, adjusting his collar and brushing up his whiskers, like a man that is getting ready to say something.

"Well, Beresford, out with it," said Vincent.

"Vincent, I have come to a very serious determination."

"I should think you might have," said Vincent, laughing. "We have been in serious circumstances lately."

"Nay, but without joking--"

"Well, without joking, then."

"I have determined to be married."

"For the two hundred and fortieth time," replied Vincent.

"Vincent, do be serious."

"Serious! have I not been dolefully serious, ever since I came head first into this philosophic retreat?--However, Will, proceed to particulars, for any news is better than no news."

"Well, then, Vincent, I am determined to marry this lovely little hostess of ours."

"Not old Mrs. Parsons, I presume," said Vincent, laughing, "there would be little eclat in an elopement with her."

Beresford grew angry, but as Vincent still continued to laugh, was at last obliged to join, though with a very poor grace.

"Now, Vincent," he resumed, "you may spare both your wit and your wisdom, for my determination is unalterable:--you know, of course, I mean the lovely Mary."

"Pshaw!" said Vincent, growing serious in his turn. "Now, Beresford, is not this just like you? Because you are here, in a stupid place, and in want of amusement, must you set yourself to ruin the peace of an honest, artless country girl:--it's too bad,--I'm ashamed of you."

"Ashamed! too bad! what do you mean? Did I not tell you that I am going to marry her?"

"And do I not know you will do no such thing!" replied Vincent,--"did you ever see a handsome woman, of honorable principles, that you have not had a six-weeks' vow of marrying?"

"But, Vincent--"

"But, Beresford," interrupted Vincent, "do you not know well enough, that all your vows and promises will wear only till you get to Quebec--and after the first ball then comes the old story,--unavoidable alteration--cruel necessity must prevent, and so forth,--and so the poor girl who has been the dupe of your good looks and fair speeches, is forgotten. Now, Beresford, you know all this as well as I do."

"But, Vincent, you do not understand the case."

"So you have told me regularly in every flirtation since you have been in the country. Come, now, Will, for once be advised, and let this affair alone. Besides, think of the absurdity of the thing,--introducing a wife whom you have picked up, like a partridge, on a shooting tour--nobody knows when or where."

"Oh, as to that," replied Beresford, "I can take her to Quebec and put her into a convent, to acquire accomplishments. She has an air and manner worthy of a countess, now--and then one can make up some little romance as to her parentage,--at all events, marriage is the only terms on which she can be gained, so marry her I will."

"And have you gained her consent, and that of her parents, to this wise scheme?"

"Her consent!" said Beresford,--"of course, she will consent, though I have not yet opened the subject with her."

"And pray how do you know that?"

"How do I know! why, I shall tell her who I am, and plead the cause officially, you see,--and, with all deference to the élite of this region, such offers do not occur every day,--she must see this, of course."

"Well," replied Vincent, "I have seen little of her, to be sure, but from the sobriety of mind and good sense that seem to characterize the family, I have some hopes that you will not succeed."

"That's past praying for, I fear," said Beresford, "if I may judge from certain little indications, and so forth,"-- and Beresford turned on his heel and whistled himself out of the room, with a very contented and assured appearance.

His confident expectations had arisen simply from the fact that our heroine, from the joint influence of acquaintance- ship and natural good humour, had grown, of late, much more approachable; besides which, for a few days past a more marked change of manner had supervened:--Mary had become absent, occasionally melancholy and more than usually ex- citable,--her color was varying, her eye restless, and there was a nervous tremor of manner, entirely different from any thing she had ever before exhibited. The truth was, that she was wholly engrossed by certain little perplexities and sorrows of her own; but, as Beresford knew nothing of the kind, he formed for himself a very natural and satisfactory theory, as to the cause of her altered manner.

Accordingly, at the close of a still afternoon, when Mary's mother and sisters were absent, Beresford stole suddenly upon her, as she was sitting by an open window curtained by green vines. He commenced his enterprise by a series of complimentary remarks, in just that assumed, comfortable way, that is inexpressibly vexatious to an inexperienced and sensitive woman--a manner that seems to say, "I understand all about you, and can manage you to admiration." Mary felt annoyed, yet conscious of her own inability to meet, on his own ground, the practised and ready man of the world, who addressed her.

"Mr. Beresford," she said at length, after some silence, "I presume that all this is very fine in its way, but I beg you will not waste it upon me, --I really have not the cultivation to appreciate it."

Beresford protested that he was entirely and devoutly serious in every word.

"I am very sorry for it, if you are," said Mary, smiling.

Beresford proceeded to reveal his name and title, and to make an offer in regular form.

With some surprise, but with great simplicity and decision, our heroine declined the proposal.

Beresford pleaded the advantages of station he had to offer, his own disinterestedness, and so forth.

"Indeed, Mr. Beresford," replied Mary, "I do not know enough about these things to feel in the least honored or tempted by them. It may, very possibly, seem to you that you do me a great honor by this proposal, but I have no such feeling. You are accustomed to such a different kind of society, such a different manner of estimating things, from any thing I have ever known, that I cannot very well understand your feelings. If I ever marry, it will be one who can fully appreciate the affection I give, for its own sake, and not one who will always look upon me as a sort of ornamental appendage to his station, and so forth."

"Some Yankee pedler or tinker, perhaps," replied Beresford, angrily.

"Very possibly," replied Mary, calmly, "and yet he may be more truly noble, than the only earl I ever had the honor of knowing,"--and our heroine left the room.

"Handsomely done, that!" said the earl, walking up and down the room--"'pon my word, a dutchess could not have executed the thing better. I was a fool for being angry with her, for, after all, it would have been awkward if she had consented,"--and the earl, who never in his life troubled himself five minutes about any thing, made up his mind to pass off the whole as a good joke; and in less than three weeks from this time, he was desperately in love with a captivating little opera dancer at Quebec.

And yet on the evening of that very day, you might have caught glimpses of the white dress of Mary, as she stood beneath the old vine arbour, in the garden, alone with one other, listening to the oft told tale again. But this time one might perhaps see that she listens with no unwilling ear, while a manly hand clasps hers, and words of passionate feeling are poured forth.

"I must go, Mary--brightest, dearest, loveliest,-- with such a form and face, such a soul, what might you not demand in one that dared hope for you, and I have nothing to offer--nothing."

"And do you think that I count a heart and soul like yours for nothing?" said Mary.

"Yes, but there is so long an uncertainty before me-- so much to be done single-handed, and not a soul thinks I shall succeed--not a soul--not even my own mother."

"Yes, George, you know I do," said Mary, "and you know what I say is worth more than all put together."

"Indeed I do--indeed I do,--or I should have given up in despair long ago, my life, my angel."

"To be sure I am an angel," said Mary, "and so I beg of you, believe every word I say,--that six or seven years from this time, you will come back here the great Mr. George Evarts, and everybody will be making bows and shaking hands."

"Ah, Mary!" said the young man, smiling, --and immediately after his face changed; an anxious and thoughtful cloud again seemed to settle upon it, --he took her hand and spoke with an expression of sorrow, such as she had never before seen.

"Mary, I fear I have done you wrong, to involve you in my uncertainties--to make your happiness in any respect dependent on my doubtful success in a long, hard struggle. I ought not to leave you bound to me by any promise. If, during these future years, you see one who makes you an immediate offer of heart and hand--one worthy of you--and you think that if it were not for me--"

"I am to take him, of course," said Mary. "Well, I will remember it. Oh, George, this is just like you, -- always desponding, when you hope most. Come back to me five or ten years hence, and if you have any advice of the kind to give then--why, I'll think of it."

But what was said after this we will not stop to relate; we will only pause a little in our story, to explain the "who and what" of the last scene.

There dwelt in the village, a poor, pale, sickly, desponding widow, whose husband had been a carpenter, but being suddenly killed by a fall, had left to his wife no other treasure than a small house and garden, and as bright and vigorous a shoot of boyhood as ever grew up, fair and flourishing by an old, decaying stock. Little George was a manly, daring, resolute fellow, with a heart running over with affection and protecting zeal for his mother, and for a while he hoed in the garden, drove the cow, milked, and helped in various matters in-doors, with an energy and propriety that caused him to be held up as a pattern in the neighbourhood. But when the days drew on that he should be put to some effective way of making a living, the various wise advisers of his mother began to shake their heads, --for with a deal of general ability he seemed to have no elective affinity for any thing in particular.

There was a good natured shoemaker, who offered fully to teach him the mysteries of his craft, and his mother looked upon it as a providential opening, and George was persuaded to essay upon the lapstone; but it would not do. Then Jonathan Parsons, being a neighbourly, advising man, thought he knew what was best for the boy, and offered to take him

on his farm and make something of him; and so George
wielded spade and hoe and axe, and a very capable young
farmer he promised to be; but after a while he declared off
from this also. In short, he seemed in the eyes of many to
be in danger of falling into that very melancholy class of instances of clever people, who, in common phrase, "don't
seem to stick to any thing."

But the gossips of the place were for once mistaken,
for there was that which George did stick to, after all. He
had in his veins that instinctive something or other, which
leads one to feel after and find what he is made for. George
had come across various odd volumes of books--history,
travels, biography,--and these had awakened in his mind a
burning desire to do or be something in the world--some-
thing, he scarce knew what, and so he determined he would
go to college. And what a sighing and wondering there was
from his old mother, and what talking and amazement among
the village worthies. Jonathan Parsons gave the young man
a faithful and fatherly lecture, from the top of a codfish barrel, on the subject of tempting Providence, and other kindred
topics, enforcing his remarks by alluding to the example of
Jack Simpson, a poor nondescript, who was generally reported to have lost his wits in the attempt to study Latin,
as a most forcible illustration of his argument. Poor George
had but one friend to encourage him amid all this opposition,
and that was our warm-hearted and trusting Mary. He had
become acquainted with her during his stay at her father's,
and she had entered warmly into all his plans, and encouraged his scheme with all a girl's confident, undoubting enthusiasm. They had never, until the evening interview we
relate, settled any definite expectations for the future, for
both knew that it was not a subject to be mentioned to Jonathan Parsons, who would set it down as a clear indication
of lunacy on the part of Mary, and of something worse upon
that of the gentleman.

We will not tell of the year-long efforts that had been
made by our hero, up to the date of his last interview--of
the ragged Latin Grammar studied by firelight at his mother's
hearth--the Euclid pored over during the long hours of the
night, while he was tending a saw-mill for a neighbouring
farmer. Suffice it to say, that alone and unassisted, he had
now conquered the preparatory studies necessary to fit him
for college, and had earned, beside, a small stock of money.
This, his little all, he laid out in a pedler's box and the
necessary outfit for it, and after bidding adieu to Mary, and

promising his mother to send her a portion of all his earnings, he left his native village with the determination never to return, till he had fulfilled the destiny he appointed for himself.

Six years from this time, and Mary was a beautiful woman of three-and-twenty, and not only beautiful, but educated and accomplished; for her own efforts had procured for her advantages of culture superior to what it is the lot of many to attain. George returned to his native village, a newly admitted lawyer, with the offer of a partnership in a very extensive business in Boston. Of course, everybody in the village altered their minds about him directly. His old mother laughed and almost blushed when complimented on her son, and said that somehow George always did seem to have it in him, and his neighbours, one and all, remembered how they had prophesied that George would be a remarkable man. As to Jonathan Parsons, he shook hands with him in extra style, invited him to drop in and see him any time, and even inquired his opinion as to one or two measures of Congress, about which he professed he had not yet made up his mind; and Mary------ah, well! Mr. George and Miss Mary had a deal of business by themselves in the little front room, from which came in time as gay a wedding as ever made an old house ring with merriment; and then they took a house in Boston, and Mr. George Evarts began to make a figure in the papers, as a leading young man in the political world, which made Jonathan Parsons a more zealous reader of them than ever; for, as he often took occasion to remark, "he felt that he had some hand in forming that young man's mind."

Many years after this, the Earl of Beresford and our heroine again met at a court drawing room in his own land, and to her, as the wife of the American Minister, his Lordship was formally presented. He was now a regular married man, somewhat gouty, and exceedingly fastidious in the matter of women, as his long experience on these subjects had entitled him to be. He was struck, however, with the noble simplicity of Mary's manners, and with a beauty which, though altered in style, time had done little to efface; nor did he know, till the evening was over, that he had been in close attendance on the little village beauty of New Hampshire and the wife of a Yankee Pedler.

From "WHAT IS AND WHAT IS NOT THE POINT IN THE
WOMAN QUESTION," Hearth and Home, August 28, 1869

John Stuart Mill says all popular reforms have to go through
three stages--Ridicule, Discussion, Acceptance.

The question of Woman's Rights is just passing out of
the stage of ridicule into that of fair, respectful discussion.
Superficial flings, taunts, and jokes are now less and less
the weapons used, and instead we see such treatises as those
of John Stuart Mill and Dr. Bushnell, which, whatever we
may think of their arguments, are certainly specimens of
earnest thinking.   All the leading magazines of the country
have been opened to one or more distinct, and oftentimes
quite powerful presentations of the question on the woman's
side, and some of the leading editors, such as George W.
Curtis, have declared themselves decidedly in its favor.

But a question of this kind covers so wide a ground,
that it is peculiarly liable to become confused and mixed with
false issues on both sides.   The advocates of reform are apt
to give undue prominence to unessential things, and, in their
intensity, to make over-claims which, in turn, furnish a mark
for the attack on the other side.

We are very desirous that our readers should understand this matter fully for themselves.   We have, of course,
our own private opinions about it; but we are not so much
anxious to bring persons to our way of thinking as to induce
them to think seriously and earnestly for themselves upon the
whole matter.   We believe it to be the present immediate duty
of every thoughtful man and woman to give this question a
careful examination under the best lights they have at command.   For this purpose, the conductors of Hearth and Home
have made arrangements to present to their readers, from
week to week, articles by the best writers whom they can
engage on both sides of the question, and we trust in that
good sense and shrewdness which characterize our American
people to come to just conclusions.

But, in order that they may have a just and clear idea,

in the outset, what is and what is not the question under consideration, we shall just state it in brief.

The practical question now before the American people is this:

Have women the same right to suffrage that men have?

In discussing this question, the only logical way is to determine what are the qualifications that give men a right to exercise suffrage, and to show that women have or have not those qualifications.

This is the course pursued in the Hon. G. F. Hoar's speech before the Massachusetts Legislature. Mr. Hoar quotes from the Massachusetts Bill of Rights, the ninth article, the following words:

> All the inhabitants of this Commonwealth having such qualifications as they (that is, all the inhabitants) shall establish, have an equal right to elect officers, and to be elected to public employment. Every individual of this society has a right to be protected by it, in the enjoyment of his life, liberty, and property, according to standing laws. He is consequently to contribute his share to the expense of this protection; and no part of the property of any individual can with justice be taken from him, or applied to public uses, without his own consent or that of the representative body of the people.

From this declaration of the Bill of Rights of Massachusetts, Mr. Hoar proceeds in a direct logical line to argue the equal rights of women in the State; and we have yet to see any thing like an attempt on the other side to meet this logical argument. It would be difficult to show that women are not individuals and inhabitants of the land, and that they do not pay taxes to support government; and the question therefore is, Which is in the wrong, the principles laid down in the Massachusetts Bill of Rights, or the customs of the laws of Massachusetts in regard to women?

All arguments upon this subject based on the supposed ill effects of political power and liberty on women are nothing to the purpose. They are something like this. Suppose a worthy, industrious farming family, living in a hard but hon-

est way, down on Cape Cod, are discovered, by the researches of some lawyer, to be the heirs to a property of
seven million. But they are very simple people, uninformed
of their rights--rather incredulous--not particularly disposed
to enter into a troublesome and expensive investigation.
Now, say some of the present owners, why disturb these
good people? They are living a plain, healthy, industrious
life--they are perfectly satisfied as they are--they don't
want it. If they should get this sudden fortune, these boys,
now so industrious and sober, would become dissipated and
go to the devil, and these worthy matrons would become
shoddy-fine women. But, says the lawyer, that's neither
here nor there. The only question is, who owns that property and by what title?

Now, it has been generally said that women are il-
logical reasoners, that they mistake poetry for argument,
and instinct for reason.

To us, so far, it really does appear that, in the consideration of this question, the logic has all been talked on
the woman's side, and the tropes and metaphors and poetry
have been wholly on the side of our much-revered and highly
educated brethren. Men are so accustomed to talking down
to women that they really have not as yet seemed to think it
worth while to meet the questions raised by them logically.

The only attempt Dr. Bushnell makes on this vital
point, where all turns, is to say that "nobody has any inherent right to vote." Supposing that, yet can the Doctor
state any reason why he or any other man should vote that
does not apply equally to women? If so, what is it? It is
nothing to the purpose whether there are or are not inherent
political rights. It is sufficient, in this American government, that our fathers supposed there were, and founded
their government on this supposition. They established, in
the Declaration of Independence, and in the State bills of
right, certain axioms, such as these:

> Governments owe their just power to the consent
> of the governed.
> Taxation without representation is tyranny.

We do not propose to raise the question whether they
were right or wrong in these axioms of government: the
simple question is, whether these axioms do not logically
lead to woman's suffrage?

When Choate had to defend the fugitive-slave law, he called the Declaration of American Independence a system of glittering generalities. When Dr. Bushnell would attack the suffrage of women, he refers with approbation to this language. In both cases, we understand this language to be a concession that the great national documents on which our government is founded were against them. But our government, such as it is, is founded and is a fixed fact. Our Declaration of Independence is still before the world as much a part of America as the stars and stripes. Whether it be glittering generalities or not, it is the foundation of all things; it is the justification which our fathers published for their conduct; it is the document on which Lincoln founded the Republican party; and it is now too late to raise the question whether its principles are true, and more to the point to inquire whether these principles, logically interpreted, do not lead to woman's suffrage.

It appears, by a certificate of the tax-assessor in the city of St. Louis, that in that city alone two thousand women pay taxes on the amount of fourteen million four hundred and ninety thousand, one hundred and ninety-nine dollars. Similar results might be gathered from the tax-lists all over the country.

Now, the question arises, Which is in fault, the Declaration of Independence, or the customs and laws of America as to women? Is taxation without representation tyranny or not?

In order further to illustrate our assertion that the course of the women upon this subject has been a strict logical sequence from the fundamental documents of our government, we will copy here the resolutions presented in the first Woman's Rights Convention held at Worcester in the year 1851:

> 1. Whereas, According to the Declaration of Independence of the United States, all men are created equal, and endowed with inalienable rights to life, liberty and the pursuit of happiness; therefore, Resolved, That we protest against the injustice done to woman by depriving her of that liberty and equality which can alone promote happiness, as contrary alike to the principles of humanity and the Declaration of Independence.
> 2. And, whereas, According to an acknowledged

principle of this Republic, taxation without representation is tyranny; and, whereas, the property of
woman is taxed like that of man; therefore, Resolved, That it is an act of the greatest tyranny
and usurpation to deprive woman of her rights of
being represented, of participating in the formation
of the laws, and enjoying all civil privileges in an
equal degree with man.

3. Resolved, That while we would not under-
value other methods, the right of suffrage for women is, in our opinion, the corner-stone of this
enterprise, since we do not seek to protect woman,
but rather to place her in a position to protect herself.

4. Resolved, That it will be woman's fault if,
the ballot once in her hand, all the barbarous, de-
moralizing, and unequal laws relating to marriage
and property do not speedily vanish from the
statute-book; and while we acknowledge that the
hope of a share in the higher professions and prof-
itable employments of society is one of the strongest motives to intellectual culture, we know, also,
that an interest in political questions is an equally
powerful stimulus; and we see beside that we do
our best to insure education to an individual, when
we put the ballot into his hands; it being so clearly
the interest of the community that one, upon whose
decisions depend its welfare and safety, should both
have free access to the best means of education,
and be urged to make use of them.

We are curious to see a fair, dispassionate argument
on the other side, that shall meet this statement of the case.
None such as we know of has been offered.

MARY ASHTON RICE LIVERMORE

(1820-1905)

Mary Ashton Rice Livermore was born in Boston to Timothy
Rice, a laborer, and Zebiah (Ashton) Rice, the daughter of
a ship's captain. She was brought up in the Baptist faith of
her father and was educated in various schools in Boston and
environs, becoming sufficiently versed in Latin, French, and
Italian to teach these languages for several years in the "female seminary" in Charlestown near Boston, from which she
had graduated in 1836. Serving later as a tutor in a Virginia
family, she acquired an abhorrence of slavery and became an
ardent abolitionist.

In 1845 she married Daniel Parker Livermore, a Universalist minister at Leicester, Massachusetts. After living
in a number of New England and New York communities
where Daniel Livermore served as pastor, the couple finally
settled in Chicago upon the appointment of her husband to the
pastorate of the Second Universalist Church there. Before
this time Mary Livermore had become active in the temperance movement and had been writing stories exposing the
evils of alcohol. In Chicago she continued writing on this
and other subjects and helped her husband edit the magazine
The New Covenant, which he had founded. During the Civil
War she did valuable service, recognized by the federal government, in organizing, provisioning, financing, and over-
seeing facilities for the care of wounded soldiers.

After the war Mary Livermore threw herself into the
women's suffrage movement, her main interest henceforth.
In 1869 the Livermore family moved back East to the Boston
suburb of Melrose. For two years she edited the Woman's
Journal, newly founded by Lucy Stone, but left that position
to devote her energies to lecturing, at which she was a resounding success. Though she lectured on many topics, her
main subject was the "woman question" in all of its aspects.
The lecture included here, "What Shall We Do with Our

Daughters?" (published in her The Story of My Life: Or the
Sunshine and Shadow of Seventy Years), was delivered before
more than eight hundred audiences. Among those who heard
it was Louisa May Alcott. In this and other lectures Livermore took up and elaborated on themes touched on by Margaret Fuller in Woman in the Nineteenth Century (1845). Her
influence as a popular lecturer in the cause of women's
rights was immense. In addition to collections of her lectures she published two memoirs widely read in her day--
My Story of the War (1887) and The Story of My Life (1897),
which are the best sources of information concerning her
career.

From THE STORY OF MY LIFE: OR THE SUNSHINE AND
SHADOW OF SEVENTY YEARS

What Shall We Do with Our Daughters?

It is more than fifty years since Margaret Fuller, standing,
as she said, "in the sunny noon of life," wrote a little book,
which she launched on the current of thought and society. It
was entitled "Woman in the Nineteenth Century"; and as the
truths it proclaimed and the reforms it advocated were far
in advance of public acceptance, its appearance was the signal for an immediate widespread newspaper controversy, that
raged with great violence. I was young then, and as I took
the book from the hands of the bookseller, wondering what
the contents of the thin little volume could be, to provoke so
wordy a strife, I opened at the first page. My attention was
immediately arrested, and a train of thought started, by the
two mottoes at the head of the opening chapter,--one underneath the other, one contradicting the other.

The first was an old-time adage, endorsed by Shakes-
peare, believed in by the world, and quoted in that day very
generally. It is not yet entirely obsolete. "Frailty, thy
name is Woman." Underneath it, and unlike it, was the
other,--"The Earth waits for her Queen." The first described

woman as she has been understood in the past; as she has masqueraded in history; as she has figured in literature; as she has, in a certain sense, existed. The other prophesied of that grander type of woman, towards which to-day the whole sex is moving, --consciously or unconsciously, willingly or unwillingly, --because the current sets that way, and there is no escape from it.

No one who has studied history, even superficially, will for a moment dispute the statement, that, during the years of which we have had historic account, there has brooded very steadily over the female half of the human family an air of repression, of limitation, of hindrance, of disability, of gloom, of servitude. If there have been epochs during which women have been regarded equal to men, they have been brief and abnormal. Among the Hindoos, woman was the slave of man, forbidden to speak the language of her master, and compelled to use the patois of slaves. The Hebrews pronounced her an after-thought of the Deity, and the mother of all evil. The Greek law regarded her as a child, and held her in life-long tutelage. The Greek philosophers proclaimed her a "monster," "an accidental production." Mediaeval councils declared her unfit for instruction. The early Christian fathers denounced her as a "noxious animal," a "painted temptress," a "necessary evil," a "desirable calamity," a "domestic peril." From the English Heptarchy to the Reformation, the law proclaimed the wife to be "in all cases, and under all circumstances, her husband's creature, servant, slave." To Diderot, the French philosopher, even in the eighteenth century, she was only a "courtesan"; to Montesquieu, an "attractive child"; to Rousseau, "an object of pleasure to man." To Michelet, nearly a century later, she was a "natural invalid." Mme. de Stael wrote truly, "that, of all the faculties with which Nature has gifted woman, she had been able to exercise fully but one, -- the faculty of suffering."

The contemptuous opinion entertained of woman in the past has found expression, not alone in literature, but also in unjust laws and customs. "In marriage she has been a serf; as a mother she has been robbed of her children; in public instruction she has been ignored; in labor she has been a menial, and then inadequately compensated; civilly she has been a minor, and politically she has had no existence. She has been the equal of man only when punishment and the payment of taxes were in question."

Born and bred for generations under such conditions
of hindrance, it has not been possible for women to rise
much above the arbitrary standards of inferiority persistently
set before them. Here and there through the ages, some
woman, endowed with phenomenal force of character, has
towered above the mediocrity of her sex, hinting at the qualities imprisoned in the feminine nature. It is not strange
that these instances have been rare; it is strange, indeed,
that women have held their own during these ages of degra-
dation. And as, by a general law of heredity, "the inheri-
tance of traits of character is persistent in proportion to the
length of time they have been inherited," it is easy to account for the conservatism of women to-day, and for the indifference, not to say hostility, with which many regard the
movements for their advancement.

For humanity has moved forward to an era where
wrong and slavery are being displaced, and reason and justice are being recognized as the rule of life. Science is extending immeasurably the bounds of knowledge and power; art
is refining life, giving to it beauty and grace; literature
bears in her hands whole ages of comfort and sympathy; industry, aided by the hundred-handed elements of nature, is
increasing the world's wealth, and invention is economizing
its labor. The age looks steadily to the redressing of wrong,
to the righting of every form of error and injustice; and the
tireless and prying philanthropy, which is almost omniscient,
is one of the most hopeful characteristics of the time.

It could not be possible in such an era, but that women should share in the justice and kindliness with which the
time is fraught. A great wave is lifting them to higher lev-
els. The leadership of the world is being taken from the
hands of the brutal and low, and the race is making its way
to a higher ideal than once it knew. It is the evolution of
this tendency that is lifting women out of their subject condition, that is emancipating them from the seclusion of the
past, and adding to the sum total of the world's worth and
wisdom, by giving to them the cultivation human beings need.
The demand for their education, --technical and industrial,
as well as intellectual, --and for their civil and political
rights, is being urged each year by an increasing host, and
with more emphatic utterance.

The doors of colleges, professional schools, and uni-
versities, closed against them for ages, are opening to them.

They are invited to pursue the same courses of study as their brothers, and are graduated with the same diplomas. Trades, businesses, remunerative vocations, and learned professions seek them; and even the laws, which are the last to feel the change in public opinion, --usually dragging a whole generation behind, --even these are being annually revised and amended, and then they fail to keep abreast of the advancing civilization.

All this is but prefatory and prophetic of the time when, for women, law will be synonymous with justice, and no opportunity for knowledge or effort will be denied them on the score of sex.

As I listen to the debates that attend their progress, and weigh the prophecies of evil always inspired by a grow- ing reform, as I hear the clash of the scientific raid upon women by the small pseudo-scientists of the day, --who weigh their brains and measure their bones to prove their inferior- ity to men, --my thoughts turn to the young women of the present time. "What shall we do with our daughters?" is really the sum and substance of what, in popular phrase, is called "the woman question." For if to-morrow all should be done that is demanded by the wisest reformer and the truest friend of woman, it would not materially affect the condition of the adult women of society. Their positions are taken, their futures are forecast, and they are harnessed into the places they occupy, not unfrequently by invisible, but om- nipotent ties of love or duty. Obedience to the behests of duty gives peace, even when love is lacking; and peace is a diviner thing than happiness.

It is for our young women that the great changes of the time promise the most; it is for our daughters, --the fair, bright girls who are the charm of society and the delight of home; the sources of infinite comfort to fathers and mothers, and the sources of great anxiety also. What shall we do with them, --and what shall they do with and for themselves?

"New occasions teach new duties,
Time makes ancient good uncouth, "--

and the training of fifty years ago is not sufficient for the girls of to-day. The changed conditions of life which our young women comfront compel greater care and thought on the part of those charged with their education, than has here- tofore been deemed necessary. They are to be weighted with larger duties, and to assume heavier responsibilities; for the days of tutelage seem to be ended for civilized women, and they are to think and act for themselves.

Let no one, therefore, say this question of the training of our daughters is a small question. No question can be small that relates to half the human race. The training of boys is not more important than that of girls. The hope of many is so centered in the "coming man," that the only questions of interest to them are such as those propounded by James Parton in "The Atlantic Monthly,"--"Will the Coming Man Smoke?" "Will He Drink Wine?" and so on to the end of the catechism. But let it not be forgotten that before this "coming man" will make his appearance, his mother will always precede him, and that he will be very largely what his mother will make him. Men are to-day confessing their need of the aid of women by appointing them on school committees, boards of charities, as prison commissioners, physicians to insane asylums, positions which they cannot worthily fill without preparation.

Therefore, not only for their own sakes, but for the sake of the human family, of which women make one-half, should we look carefully to the training of our daughters. Nature has so constituted us that the sexes act and react upon each other, making every "woman's cause" a man's cause, and every man's cause a woman's cause; so that we

"Rise or sink
Together, dwarfed or godlike, bond or free."

And they are the foes of the race, albeit not always intentional, who set themselves against the removal of woman's disabilities, shut in their faces the doors of education or opportunity, or deny them any but the smallest and most incomplete training. For it is true that "who educates a woman educates a race."

Good health is a great prerequisite of successful or happy living. To live worthily or happily, to accomplish much for one's self or others when suffering much from pain and disease, is attended with difficulty. Dr. Johnson used to say that "every man is a rascal when he is sick." And very much of the peevishness, irritability, capriciousness, and impatience seen in men and women has its root in bodily illness. The very morals suffer from disease of the body. Therefore I would give to "our daughters" a good physical education.

142

We shall by-and-by come to recognize the right of
every child to be well born, --sound in body, with inherited
tendencies towards mental and moral health. We have learned
that it is possible to direct the operations of nature so as to
have finer breeds of horses, cattle, and fowls, to improve
our fruits, flowers, and grains. Science searches for the
prenatal laws of being, and comes to the aid of all who wish
to improve the lower creation. When shall an enlightened
public sentiment demand that those who seek of God the gift
of little children shall make themselves worthy the gift, by
healthful and noble living, practical acquaintance with prenatal laws of being, and all that relates to the hereditary
transmission of qualities.

If we would give to our daughters a good physiological
training we must attend carefully to their dress. The dress
of women at the present time is about as unhygienic as it
well can be. And many of our girls are made the victims
of disease and weakness for life, through the evils of the
dress they wear from birth. The causes of their invalidism
are sought in hard study, co-education, too much exercise,
or lack of rest and quiet in certain periods when nature demands it. All the while the medical attendant is silent concerning the "glove-fitting," steel-clasped corset; the heavy,
dragging skirts, the bands engirding the body, and the pinch-
ing, distorting boot. These will account for much of the
feebleness of women and girls; for they exhaust energy, make
freedom of movement a painful impossibility, and frequently
shipwreck our young daughter before she gets out of port.

While it is undoubted true that the practice of tight
lacing is regarded with growing disfavor, it is also true that
the corsets in vogue, at present, are more objectionable than
those worn even half a century ago. For those were home-
made, and, while they could be very tightly laced, did not
fit the figure well, were free from the torture of whalebones
and steel front pieces, all stitched in; while broad straps
passing over the shoulders supported them, and the clothing
hung upon them. But the modern corset is so ingeniously
woven that it presses in upon the body, the muscular walls,
the floating ribs, the stomach, the hips, and the abdomen,
compelling them to take the form the corset-maker has de-
vised, in lieu of that God has given. Stiff whalebones behind,
and finely "tempered steel-fronts" pressing into the stomach
and curving over the abdomen, keep the figure of the girl
erect and unbending, while Nature has made the spine supple
with joints.

Physicians have persistently condemned the corset for half a century, even when it was not so harmful an article of dress as it is to-day. The educated women physicians, who are gaining in numbers, influence, and practice, denounce it unqualifiedly, lay to its charge no small amount of the dire diseases on whose treatment gynaecologists fatten, and declare that it enhances the peril of maternity, and inflicts upon the world inferior children. Men condemn corsets in the abstract, and sometimes are brave enough to insist that the women of their households shall be emancipated from them; and yet their eyes have been so generally educated to the approval of the small waist, and the hourglass figure, that they often hinder women who seek a hygienic style of dress.

It is a mistake on the part of our daughters that the corset will give them beauty of figure. The young American girl is usually lithe and slender, and requires no artificial intensifying of her slightness. The corset will give her only stiffness of appearance, and interferes with that grace of motion, which is one of the charms of young girls. The basque under-waist, made as a substitute for the corset, and beginning to supersede it, fits the figure trimly, revealing its graceful contour, and is kept in place,--not by bones, or slips of steel, or thickly stitched-in stiff cords,--but by the weight of the skirts buttoned on the lower part. Over this under-waist the outer dress can be fitted; and its waist will be smooth and unwrinkled,--a desideratum to most women.

The stout woman, who wears a corset to diminish her proportions, only distorts her figure; for her pinched waist causes her broad shoulders and hips to look broader by contrast, while the pressure upon the heart and blood-vessels gives to her face that permanent blowzy flush, that suggests apoplexy.

John Burroughs, in his "Winter Sunshine," expresses the fear that "the American is becoming disqualified for the manly art of walking, by a falling-off in the size of his foot. ... A small, trim foot," he tells us, "well booted or gaitered, is the national vanity. How we stare at the big feet of foreigners, and wonder what may be the price of leather in those countries, and where all the aristocratic blood is, that these plebeian extremities so predominate!"

The prevailing French boots made for women, and exhibited in the shop-windows, are painfully suggestive. Pointed and elongated, they prophesy cramped and atrophied toes; while the high and narrow heel, that slides down under the instep, throws the whole body into an unnatural position in walking, creating diseases which are difficult of cure. "Show me her boots!" said a physician, called to a young lady suffering from unendurable pain in the back and knee-joints, which extended and engirt her, till, to use her own language, "she was solid pain downwards from the waist." "There's the trouble!" was his sententious comment, as he tossed the fashionable torturing boot from him after examination.

While the clothing of our daughters should not deform the figure nor injure the health, it need be neither inelegant nor inartistic. No particular style of dress can be recommended, but each one should choose what is most becoming and appropriate in fashion and material. With sacred regard to the laws of health, and without too large expenditure of time and money, every woman should aim to present an attractive exterior to her friends and the world. So, indeed, should every man; for it is the duty of all human beings to be as beautiful as possible.

I have spoken at length of dress, because of the physical discomfort and hindrance caused by the prevailing dress of women, and because it is also a prolific source of disease, which becomes chronic and incurable. But food, sleep, exercise, and other matters demand attention when one is intrusted with the education of girls. American children, unlike those which we see abroad, generally sit at table with their parents, eat the same food, keep the same late hours, and share with them the excitement of evening guests, evening meetings and lectures, and the dissipation of theatres, operas, balls, and receptions. This is unwise indulgence. Children require simple food, early hours for retiring, and abundance of sleep, as well as freedom from social and religious excitements.

Signs multiply about us that the women of the future will have healthy and strong physiques. Dress-reform associations are organized in the principal American cities, and agencies established to furnish under-garments, or patterns for them, demanded by common sense and vigorous health. For it is the under-garments that the dress-reform proposes to change. The outer garments may be safely left to the taste of the individual who has accepted the principles of the dress-reform in the construction of the under-garments.

Health is a means to an end. It is an investment for
the future. That end is worthy work and noble living. And
life has little to offer the young girl who has dropped into
physical deterioration, which cuts her off from the activities
of the time, and makes existence to her synonymous with
endurance.

It is hardly necessary that anything should be said, in
advocacy of the higher intellectual education of our daughters.
For the question of woman's collegiate education is practically
settled; and it is almost as easy to-day for a woman to obtain the highest university education, as it is for a man.

But no phase of the great movement for the advancement of women has progressed so slowly, as that which demands their technical and industrial training. To be sure,
the last fifty years, which have brought great changes to the
women of America, have largely increased the number of remunerative employments they are permitted to enter. When
Harriet Martineau visited America in 1840, she found but
seven employments open to women. At the present time,
according to Hon. Carroll D. Wright, Chief of the National
Bureau of the Statistics of Labor, there are about three hundred and fifty industrial occupations open to women.

And yet it is true, however, that women have received
very little special industrial training to fit them for the work
they are doing, or for a higher kind of work which will give
them better pay. Perhaps almost the same may be said concerning the technical training of men in this country.

I cannot leave this topic of women's industrial training, without speaking of our culpability in neglecting to give
our daughters some knowledge of business affairs. With utter
indifference on our part, they are allowed to grow to womanhood unfamiliar with the most ordinary forms of business
transactions,--how to make out bills and to give receipts;
how to draw bank-checks; how to make notes, and what are
the cautions to be observed concerning them; what is the
best method of transmitting funds to a distance, whether by
postal orders or bank drafts; what are safe rates of interest;
how to purchase a life annuity, or effect an insurance on life
or property, and so on.

If property is to pass into their possession, our daughters certainly need to know much more than this, that they

may be able to manage it with wisdom, or even to retain it securely. They need to know what are the elements of financial security; what may be considered safe investments; how to rent, improve, or sell property; what margin of property above the amount of the loan should be required, when it is made on real estate; what constitutes a valid title to property; what cautions are to be observed concerning mortgages; what are the property-rights of married women in the states of their residence, with other like information.

We talk much of preparing our daughters to be good wives, mothers, and home-makers. Do we systematically attempt this? Do we conduct the education of girls with this object? Do we not trust almost entirely to natural instinct and aptitude, which, in the woman, is incomparably strong in the direction of wifehood, motherhood, and the home? For the mighty reason that the majority of women will always, while the world stands, be wives, mothers, and mistresses of homes, they should receive the largest, completest, and most thorough training. It is not possible to state this too strongly; for these positions are the most important that woman can occupy. Education, religion, human affection, and civil law, all should conspire to aid her in these departments, to do the best work of which she is capable.

The very highest function of woman is to raise and train the family; it is the very highest function of man also. Indeed, civilization has but this end in view, --the perpetuation and improvement of the race. The establishment of homes, the rearing of families, the founding of schools and colleges, the planting of institutions, the maintaining of governments, all are but means to this end. As Humboldt said years ago, "Governments, religion, property, books, are but the scaffolding to build men. Earth holds up to her Master no fruit, but the finished man."

The duties of the mother begin long before her child comes into life, --ay, and the duties of the father also. She needs to know all that science can teach of the prenatal laws of being, and of the laws of heredity. Her acquaintance with physiology should not be the superficial knowledge, given in the ordinary school or college even. It should be a thorough exposition of the mysteries of her own physical being, with a clear statement of the hygienic laws she must obey, if she would grow into healthy, enduring, glorious womanhood. She should be taught the laws of ventilation and nutrition; what

constitutes healthful food; the care of infancy; the nursing of
the sick; and in what that vigilant and scrupulous cleanliness
consists, which almost prohibits certain forms of disease
from passing under one's roof.   Intelligence, system, economy, industry, patience, good nature, firmness, good health,
a fine moral sense, all these are called into action.   So is
a knowledge of cooking, laundry work, how to make and re-
pair clothing, together with the other industries of domestic
life, even when one has means to employ servants to perform this work; for a woman cannot tell when she is well
served, unless she knows what good work is.   It requires
a very high order of woman to be a good wife, mother, and
housekeeper; and she who makes a success in these departments possesses such a combination of admirable qualities,
both mental and moral, that, with proper training, she might
make a success in almost any department.

We should never forget that moral and religious training underlies and permeates all other training when it is
wisely and judiciously given.   The education of the will to
the customs and habits of good society begins long before
the child is old enough to reason on the subject.   But its
education to the law of right, its submission to the will of
God, while it must be begun early, cannot be carried on to
perfection until the child's reason is developed and its moral
nature evolved sufficiently to feel how paramount to all other
demands are those of right and duty.

Let our sons and daughters be taught that they are
children of God, so divine in ancestry, so royal of parentage, that they must carry themselves nobly, and not consent
to meanness, low, selfish lives, and vice.   Let them be
taught that to love God is to love whatever is good and just
and true; and that loving brothers, sisters, schoolmates, and
humanity as a whole, is also loving God, since God is our
common Father, and "we are all brethren."

They should be trained to regard earthly life as the
first school of the soul, where there are lessons to be
learned, tasks to be mastered, hardships to be borne, and
where God's divinest agent of help is often hindrance; and
that only as we learn well the lessons given us here, may
we expect to go joyfully forward to that higher school to
which we shall be promoted, where the tasks will be nobler,
the lessons grander, the outlook broader, and where life
will be on a loftier plane.   While the coldness of skepticism
seems to be creeping over the age, --mainly, I believe, be-

cause of its great immersion in materialism of life and activity,--it is possible to train children to such a far-reaching, telescopic religious vision that they will overlook all fogs and mists of doubt. The low fears and dismaying presages that weigh down so many souls, will be dispelled by the clear atmosphere in which they will dwell; and with hearts throbbing evenly with the heart of God, they will say confidently, "Because He lives, I shall live also."

LUCY LARCOM

(1824-1893)

The daughter of a Beverly, Massachusetts, sea-captain and
merchant, Lucy Larcom was born in 1824. When Lucy was
eleven years old, her widowed mother moved with her and
several others of her many children to Lowell, Massachusetts, to take on the duties of matron of one of the boarding
houses established by the textile manufacturers of that city
for the accommodation of the girls and young women who
worked in the mills. As Larcom relates in an Atlantic
Monthly article (November 1881), "Among Lowell Mill-Girls:
A Reminiscence," and in the excerpt from A New England
Girlhood (1889) that follows, most of the mill-girls were
from up-country New England farms. Their employment
was usually only for a few years and thus they did not constitute a distinct proletarian group. The mill-owners apparently felt it their responsibility to supervise closely the
lives of these daughters, many of them in their early teens,
of respectable though poor New England families. Though
they worked fourteen hours a day for an average wage of
two dollars a week, the girls' morals and reputations were
thought to be of value, and thus they lived under rigid re-
strictions--10 p.m. lights-out, church on Sundays, attendance
at school part of the year for the youngest ones.

When twelve years old, Lucy Larcom went to work in
the mills and continued to work in them for the next ten
years. She was a contributor to The Lowell Offering, a
magazine written, edited, and published by the girls. In
1846 she left Lowell for Illinois, where she taught school for
three years and then attended Monticello Seminary in Godfrey,
graduating in 1852. Returning East, she taught English for
eight years at Wheaton College at Norton, Massachusetts.
The remainder of her life she devoted to writing poetry and
prose, much of it for juvenile periodicals. Before she died,
she had published four volumes of verse, one of them, An
Idyl of Work (1875), being a lengthy narrative treatment of

life among the mill-girls. Her best book--and the only one
that commands serious interest today--is the autobiographical
A New England Girlhood, intended for young readers but highly
readable for all ages and both sexes.

Larcom was deeply religious, first within her ancestral Congregationalist Church, and later as an Episcopalian.
Though she was a firm abolitionist, her views concerning the
problems of labor were conservative (she would not countenance strikes) and she remained aloof from the feminist
movement. She accepts the stereotyped female role of the
helping, supportive woman, but seems to have basic pride in
herself and in all types of work that women do.

A New England Girlhood (1889) is an obvious source
of information regarding Larcom's early life. For further
biographical detail, see D. D. Addison, Lucy Larcom: Life,
Letters and Diary (1894), and for a critical assessment see
Perry D. Westbrook, Acres of Flint: Sarah Orne Jewett and
Her Contemporaries, rev. ed. (1981).

From Chapter IX, A NEW ENGLAND GIRLHOOD

The girls who toiled together at Lowell were clearing away
a few weeds from the overgrown track of independent labor
for other women. They practically said, by numbering themselves among factory girls, that in our country no real odium
could be attached to any honest toil that any self-respecting
woman might undertake.

I regard it as one of the privileges of my youth that
I was permitted to grow up among those active, interesting
girls, whose lives were not mere echoes of other lives, but
had principle and purpose distinctly their own. Their vigor
of character was a natural development. The New Hampshire
girls who came to Lowell were descendants of the sturdy
backwoodsmen who settled that State scarcely a hundred years
before. Their grandmothers had suffered the hardships of

frontier life, had known the horrors of savage warfare when
the beautiful valleys of the Connecticut and the Merrimack
were threaded with Indian trails from Canada to the white
settlements. Those young women did justice to their inheri-
tance. They were earnest and capable; ready to undertake
anything that was worth doing. My dreamy, indolent nature
was shamed into activity among them. They gave me a
larger, firmer ideal of womanhood.

Often during the many summers and autumns that of
late years I have spent among the New Hampshire hills,
sometimes far up the mountain sides, where I could listen
to the first song of the little brooks setting out on their
journey to join the very river that flowed at my feet when
I was a working-girl on its banks, --the Merrimack, --I have
felt as if I could also hear the early music of my work-
mates' lives, those who were born among these glorious
summits. Pure, strong, crystalline natures, carrying down
with them the light of blue skies and the freshness of free
winds to their place of toil, broadening and strengthening as
they went on, who can tell how they have refreshed the world,
how beautifully they have blended their being with the great
ocean of results? A brook's life is like the life of a maiden.
The rivers receive their strength from the rock-born rills,
from the unfailing purity of the mountain-streams.

A girl's place in the world is a very strong one: it
is a pity that she does not always see it so. It is strongest
through her natural impulse to steady herself by leaning upon
the Eternal Life, the only Reality; and her weakness comes
also from her inclination to lean against something, --upon an
unworthy support, rather than none at all. She often lets
her life get broken into fragments among the flimsy trellises
of fashion and conventionality, when it might be a perfect
thing in the upright beauty of its own consecrated freedom.

Yet girlhood seldom appreciates itself. We often hear
a girl wishing that she were a boy. That seems so strange!
God made no mistake in her creation. He sent her into the
world full of power and will to be a helper; and only He
knows how much his world needs help. She is here to make
this great house of humanity a habitable and a beautiful place,
without and within, --a true home for every one of his children. It matters not if she is poor, if she has to toil for
her daily bread, or even if she is surrounded by coarseness
and uncongeniality: nothing can deprive her of her natural
instinct to help, of her birthright as a helper. These very

hindrances may, with faith and patience, develop in her a
nobler womanhood.

No; let girls be as thankful that they are girls as that
they are human beings; for they also, according to his own
loving plan for them, were created in the image of God.
Their real power, the divine dowry of womanhood, is that
of receiving and giving inspiration. In this a girl often sur-
passes her brother; and it is for her to hold firmly and
faithfully to her holiest instincts, so that when he lets his
standard droop, she may, through her spiritual strength, be
a standard-bearer for him. Courage and self-reliance are
now held to be virtues as womanly as they are manly; for
the world has grown wise enough to see that nothing except
a life can really help another life. It is strange that it
should ever have held any other theory about woman.

That was a true use of the word "help" that grew up
so naturally in the rendering and receiving of womanly service in the old-fashioned New England household. A girl came
into a family as one of the home-group, to share its burdens,
to feel that they were her own. The woman who employed
her, if her nature was at all generous, could not feel that
money alone was an equivalent for a heart's service; she
added to it her friendship, her gratitude and esteem. The
domestic problem can never be rightly settled until the old
idea of mutual help is in some way restored. This is a
question for girls of the present generation to consider, and
she who can bring about a practical solution of it will win
the world's gratitude.

We used sometimes to see it claimed, in public prints,
that it would be better for all of us mill-girls to be working
in families, at domestic service, than to be where we were.

Perhaps the difficulties of modern housekeepers did
begin with the opening of the Lowell factories. Country girls
were naturally independent, and the feeling that at this new
work the few hours they had of every-day leisure were entirely their own was a satisfaction to them. They preferred
it to going out as "hired help." It was like a young man's
pleasure in entering upon business for himself. Girls had
never tried that experiment before, and they liked it. It
brought out in them a dormant strength of character which
the world did not previously see, but now fully acknowledges.
Of course they had a right to continue at that freer kind of
work as long as they chose, although their doing so increased

the perplexities of the housekeeping problem for themselves
even, since many of them were to become, and did become,
American house-mistresses.

It would be a step towards the settlement of this vexed
and vexing question if girls would decline to classify each
other by their occupations, which among us are usually only
temporary, and are continually shifting from one pair of hands
to another. Changes of fortune come so abruptly that the
millionaire's daughter of to-day may be glad to earn her living by sewing or sweeping tomorrow.

It is the first duty of every woman to recognize the
mutual bond of universal womanhood. Let her ask herself
whether she would like to hear herself or her sister spoken
of as a shop-girl, or a factory-girl, or a servant-girl, if
necessity had compelled her for a time to be employed in
either of the ways indicated. If she would shrink from it a
little, then she is a little inhuman when she puts her unknown
human sisters who are so occupied into a class by themselves,
feeling herself to be somewhat their superior. She is really
the superior person who has accepted her work and is doing
it faithfully, whatever it is. This designating others by their
casual employments prevents one from making real distinctions, from knowing persons as persons. A false standard
is set up in the minds of those who classify and of those who
are classified.

Perhaps it is chiefly the fault of ladies themselves
that the word "lady" has nearly lost its original meaning (a
noble one) indicating sympathy and service;--bread-giver to
those who are in need. The idea that it means something
external in dress or circumstances has been too generally
adopted by rich and poor; and this, coupled with the sweeping notion that in our country one person is just as good as
another, has led to ridiculous results, like that of sales-
women calling themselves "salesladies." I have even heard
a chambermaid at a hotel introduce herself to guests as "the
chamberlady."

I do not believe that any Lowell mill-girl was ever
absurd enough to wish to be known as a "factory-lady," although most of them knew that "factory-girl" did not repre-
sent a high type of womanhood in the Old World. But they
themselves belonged to the New World, not to the Old; and
they were making their own traditions, to hand down to their
Republican descendants,--one of which was and is that honest

work has no need to assert itself or to humble itself in a nation like ours, but simply to take its place as one of the foundation-stones of the Republic.

The young women who worked at Lowell had the advantage of living in a community where character alone commanded respect. They never, at their work or away from it, heard themselves contemptuously spoken of on account of their occupation, except by the ignorant or weak-minded, whose comments they were of course too sensible to heed.

We may as well acknowledge that one of the unworthy tendencies of womankind is towards petty estimates of other women. This classifying habit illustrates the fact. If we must classify our sisters, let us broaden ourselves by making large classifications. We might all place ourselves in one of two ranks--the women who do something, and the women who do nothing; the first being of course the only creditable place to occupy. And if we would escape from our pettinesses, as we all may and should, the way to do it is to find the key to other lives, and live in their largeness, by sharing their outlook upon life. Even poorer people's windows will give us a new horizon, and often a far broader one than our own.

ROSE TERRY COOKE

(1827-1892)

Rose Terry Cooke was born on a farm near Hartford, Connecticut, in 1827. Both of her parents--Henry Wadsworth
and Anne Wright Hurlburt Terry--were of old and prosperous
Connecticut families, but her father's work as a landscape
gardener was financially unrewarding, so that when Rose was
six years old, the family moved into Hartford to live in her
grandmother Terry's mansion. A precocious child, Rose
learned to read at the age of three. At sixteen she graduated from Hartford Female Seminary and, the same year,
experienced the religious conversion prerequisite to full membership in the Congregational Church. After four years of
teaching in New Jersey, she returned to Hartford. Soon she
was placing poems in the best periodicals of the day. Though
by preference she wrote poetry, she had more talent for fiction, and from 1855 until near the end of her life she had no
difficulty in publishing numerous stories. Always a staunch
churchwoman, she encumbered much of her work with moral
or religious messages. Her forte, however, was in her insistence on representing scenes and characters realistically.
Since a major source of her material was the lives of farm
and village folks on the sterile and economically depressed
Connecticut countryside, her realism resulted in depictions
of spiritual and social, not to mention physical, deprivation.
Much of her writing of this nature is collected in Somebody's
Neighbors (1881), The Sphinx's Children and Other People's
(1886)--from which the story that follows is taken--and Huck-
leberries Gathered from New England Hills (1891).

In 1873, when she was forty-six years old, Rose married Rollin H. Cooke, a widower sixteen years younger than
she and the father of two daughters. Rollin Cooke, though
intelligent and affable, was temperamentally incapable of holding a steady, income-producing job, and thus most of the support of the family was shouldered by Rose. As Rose grew
older, she began to experience some difficulty in selling her

writings. During the last years of her life she and her husband lived precariously in Pittsfield, Massachusetts, where she completed a financially disappointing novel, Steadfast (1889), and he failed in his business ventures. She died of influenza in Pittsfield in 1892.

No book-length biography or critical study of Cooke has been published. Those interested should consult Notable American Women and Perry D. Westbrook, Acres of Flint: Sarah Orne Jewett and Her Contemporaries, rev. ed. (1981).

From THE SPHINX'S CHILDREN AND OTHER PEOPLE'S

Too Late

"'Tis true 'tis pity! pity 'tis, 'tis true!"

In one of those scanty New England towns that fill a stranger with the acutest sense of desolation, more desolate than the desert itself, because there are human inhabitants to suffer from its solitude and listlessness, there stood, and still stands, a large red farmhouse, with sloping roof, and great chimney in the middle, where David Blair lived. Perhaps Wingfield was not so forlorn to him as to another, for he had Scotch blood in his veins, and his shrewd thrift found full exercise in redeeming the earth from thorns and briars, and eating his bread under the full force of the primeval curse. He was a "dour" man, with a long, grim visage that would have become any Covenanter's conventicle in his native land; and his prayers were as long and grim as his face. Of life's graces and amenities he had no idea; they would have been scouted as profane vanities had they blossomed inside his threshold. Existence to him was a heavy and dreadful responsibility; a drear and doubtful working out of his own salvation; a perpetual fleeing from the wrath to come, that seemed to dog his heels and rear threatening heads at every turn. A cowardly man, with these ever-present terrors, would have taken refuge in some sweet and

lulling sin or creed, some belief of a universal salvation,
some epicurean "let us eat and drink, for to-morrow we
die, " or some idea in nothing beyond the grave.

But David Blair was full of courage. Like some
knotty, twisted oak, that offers scant solace to the eye, he
endured, oaklike, all storms, and bent not an atom to any
fierce blast of nature or Providence; for he made a distinction between them. His wife was a neat, quiet, subdued
woman, who held her house and her husband in as much
reverence as a Feejee holds his idols. Like most women,
she had an instinctive love for grace and beauty, but from
long repression it was only a blind and groping instinct.
Her house was kept in a state of spotless purity, but was
bald as any vineless rock within. Flies never intruded
there; spiders still less. The windows of the "best room"
were veiled and double veiled with green paper shades and
snow white cotton curtains, and the ghastly light that strayed
in through these obstructions revealed a speckless but hideous homespun carpet, four straight-backed chairs, with
horsehair seats, an equally black and shining sofa, and a
round mahogany table with a great Bible in the midst. No
vases, no shells, no ornament of useless fashion stood on
the white wooden mantelpiece over the open fireplace; no
stencil border broke the monotonous whitewash of the walls.
You could see your face in a state of distortion and jaundice
anywhere in the andirons, so brilliant were their brassy col-
umns; and the very bricks of the chimney were scraped and
washed from the soot of the rare fire. You could hardly
imagine that even the leaping, laughing wood fire could impart any cheer to the funereal order of that chill and musty
apartment. Bedroom, kitchen, shed, woodhouse--all shared
this scrupulous array. The processes that in other households are wont to give cheery tokens of life, and bounty, and
natural appetites and passions, seemed here to be carried
on under protest. No flour was spilled when Thankful Blair
made bread; no milk ever slopped from an overfull pail; no
shoe ever brought in mud or sand across the mats that lay
inside and outside of every door. The very garret preserved
an aspect of serenity, since all its bundles of herbs hung
evenly side by side, and the stores of nuts had each their
separate boundaries, lest some jarring door or intrusive
mouse should scatter them.

In the midst of all this order there was yet a child,
if little Hannah Blair ever was a child in more than name.
From her babyhood she was the model of all Wingfield ba-

bies; a child that never fretted, that slept nights through all
the pangs and perils of teething, that had every childish disease with perfect decency and patience, was a child to be
held up to every mother's admiration.   Poor little soul!
The mother love that crushed those other babies with kisses,
that romped and laughed with them, when she was left
straight and solemn in her cradle, that petted, and slapped,
and spoiled, and scolded all those common children, Thankful Blair kept under lock and key in her inmost heart.

"Beware of idols!" was the stern warning that had
fallen on her first outburst of joy at the birth of one living
child at last, and from that time the whole tenor of her
husband's speech and prayer had been that they both might
be saved from the awful sin of idolatry, and be enabled to
bring up their child in the fear of the Lord, a hater of sin
and a follower of the law: the gospel that a baby brought to
light was not yet theirs!   So Hannah grew to girlhood, a
feminine reproduction of her father.   Keen, practical insight
is not the most softening trait for a woman to possess.   It
is iron and steel in the soul that does not burn with love
mighty and outflowing enough to fuse all other elements in its
own glow, and as Hannah grew older and read her mother's
repressed nature through and through, the tender heart, the
timid conscience, the longing after better and brighter things
than life offered to her only moved her child to an unavowed
contempt for a soul so weak and so childish.   In a certain
way Hannah Blair loved her mother, but it was more as if
she had been her child than her parent.   Toward her father
her feelings were far different.   She respected him; he was
her model.   She alone knew, from a like experience, what
reserved depth of feeling lay unawakened under his rigid ex-
terior--she knew, for there were times when her own granite
nature shuddered through and through with volcanic forces,
when her only refuge against generous indignation or mighty
anger was in solitary prayer and grievous wrestlings of the
flesh against the spirit as well as the spirit against the flesh.
So Hannah grew up to womanhood.   Tall and slight as any
woodland sapling, but without the native grace of a free
growth, her erect and alert figure pleased only by its alacrity and spotless clothing.   She was "dredful spry," as old
Moll Thunder, the half-breed Indian woman, used to say--
"dredful spry; most like squaw--so still, so straight; blue
eyes, most like ice.   Ho! Moll better walk a chalk 'fore
Miss Hanner!"

And Moll spoke from bitter experience, for old Deacon

Campbell himself never gave her severer lectures on her un-
godly life and conversation than dropped with cutting distinctness from those prim, thin, red lips. Yet Hannah Blair was
not without charms for the youth of Wingfield. Spare as she
was, her face had the fresh bloom of youth upon its high,
straight features; her eyes were blue and bright, her hair,
smoothed about her small head, glittered like fresh flax, and
made a heavy coil, that her slender white throat seemed over
small to sustain. She was cool, serene, rather unapproacha-
ble to lovers or love makers, but she was David Blair's only
child, and his farm lay fair and wide on the high plains of
Wingfield. She was well-to-do and pious--charms which hold
to this day potent sway over the youth of her native soil--and
after she was eighteen no Saturday night passed in solitude in
the Blair keeping-room, for young men of all sorts and sizes
ranged themselves against the wall, sometimes four at once,
tilted their chairs, twirled their thumbs, crossed one foot
and then the other over their alternate knees, dropped sparse
remarks about the corn, or the weather, or the sermon,
sometimes even the village politics, but one and all stared
at Hannah as she sat upright and prim by the fireplace or
the window, arrayed in a blue stuff gown or a flowered chintz,
as the season might be, and sitting as serene, as cool, as
uninteresting as any cherub on a tombstone, till the old Dutch
clock struck nine, the meeting-house bell tolled, and the
young men, one and all, made their awkward farewells and
went home, uttering, no doubt, a sigh of relief when the
painful pleasure was over.

By and by the Wingfield store, long kept by Uncle Gid
Mayhew, began to have a look of new life, for the old man's
only son, Charley Mayhew, had come home from Boston,
where he had been ten years in a drygoods shop, to take the
business off his father's hands. Just in time, too, for the
store was scarce set to rights in symmetrical fashion when
Uncle Gid was struck with paralysis and put to bed for all
the rest of his life--a brief one at that. Wingfield gossips
shook their heads and muttered that the new order of things
was enough to kill him. After so many years of dust and
confusion, to see the pepper corns, candy, and beeswax
sorted out into fresh, clean jars; the shoes and ribbons, cut
nails and bar soap neatly disentangled and arranged; the
plows, harrows, cheeses, hoes, and bales of cotton and calico divorced and placed at different ends of the store; the
grimy windows washed, and the dirty floor cleaned and swept,
was perhaps a shock to the old man, but not enough to kill
him. His eighty years of vegetation sufficed for that; but he

left behind him this son, so full of life, and spirit, and fun, so earnest at work, so abounding in energy, but withal so given over to frolic in its time, that it seemed as if even Wingfield stagnation never could give him a proper dulness or paralyze his handsome face and manly figure. Of course Charley Mayhew fell in love with Hannah Blair.

A mischievous desire at first to wake up those cold blue eyes and flush that clear-set face with blushes soon deepened into a very devoted affection. The ranks of Saturday night lovers began to look at him with evil eyes, for not even the formality of the best parlor restrained his fun, or the impassive visage of David Blair awed him into silence. Even Hannah began to glow and vivify in his presence; a warmer color flushed her cheeks, her thin lips relaxed in real smiles, her eyes shone with deeper and keener gleams than the firelight lent them, and, worst of all, the sheepish suitors themselves could not help an occasional giggle, a broad grin, or even a decided horse laugh, at his sallies; and when at last David Blair himself relaxed into an audible laugh, and declared to Charley he was "a master hand at telling stories," the vexed ranks gave it up, allowed that the conquering hero had come, and left Charley Mayhew a free field thereafter, which of course he improved. But even after Hannah Blair had promised in good set terms to be his wife, and David had given his slow consent, it was doubtful to Charley if this treasure was his merely out of his own determined persistence or with any genuine feeling of her own, any real response of heart, for the maiden was so inaccessible, so chill, so proper, that his warm, impulsive nature dashed against hers and recoiled as the wild sea from a rocky coast. Yet after many days the rock does show signs of yielding; there are traces on its surface, though it needs years to soften and disintegrate its nature. They were a handsome couple, these two, and admiring eyes followed them in their walks. Never had Hannah's face mantled with so rich a color, or her eyes shone with so deep and soft a blue; the stern, red lips relaxed into a serene content, and here and there a tint of gaiety about her prim dress--a fresh ribbon, a flower at her throat, a new frill--told of her shy blossom time. She was like one of those prim, old-fashioned pinks, whose cold color, formal shape, stiff growth, and dagger-shaped gray-green leaves stamp them the quaint old-maid sisterhood of flowers, yet which hold in their hearts a breath of passionate spice, an odor of the glowing Orient or the sweet and ardent South, that seems fitter for the open-breasted roses, looking frankly and fervently up to the sun.

No, not even her lover knew the madness of Hannah
Blair's hungry heart, now for the first time fed--a madness
that filled her with sweet delirium, that she regarded as
nothing less than a direct satanic impulse, against which she
fought and prayed, all in vain: for God was greater than her
heart, and He had filled it with that love which every wife
and mother needs, strong enough to endure all things, to be
forever faithful and forever fresh.   But no vine-planted and
grass-strewn volcano ever showed more placidly than Hannah
Blair.   Her daily duties were done with such exactness and
patience, her lover's demands so coolly set aside till those
duties were attended to, her face kept so calm even when the
blood thrilled to her fingertips at the sound of his voice,
that, long as her mother had known her, she looked on with
wonder, and admired afar off the self-control she never could
have exhibited.   For Hannah's wooing was carried on in no
such style as her mother's had been.   Thankful Parsons had
accepted David Blair from a simple sense of duty, and he
had asked her because she was meek and pious, had a good
farm and understood cows; no troublesome sentiment, no
turbulent passion disturbed their rather dull courtship.   A
very different wooer was this handsome, merry young fellow,
with his dark curls and keen, pleasant eyes, who came into
the house like a fresh, dancing breeze, and stirred its dusty
stagnation into absolute sparkle.   Mrs. Blair loved him
dearly already; her repressed heart opened to him all its
motherly instincts.   She cooked for him whatever she observed he liked, with simple zeal and pleasure.   She unconsciously smiled to hear his voice.   Deeply she wondered at
Hannah, who, day by day, stitched on her quilts, her sheets,
her pillow-cases, and her napery, with as diligent sternness
as ever she applied to more irksome tasks, and never once
blushed or smiled over the buying or shaping of her personal
bridal gear, only showing if possible a keener eye for business, a more infallible judgment of goods and prices, wear
and tear, use and fitness, than ever before.

So the long winter wore away.   Hannah's goods lay
piled in the "spare chamber"--heaps of immaculate linen,
homespun flannel, patchwork of gayest hues, and towels
woven and hemmed by her own hands; and in the clothes-
press, whose deep drawers were filled with her own garments in neat array, hung the very wedding dress of dove-
colored paduasoy, the great Leghorn bonnet, with white satin
ribbons, and the black silk cardinal.   Hannah had foregone
all the amusements of the past months, at no time consonant
to her taste, in order to construct these treasures for her

new life. In vain had Charley coaxed her to share in the
sleighing frolics, the huskings, the quilting bees of the neighborhood. It did not once enter into his mind that Hannah had
rather be alone with the fulness of her great joy than to have
its sacred rapture intermeddled with by the kindly or unkindly
jokes and jeers of other people. He never knew that her delight was full even to oppression, when she sat by herself
and sewed like an automaton, setting with every stitch a hope
or a thought of her love and life.

It was spring now. The long, cold winter had passed
at last; the woods began to bud, the pastures grew green
even in Wingfield, and brave little blossoms sprung up in the
very moisture of the just melted snowdrifts. May had brought
the robins and the swallows back; here and there an oriole
darted like a flake of fire from one drooping elm to another;
the stiff larches put out little crimson cones; the gracious
elm boughs grew dusk and dense with swelling buds, and the
maple hung out its dancing yellow tassels high in air. The
swamps were transfigured with vivid verdure and lit with
rank yellow blossoms.

"The wild marsh marigold shone like fire, "

and the quaint, sad-colored trillium made its protest in fence
corners and by the low buttresses of granite on the hills far
and near, and the rough-leaved arbutus nestled its baby faces
of sweetest bloom deep in the gray grass and stiff moss beds.
The day drew near for the wedding. It was to be the last
Wednesday in May.

"Darned unlucky, " muttered Moll Thunder, drying her
ragged shoes before Mrs. Blair's kitchen fire, having just
brought a fagot of herbs and roots for the brewing of root-
beer--even then a favorite beverage in New England, as it
is today. "Darned unlucky! Married in May, repent alway.
Guess Hanner pretty good like ter set up 'gainst old debbil
heself. No good, no good; debbil pretty good strong. Moll
knows! He! he! he!"

Mrs. Blair shivered. She was superstitious, like all
women, and old Moll was a born witch, everybody knew.
But then her daughter's pure, fair, and resolute face rose
up before her, and the superstitious fear flickered and went
out. She thought Hannah altogether beyond the power of "ole
debbil. " At last the last Wednesday came--a day as serene
and lovely as if new created: flying masses of white cloud

chased each other through the azure sky, and cast quick
shadows on the long, green range of hills that shut in Wingfield on the west.   Shine and shadow added an exquisite
grace of expression to the shades of tender green veiling
those cruel granite rocks; a like flitting grace at last transfigured Hannah Blair's cold-featured face.   The apple trees
blossomed everywhere with festive garlands of faint pink
bloom, and filled the air with their bitter-sweet, subtle
odor, clean and delicate, yet the parent of that luscious,
vinous, oppressive perfume that autumn should bring from
the heaps of gold and crimson fruit as yet unformed below
those waxen petals.

Today at last Hannah had resolved to give her beating
heart one day of freedom--one long day of unrestrained joy--
if she could bear the freedom of that ardent rapture so long,
so conscientiously repressed.   For once in her life she sung
about her work; psalm tunes, indeed, but one can put a deal
of vitality into Mear and Bethesda; and Cambridge, with its
glad, exultant repeat, has all the capacity of a love song.
Mrs. Blair heard it from the kitchen where she was watching the last pan of cake come to crisp perfection in the
brick oven.   The old words had a curious adaptation to the
sweet, intense triumph of the air, and Hannah carried the
three parts of the tune as they came in with a flexibility of
voice new to her as to her sole hearer:

> "'Twas in the watches of the night
> I thought upon thy power;
> I kept thy lovely face in sight
> Amid the darkest hour!"

What a subdued ectasy rose and fell in her voice as she
swept and garnished the old house.   "Amid the darkest hour!"
Oh, there never could be a dark hour for her again, she
thought--never a doubt, or fear, or trouble.   "My beloved
is mine, and I am his" rose to her lips from the oldest of
all love songs.   Half profane, she seemed to herself, but
today her deeper nature got the better of her deep prejudices;
she was at heart for once a simple, love-smitten girl.

The quiet wedding was to be after tea.   Nobody was
asked, for the few relatives David Blair possessed were almost strangers to him, and lived far away.   His wife had
been an only child, and Hannah had made no girl friends in
the village.   The minister was to come at eight o'clock, and
the orthodox cake and wine handed round after the ceremony.

The young couple were to go to their own house, and settle
down at once to the duties and cares of life. Charley had
been ordered not to appear till tea-time, and after the dinner was eaten and everything put to rights Mrs.
Blair went
to her room to plait a cap ruffle, and Hannah sat down in
the spare room by herself, to rest, she said--really to
dream, to hope, to bury her face in her trembling hand,
and let a mighty wave of rapture overflow her whole en-
tranced soul. The cap ruffle troubled Mrs. Blair much.
Twice it had to be taken from the prim plaits and relaid,
then to be sprinkled and ironed out. This involved making
a fresh fire to heat the flatiron, and it got to be well on in
the afternoon, and Mrs. Blair was tired. There was nobody
to reflect on her waste of time, so she lay down a moment
on the bed. David had gone to plow a lot on the furthest
part of the farm. He neglected work for no emergency. As
a godless neighbor said once, "Dave Blair would sow rye on
the edge of hell if he thought he could get the cattle there to
plow it up!" A daughter's wedding day was no excuse for
idleness in him. So Mrs. Blair was safe in her nap.

Meantime, as Hannah sat a little withdrawn from the
open window where for once the afternoon sun streamed in
unguardedly, and the passionate warble of the song-sparrows,
and the indescribable odor of spring followed too, she was
suddenly half aware of an outside shadow, and a letter
skimmed through the window, and fell at her feet. Scarce
roused from her dream, she looked at it fixedly a moment
before she stooped to pick it up. Its coming was so sudden,
so startling, it did not once occur to her to look out and see
who brought it. She hesitated before she broke the broad,
red seal, and swept her hand across her eyes as if to brush
away the dreams that had filled and clouded them. But the
first few words brought back to those eyes their native steely
glint, and as she read on life, light, love withdrew their
tender glories from her face. It settled into stone, into
flint. Her mouth set in lines of dreadful, implacable por-
tent, her cheek paled to the whiteness of a marble monu-
ment, and the red lips faded to pale, cold purple. What
she read in that letter neither man nor woman save the
writer and the reader ever knew, for when it was read Hannah Blair walked, like an unrepentant conspirator to the
stake, fearless, careless, hopeless, out into the small, silent kitchen, and laying that missive of evil on the smolder-
ing coals, stood by stark and stiff till every ash was burned
or floated up the chimney. Then she turned, and said in the
voice of one who calls from his grave,

"Mother!"

Mrs. Blair sprung from her doze at the sound. Her
mother instinct was keen as the hen's who hears the hawk
scream in the sky, and knows her brood in danger. She
was on the threshold of the kitchen door almost as soon as
Hannah spoke, but her heart sank to its furthest depth when
she saw the face before her. Death would have left no such
traces--given her no such shock. This was death in life,
and it spoke, slowly, deliberately, with an awful distinctness.

"Mother, when Charles Mayhew comes here tonight,
you must tell him I will not marry him."

"What?" half screamed the terrified woman, doubtful
of her own hearing. Again the cold, relentless tones, in
accents as clear and certain as the voice of fate itself:

"When Charles Mayhew comes here tonight, you must
see him, and tell him I will not marry him."

"Hanner, I can't! I can't! What for? What do you
mean? What is it?"

The words syllabled themselves again out of the thin,
rigid lips:

"I will not marry him."

"Oh, I can't tell him! he will die! I cannot, Hanner.
You must tell him yourself--you must! you must!"

Still the same answer, only the words lessening each
time:

"I will not!"

"But, Hanner, child, stop and think--do. All your
things made; you're published; the minister's spoke to. Why
do you act so? You can't, Hanner. Oh, I never can tell
him! What shall I say? What will he do? Oh, dear! You
must tell him yourself; I can't--I won't! I ain't goin' to;
you must!"

A shade of mortal weariness stole across the gray,
still face, most like the relaxation of the features after death;
but that was all the shrill tirade produced, except the dull,
cold repetition:

"I will not!"

And then Hannah Blair turned and crept up the narrow stairway to her bedroom; her mother, stunned with terror and amazement, still with a mother's alert ear, heard the key grate in the lock, the window shut quietly down, and heard no more. The house was silent even to breathlessness. In her desperation Mrs. Blair began to wish that David would come; and then the unconscious spur of lifelong habit stung her into action. It was five o'clock, and she must get tea; for tea must be prepared though the crack of doom were impending. So she built the fire, filled the kettle, hung it on the crane, laid the table, all with the accuracy of habit, her ear strained to its utmost to hear some voice, some sigh, some movement from that bolted chamber above. All in vain. There might have been a corpse there for any sound of life, and Mrs. Blair felt the awe of death creep over her as she listened. For once it was glad relief to hear David coming with the oxen; to see them driven to their shed; to watch his gaunt, erect figure come up the path to the back door; but how hard it was to tell him. He asked no question, he made no comment, but the cold, gray eye quickened into fire like the sudden glitter of lightning, and without a word he strode up the stair to Hannah's room.

"Hannah!"

There was no answer. David Blair was ill-used to disobedience. His voice was sterner than ever as he repeated the call:

"Hannah, open your door!"

Slowly the key turned, slowly the door opened, and the two faced each other. The strong man recoiled. Was this his child--this gray, rigid masque, this old woman? But he had a duty to do.

"Hannah, why is this?"

"I cannot tell you, father."

"But you must see Charles Mayhew."

"I will not!"

Still calm, but inexpressibly bitter and determined,

like one repeating a dreadful lesson after some tyrant's torture. David Blair could not speak. He stood still on that threshold without speech or motion, and softly as it had opened the door closed in his face, the key turned, he was shut out--not merely from the chamber, but forever from the deepest recess of Hannah's heart and life, if indeed he had ever, even in imagination, entered there. He stood a moment in silent amazement, and then went down into the kitchen utterly speechless. He swallowed his supper mechanically, reached down his hat, but on the doorstep turned and said:

"Thankful, you must tell Charles Mayhew: Hannah will not; I cannot. It is women's work--yea, it was a woman that first time in Paradise!"

And with this Scriptural sneer he left his frightened wife to do the thing he dared not. Not the first man who has done so, nor the last. An hour later the joyful bridegroom came in, his dark eyes full of happy light, his handsome figure set off by a new suit of clothes, the like of which Wingfield never had seen, much less originated; his face fairly radiant; but it clouded quickly as a storm-reflecting lake when he saw the cold, wet face of Mrs. Blair, the reddened eyes, the quivering lips, and felt the close yet trembling pressure of the kind old arms, for the first time clasped round his neck as he stooped toward her. How Thankful Blair contrived to tell him what she had to tell she never knew. It was forced from her lips in incoherent snatches; it was received at first with total incredulity, and she needed to repeat it again and again--to recall Hannah's words, to describe, as she best might, her ghastly aspect, her hollow, hoarse voice, her reply to her father. At last Charles Mayhew began to believe--to rave, to give way to such passionate, angry grief that Thankful Blair trembled and longed for Parson Day to come, or for David to return. But neither thing happened, for David had warned the parson, and then hidden his own distress and dismay as far as he could get from the house in his own woodland, sitting on a log for hours lest in coming back to the house he should face the man he could not but pity and fear both; for what reason or shadow of excuse could he offer to him for his daughter's cruel and mysterious conduct? So Mrs. Blair had to bear the scene alone. At last the maddened man insisted on going upstairs to Hannah's door, but that her mother withstood. He should not harass Hannah; she would keep her from one more anguish, if she stood in the doorway and resisted physically.

"But I will see her! I will speak to her! I will know myself what this means! I am not a fool or a dog, to be thrown aside for nothing!"

And with this he rushed out of the kitchen door, round the end of the house, to the grass-plat below Hannah's window. Well he knew that little window, with its prim white curtain, where he had so often watched the light go out from the hillside, where he always lingered in his homeward walks. The curtain was down now, and no ray of light quivered from behind it.

"Hannah! Hannah! my Hannah!" he called with anguish in every tone. "Hannah, look at me! only just look at me! tell me one word!" And then came the fondest pleadings, the most passionate remonstrances--all in vain. He might as well have agonized by her coffin side--by her grass-grown grave. Now a different mood inspired him, and he poured out threats and commands till the cool moonlight air seemed quivering with passion and rage. Still there was no voice or answer, nor any that replied. The calmness of immortal repose lay upon this quiet dwelling, though the torment and tumult without stormed like a tempest. Was there then neither tumult nor torment within? At last, when hours --ages it seemed to the desperate man--had passed by, nature could endure no more. The apathy of exhaustion stole over him; he felt a despair that was partly bodily weariness take entire possession of him; he ceased to adjure, to remonstrate, to cry out.

"Good-by, Hannah, good-by!" he called at length. The weak, sad accents beat like storm-weary birds vainly against that blank, deaf window. Nothing spoke to him, not even the worn-out and helpless woman who sat on the kitchen doorstep with her apron over her head, veiling her hopeless distress, nor lifting that homely screen to see a ruined man creep away from his own grave--the grave of all his better nature, to be seen there no more, for from that hour no creature in Wingfield ever saw or heard of him again.

There was a mighty stir among the gossips of the village for once. Not often did so piquant and mysterious a bit of scandal regale them at sewing societies, at tea-fights, even at prayer-meetings, for it became a matter of certain religious interest, since all the parties therein were church members. But in vain did all the gossips lay their heads together. Nothing was known beyond the bare facts that at the last min-

ute Hannah Blair had "gi'n the mitten" to Charley Mayhew,
and he had then and there disappeared. His store was sold
to a newcomer from Grenville Center, who was not commu-
nicative--perhaps because he had nothing to tell--and Charley
dropped out of daily talk before long, as one who is dead and
buried far away, as we all do, after how brief a time, how
vanishing a grief. As for the Blairs, they endured in stoical
silence, and made no sign. Sunday saw both the old people
in their places early; nobody looked for Hannah, but before
the bell ceased its melancholy toll, just before Parson Day
ambled up the broad aisle, her slender figure, straight and
still as ever, came up to her seat in the square pew. True,
her face was colorless; the shadow of death lingered there
yet; and though her eyes shone with keener glitter than ever,
and her lips burned like a scarlet streak, an acute observer
would have seen upon her face traces of a dreadful conflict,
lines around the mouth that years of suffering might have
grown; a relaxation of the muscles about the eye and temple;
a look as of one who sees only something afar off, who is
absent from the body as far as consciousness goes. There
she sat, through short prayer and long prayer, hymn, psalm,
and sermon, and the battery of looks both direct and furtive
that assailed her, all unmoved. And at home it was the
same--utterly listless, cold, silent, she took up her life
again; day by day did her weary round of household duties
with the same punctilious neatness and despatch--spun and
knit and turned cheeses, for her mother had been broken
down visibly for a time by this strange and sad catastrophe,
and was more incapable than ever in her life before of earnest work, so Hannah had her place to supply in part as well
as her own. We hear of martyrs of the stake, the fagot,
the arena, the hunger-maddened beasts, the rising tide, the
rack, and our souls shudder, our flesh creeps: we wonder
and adore. I think the gladdest look of her life would have
illuminated Hannah Blair's face had it been possible now to
exchange her endurance for any of these deaths; but it is women who must endure; for them are those secret agonies no
enthusiasm gilds, no hope assuages, no sympathy consoles.
God alone stoops to this anguish, and He not always, for
there is a stubborn pride that will not lift its eyes to Heaven
lest it should be a tacit acknowledgment that they were fixed
once upon poor earth. For these remains only the outlook
daily lessening to all of us--the outlook whose vista ends in
a grave.

But the unrelenting days stole on; their dead march,
with monotonous tramp, left traces on even Hannah's wretched,

haughty soul. They trampled down the past in thick dust; it
became ashes under their feet. Her life from torture subsided into pain; then into bitterness, stoicism, contempt--at
last into a certain treadmill of indifference; only not indifference from the strong cruel grasp she still found it needful
to keep upon thought and memory: once let that iron hand
relax its pressure, and chaos threatened her again; she dared
not. Lovers came no more to Hannah; a certain instinct of
their sure fate kept them away; the store of linen and cotton
she had gathered her mother's careful hands had packed away
directly in the great garret. The lavender silk, the cardinal,
the big bonnet, had been worn to church year after year in
the same spirit in which a Hindoo woman puts on her gor-
geous garments and her golden ornaments for suttee. Mrs.
Blair looked on in solemn wonder, but said not a word. Nor
were these bridal robes worn threadbare ten years after,
when another change came to Hannah's life; when Josiah Maxwell, a well-to-do bachelor from Newfield, the next village,
was "recommended" to her, and came over to try his chance.
Josiah was a personable, hale, florid man of forty; generous,
warmhearted, a little blustering perhaps, but thoroughly good,
and a rich man for those days. He had a tannery, a foundry,
and a flourishing farm. Newfield was a place of great water-
privileges, sure to grow; it was pretty, bright, and successful; the sleepy mullein-growing farms of Wingfield had in them
no such cheer or life. Hannah was thirty years old; the matter was set before her purely as a matter of business. Josiah wanted a pious, capable wife. He had been too busy to
fall in love all his life; now he was too sensible (he thought),
so he looked about him calmly, after royal fashion, and hearing good report of Hannah Blair, proceeded to make her acquaintance and visit her. She too was a rational woman;
feeling she had long set aside as a weak indulgence of the
flesh; all these long and lonely years had taught her a lesson
--more than one. She had learned too that a nature as strong,
as dominant, as full of power and pride as hers must have
some outlet or burn itself out, and here was a prospect offered that appealed to her native instincts, save and except
that one so long trodden under foot. She accepted Mr. Maxwell; listened to his desire for a short engagement favorably;
took down the stores prepared for a past occasion from the
chests in the garret, washed and bleached them with her own
hands; and purchased once more her bridal attire, somewhat
graver, much more costly than before--a plum-colored satin
dress, a white merino shawl, a hat of chip with rich white
ribbons. Moll Thunder, who served as chorus to this homely
tragedy, was at hand with her quaint shrewd comment, as she

brought Mrs. Blair her yearly tribute of hickory nuts the
week before the wedding.

"He! he! She look pretty much fine; same as cedar
tree out dere, all red vine all ober; nobody tink him ole
cedar been lightnin'-struck las' year. He! he! Hain't got
no heart in him--pretty much holler."

One bright October day Hannah was married. Parson
Day's successor performed the ceremony in the afternoon,
and the "happy couple" went home to Newfield in a gig directly. Never was a calmer bride, a more matter-of-fact
wedding. Sentiment was at a discount in the Blair family;
if David felt anything at parting with his only child, he repressed its expression; and since that day her mother never
could forget Hannah had wrought in poor Mrs. Blair's mind
a sort of terror toward her that actually made her absence
a relief, and the company of the little "bound girl" she had
taken to bring up a pleasant substitute for Hannah's stern,
quiet activity. Everybody was suited; it was almost a pleasure to Mrs. Maxwell to rule over her sunny farmhouse and
become a model to all backsliding housekeepers about her.
Her butter always "came," her bread never soured, her hens
laid and set, her chickens hatched, in the most exemplary
manner; nobody had such a garden, such a loom and wheel,
such spotless linen, such shiny mahogany; there was never
a hole in her husband's garments or a button off his shirt;
the one thing that troubled her was that her husband, good,
honest, tender man, had during their first year of married
life fallen thoroughly in love with her; it was not in his genial nature to live in the house a year with even a cat and
not love it. Hannah was a handsome woman and his wife;
what could one expect? But she did not expect it; she was
bored and put out by his demonstrations; almost felt a cold
contempt for the love he lavished on her, icy and irrespon-
sive as she was, though all the time ostensibly submissive.

Josiah felt after a time that he had made a mistake;
but he had the sense to adapt himself to it, and to be content, like many another idolater, with worship instead of response. Not even the little daughter born in the second year
of their marriage thawed the heart so long frost-sealed in
Hannah's breast; she had once worshiped a false god, and
endured the penalty; henceforward she would be warned. Baby
was baptized Dorothy, after her father's dead mother, and by
every one but Hannah that quaint style was softened into Dolly.
Never was a child better brought up, everybody said--a rosy,

sturdy, saucy little creature, doing credit to fresh air and
plain food; a very romp in the barn and fields with her
father, whom she loved with all her warm, wayward heart;
but alas! a child whose strong impulses, ardent feeling, violent temper, and stormy will were never to know the softening, tempering sweetness of real mother love. She knew
none of those tender hours of caressing and confidence that
even a very little child enjoys in the warmth of any mother-
heart, if not its own mother's; no loving arms clasped her
to a mother's bosom to soothe her baby-griefs, to rest her
childish weariness. There were even times when Hannah
Maxwell seemed to resent her existence; to repel her affection, though her duty kept her inexorably just to the child.
Dolly was never punished for what she had not done, but always for nearly everything she did do, and services were
exacted from her that made her childhood a painful memory
to all her later life. Was there butter or eggs wanted from
Wingfield on any emergency? at five years old Dolly would
be mounted on the steady old horse that Josiah had owned
fifteen years, and with saddle-bags swinging on either side,
sent over to her grandfather's at Wingfield to bring home the
supplies--a long and lonely road of five full-measured miles
for the tiny creature to traverse; and one could scarce believe the story did it not come direct to these pages from
her own lips. In vain was Josiah's remonstrance; for by
this time Hannah was fully the head of the house, and the
first principle of her rule was silent obedience. All her
husband could do was to indulge and spoil Dolly in private,
persistently and bravely. Alas for her, there was one day
in the week when even father could not interfere to help his
darling. Sunday was a sound of terror in her ears: first
the grim and silent breakfast, where nobody dared smile,
and where even a fixed routine of food, not in itself enticing,
became at last tasteless by mere habit: codfish-cakes and
tea; of these, "as of all carnal pleasure, cometh satiety at
the last," according to the monk in Hypatia; then, fixed in a
high, stiff-backed chair, the pretty little vagrant must be
still and read her Bible till it was time to ride to church--
till she was taken down and arrayed in spotlessness and
starch, and set bodkinwise into the gig between her silent
mother and subdued father.

Once at meeting, began the weariest routine of all.
Through all the long services, her little fat legs swinging from
the high seat, Dolly was expected to sit perfectly quiet; not a
motion was allowed, not a whisper permitted; she dared not
turn her head to watch a profane butterfly or a jolly bumble-

bee wandering about that great roof or tall window. Of
course she did do it instinctively, recovering herself with
a start of terror, and a glance at her mother's cold blue
eyes, always fixed on Parson Buck, but always aware of
all going on beside her, as Dolly knew too well. At noon,
after a hurried lunch of gingerbread and cheese, the child
was taken to the nearest house, there to sit through the
noon prayer-meeting, her weary legs swinging this time off
the edge of the high bed and her wearier ears dinned with
long prayers. Then, as soon as the bell tolled, off to the
meeting-house to undergo another long sermon, till, worn
out mentally and physically, the last hour of the seance became a struggle with sleep painful in the extreme, as well
in present resistance as in certainty of results; for soon as
poor Dolly reached home, after another silent drive, she
was invariably taken into the spare bedroom and soundly
whipped for being restless in meeting. And, adding insult
to injury, after dinner, enjoyed with the eager appetite of
a healthy child used to three meals on a week-day, she was
required to repeat that theological torture, the Assembly's
Catechism, from end to end. But in spite of all this, partly
because Sunday came only once a week, partly because of
her father's genial nature and devoted affection for his girl,
which grew deeper and stronger constantly, Dolly did not
miss of her life as many a morbid character might have in
her place. She grew up a rosy, sunny, practical young woman, with a dominant temper toward everybody but her mother.

Plump, healthy, and pretty, her cheeriness and usefulness would have made her popular had she been a poor
man's daughter; and by this time Josiah Maxwell was the
richest man in the town, so Dolly had plenty of lovers, and
in due time married a fine young fellow, and settled down
at home with her parents, who were almost as much pleased
with Mr. Henderson as was their daughter. But all this time
Mrs. Maxwell preserved the calm austerity of her manner,
even to her child. She did her duty by Dolly. She prepared
for her marriage with liberal hand and unerring judgment,
but no caress, no sympathetic word, no slightest expression
of affection soothed the girl's agitated heart or offered her
support in this tender yet exciting crisis of her life.

Hannah Maxwell made her life a matter of business--
it had been nothing else to her for years; it was an old habit
at sixty; and she was well over that age when one day Dolly,
rocking her first baby to sleep, was startled to see her moth-

er, who sat in her upright chair reading the county paper, fall quietly to the floor and lie there. Baby was left to fret while her mother ran to the old lady and lifted her spare thin shape to the sofa; but she did not need to do more, for Mrs. Maxwell's eyes opened and her hand clasped tight on Dolly's.

"Do not call any one," she whispered faintly, and leaning on her daughter's shoulder her whole body shook with agonized sobs. At last that heart of granite had broken in her breast; lightning-struck so long ago, now it crumbled. With her head still on Dolly's kind arm, she told her then and there the whole story of her one love, her solitary passion, and its fatal ending. She still kept to herself the contents of that anonymous letter, only declaring that she knew, and the writer must have been aware she would know, from the handwriting as well as the circumstances detailed, who wrote it, and that the information it conveyed of certain lapses from virtue on the part of Charles Mayhew must be genuine.

"Oh, Dolly," groaned the smitten woman, "when he stood under my window and called me, I was wrung to my heart's core. The pains of hell gat hold upon me. I was upon the floor, with my arms wound about the bed rail and my teeth shut like a vise, lest I should listen to the voice of nature, and going to the window to answer him, behold his face. Had I seen him I must have gone down and done what I thought a sin; so I steeled myself to resist, although I thought flesh would fail in the end; but it did not. I conquered then and after. Oh, how long it has been! I meant to do right, Dolly, but today, when I saw in the paper that he died last week in a barn over Goshen way, a lonely, drunken pauper--Dolly, my heart came out of its grave and smote me. Had I been a meeker woman, having mercy instead of judgment, I might have helped him to right ways. I might have saved him--I loved him so."

The last words struck upon her hearer with the force of a blow, so burning, so eager, so intense was the emphasis: "I loved him so!"

Ah, who could ever know the depths out of which that regretful utterance sprang!

"Dear mother, dear mother," sobbed Dolly, altogether overcome by this sudden revelation of gulfs she had never

dreamed of--a heart which, long repressed, convulsively
burst at last, and revealed its bleeding arteries.

"Dear, good mother, don't feel so--don't! You meant
right.   Try to forgive yourself.   If you made a mistake then,
try to forget it now.   Try to believe it was all for the best--
do, dear."

But all she got for answer was: "Dolly, it is too
late!"

LOUISA MAY ALCOTT
<u> </u>

(1832-1888)

Louisa May Alcott, the second of four daughters of Abigail May and Amos Bronson Alcott, was born in 1832 in Pennsylvania, where her father was teaching school. The next year the family moved back to the parents' native New England, and Bronson opened an experimental school in Boston. The self-educated son of a poor Connecticut farmer, Bronson not only had highly unconventional ideas on education but became one of the most idealistic of the so-called transcendental philosophers of New England. After the failure of the school in Boston the Alcotts moved to Concord, where Louisa May spent much of her girlhood and later life, numbering among her friends and neighbors Ralph Waldo Emerson, Henry Thoreau, and Nathaniel Hawthorne.

The pleasant and idyllic side of her life in Concord is reflected in her immensely popular book <u>Little Women</u> (1868-1869). But there were aspects of the Alcott family life that were less than idyllic. Bronson, the most impractical of the Transcendentalists, failed to provide a livelihood for his family--mainly because he was unwilling to work at any employment that violated his ideals. As a consequence the Alcotts lived in poverty, borrowing from friends and begging from Abigail's relatives, until the publication of <u>Little Women</u> enabled Louisa to support her parents and give financial aid to her sisters. The brush with actual starvation at Fruitlands, as described in one of the following selections, differed only in degree from conditions endemic in the Alcott household.

Louisa's account of the Fruitlands experience typifies her ambivalent feelings about her father's idealism and about Transcendentalism in general. Throughout her adult life she admired Bronson's dedication to principles and sorrowed with him in his numerous disappointments. But she had a greater

176

admiration for her mother's fortitude and patience, and as her irony and sarcasm in "Transcendental Wild Oats" (published in Silver Pitchers: And Independence, A Centennial Love Story, 1876) reveal, she resented the price paid in lack of comfort and security for Bronson's transcendental convictions. Yet Bronson was far from an evil or unfeeling man, and Louisa's affection for him was strong and lasting.

Endowed, or perhaps afflicted, with a relentless sense of duty, Louisa did not marry but devoted her life to trying to fill the needs of her parents and sisters. In doing this she had to suppress to a great extent her own ambitions and desires. These impulses and her anger at having to suppress them found release in a series of pseudonymously published Gothic thrillers (recently rediscovered and reprinted), peopled by femmes fatales and villainous men involved in violence and intrigue. Under her own name she wrote fiction brimming with Victorian morality and sentiment, for these were the literary money-makers of the time.

Louisa's health was permanently damaged by mercury poisoning resulting from medication for illness contracted while she had briefly served as an army nurse during the Civil War. Yet recurring invalidism did not deter her from what she considered her duties to her family, and she found additional strength to devote to the women's movement. A friend of Susan B. Anthony, Mary Livermore, and Lucy Stone, she contributed many articles to the Woman's Journal (edited by Lucy Stone in Boston). When at last the Concord women were permitted to vote in town meeting for members of the school board, Louisa did what she could to make this token suffrage meaningful. In dispatches to the Woman's Journal, she records the meager results of her efforts.

Two excellent biographical and critical studies of Alcott are Madeleine B. Stern, Louisa May Alcott (1950), and Martha Saxton, Louisa May: A Modern Biography of Louisa May Alcott (1977).

From SILVER PITCHERS

Transcendental Wild Oats
A Chapter from an Unwritten Romance

On the first day of June, 184-, a large wagon, drawn by a
small horse and containing a motley load, went lumbering
over certain New England hills, with the pleasing accompani-
ments of wind, rain, and hail. A serene man with a serene
child upon his knee was driving, or rather being driven, for
the small horse had it all his own way. A brown boy with
a William Penn style of countenance sat beside him, firmly
embracing a bust of Socrates. Behind them was an energetic-
looking woman, with a benevolent brow, satirical mouth, and
eyes brimful of hope and courage. A baby reposed upon her
lap, a mirror leaned against her knee, and a basket of pro-
visions danced about at her feet, as she struggled with a
large, unruly umbrella. Two blue-eyed little girls, with
hands full of childish treasures, sat under one old shawl,
chatting happily together.

In front of this lively party stalked a tall, sharp-
featured man, in a long blue cloak; and a fourth small girl
trudged along beside him through the mud as if she rather
enjoyed it.

The wind whistled over the bleak hills; the rain fell
in a despondent drizzle, and twilight began to fall. But the
calm man gazed as tranquilly into the fog as if he beheld a
radiant bow of promise spanning the gray sky. The cheery
woman tried to cover every one but herself with the big umbrella. The brown boy pillowed his head on the bald pate of
Socrates and slumbered peacefully. The little girls sang lul-
labies to their dolls in soft, maternal murmurs. The sharp-
nosed pedestrian marched steadily on, with the blue cloak
streaming out behind him like a banner; and the lively infant
splashed through the puddles with a duck-like satisfaction
pleasant to behold.

Thus these modern pilgrims journeyed hopefully out of
the old world, to found a new one in the wilderness.

The editors of "The Transcendental Tripod" had received from Messrs. Lion & Lamb (two of the aforesaid pilgrims) a communication from which the following statement
is an extract:--

"We have made arrangements with the proprietor of
an estate of about a hundred acres which liberates this tract
from human ownership. Here we shall prosecute our effort
to initiate a Family in harmony with the primitive instincts
of man.

"Ordinary secular farming is not our object. Fruit,
grain, pulse, herbs, flax, and other vegetable products, receiving assiduous attention, will afford ample manual occupation, and chaste supplies for the bodily needs. It is intended
to adorn the pastures with orchards, and to supersede the
labor of cattle by the spade and the pruning-knife.

"Consecrated to human freedom, the land awaits the
sober culture of devoted men. Beginning with small pecuniary
means, this enterprise must be rooted in a reliance on the
succors of an ever-bounteous Providence, whose vital affini-
ties being secured by this union with uncorrupted field and
unworldly persons, the cares and injuries of a life of gain
are avoided.

"The inner nature of each member of the Family is
at no time neglected. Our plan contemplates all such disci-
plines, cultures, and habits as evidently conduce to the puri-
fying of the inmates.

"Pledged to the spirit alone, the founders anticipate no
hasty or numerous addition to their numbers. The kingdom
of peace is entered only through the gates of self-denial; and
felicity is the test and the reward of loyalty to the unswerv-
ing law of Love."

This prospective Eden at present consisted of an old
red farm-house, a dilapidated barn, many acres of meadow-
land, and a grove. Ten ancient apple-trees were all the
"chaste supply" which the place offered as yet; but, in the
firm belief that plenteous orchards were soon to be evoked
from their inner consciousness, these sanguine founders had
christened their domain Fruitlands.

Here Timon Lion intended to found a colony of Latter

Day Saints, who, under his patriarchal sway, should regenerate the world and glorify his name for ever. Here Abel Lamb, with the devoutest faith in the high ideal which was to him a living truth, desired to plant a Paradise, where Beauty, Virtue, Justice, and Love might live happily together, without the possibility of a serpent entering in. And here his wife, unconverted but faithful to the end, hoped, after many wanderings over the face of the earth, to find rest for herself and a home for her children.

"There is our new abode," announced the enthusiast, smiling with a satisfaction quite undamped by the drops dripping from his hat-brim, as they turned at length into a cart-path that wound along a steep hillside into a barren-looking valley.

"A little difficult of access," observed his practical wife, as she endeavored to keep her various household gods from going overboard with every lurch of the laden ark.

"Like all good things. But those who earnestly desire and patiently seek will soon find us," placidly responded the philosopher from the mud, through which he was now endeavoring to pilot the much-enduring horse.

"Truth lies at the bottom of a well, Sister Hope," said Brother Timon, pausing to detach his small comrade from a gate, whereon she was perched for a clearer gaze into futurity.

"That's the reason we so seldom get at it, I suppose," replied Mrs. Hope, making a vain clutch at the mirror, which a sudden jolt sent flying out of her hands.

"We want no false reflections here," said Timon, with a grim smile, as he crunched the fragments under foot in his onward march.

Sister Hope held her peace, and looked wistfully through the mist at her promised home. The old red house with a hospitable glimmer at its windows cheered her eyes; and, considering the weather, was a fitter refuge than the sylvan bowers some of the more ardent souls might have preferred.

The new-comers were welcomed by one of the elect precious,--a regenerate farmer, whose idea of reform consisted chiefly in wearing white cotton raiment and shoes of

untanned leather.   This costume, with a snowy beard, gave
him a venerable, and at the same time a somewhat bridal
appearance.

The goods and chattels of the Society not having arrived, the weary family reposed before the fire on blocks of
wood, while Brother Moses White regaled them with roasted
potatoes, brown bread and water, in two plates, a tin pan,
and one mug; his table service being limited.   But, having
cast the forms and vanities of a depraved world behind them,
the elders welcomed hardship with the enthusiasm of new
pioneers, and the children heartily enjoyed this foretaste of
what they believed was to be a sort of perpetual picnic.

During the progress of this frugal meal, two more
brothers appeared.   One a dark, melancholy man, clad in
homespun, whose peculiar mission was to turn his name
hind part before and use as few words as possible.   The
other was a bland, bearded Englishman, who expected to be
saved by eating uncooked food and going without clothes.   He
had not yet adopted the primitive costume, however; but contented himself with meditatively chewing dry beans out of a
basket.

"Every meal should be a sacrament, and the vessels
used beautiful and symbolical," observed Brother Lamb,
mildly, righting the tin pan slipping about on his knees.   "I
priced a silver service when in town, but it was too costly;
so I got some graceful cups and vases of Britannia ware."

"Hardest things in the world to keep bright.   Will
whiting be allowed in the community?" inquired Sister Hope,
with a housewife's interest in labor-saving institutions.

"Such trivial questions will be discussed at a more
fitting time," answered Brother Timon, sharply, as he burnt
his fingers with a very hot potato.   "Neither sugar, molasses, milk, butter, cheese, nor flesh are to be used among
us, for nothing is to be admitted which has caused wrong or
death to man or beast."

"Our garments are to be linen till we learn to raise
our own cotton or some substitute for woollen fabrics," added
Brother Abel, blissfully basking in an imaginary future as
warm and brilliant as the generous fire before him.

"Haou abaout shoes?" asked Brother Moses, surveying
his own with interest.

"We must yield that point till we can manufacture an innocent substitute for leather. Bark, wood, or some durable fabric will be invented in time. Meanwhile, those who desire to carry out our idea to the fullest extent can go barefooted," said Lion, who liked extreme measures.

"I never will, nor let my girls," murmured rebellious Sister Hope, under her breath.

"Haou do you cattle'ate to treat the ten-acre lot? Ef things ain't 'tended to right smart, we shan't hev no crops," observed the practical patriarch in cotton.

"We shall spade it," replied Abel, in such perfect good faith that Moses said no more, though he indulged in a shake of the head as he glanced at hands that had held nothing heavier than a pen for years. He was a paternal old soul and regarded the younger men as promising boys on a new sort of lark.

"What shall we do for lamps, if we cannot use any animal substance? I do hope light of some sort is to be thrown upon the enterprise," said Mrs. Lamb, with anxiety, for in those days kerosene and camphene were not, and gas unknown in the wilderness.

"We shall go without till we have discovered some vegetable oil or wax to serve us," replied Brother Timon, in a decided tone, which caused Sister Hope to resolve that her private lamp should be always trimmed, if not burning.

"Each member is to perform the work for which experience, strength, and taste best fit him," continued Dictator Lion. "Thus drudgery and disorder will be avoided and harmony prevail. We shall rise at dawn, begin the day by bathing, followed by music, and then a chaste repast of fruit and bread. Each one finds congenial occupation till the meridian meal; when some deep-searching conversation gives rest to the body and development to the mind. Healthful labor again engages us till the last meal, when we assemble in social communion, prolonged till sunset, when we retire to sweet repose, ready for the next day's activity."

"What part of the work do you incline to yourself?" asked Sister Hope, with a humorous glimmer in her keen eyes.

"I shall wait till it is made clear to me. Being in
preference to doing is the great aim, and this comes to us
rather by a resigned willingness than a wilful activity, which
is a check to all divine growth, " responded Brother Timon.

"I thought so. "   And Mrs. Lamb sighed audibly, for
during the year he had spent in her family Brother Timon
had so faithfully carried out his idea of "being, not doing, "
that she had found his "divine growth" both an expensive and
unsatisfactory process.

Here her husband struck into the conversation, his
face shining with the light and joy of the splendid dreams
and high ideals hovering before him.

"In these steps of reform, we do not rely so much on
scientific reasoning or physiological skill as on the spirit's
dictates.   The greater part of man's duty consists in leaving
alone much that he now does.   Shall I stimulate with tea,
coffee, or wine?   No.   Shall I consume flesh?   Not if I
value health.   Shall I subjugate cattle?   Shall I claim property in any created thing?   Shall I trade?   Shall I adopt a
form of religion?   Shall I interest myself in politics?   To
how many of these questions--could we ask them deeply
enough and could they be heard as having relation to our
eternal welfare--would the response be 'Abstain'?"

A mild snore seemed to echo the last word of Abel's
rhapsody, for Brother Moses had succumbed to mundane
slumber and sat nodding like a massive ghost.   Forest Absalom, the silent man, and John Pease, the English member,
now departed to the barn; and Mrs. Lamb led her flock to
a temporary fold, leaving the founders of the "Consociate
Family" to build castles in the air till the fire went out and
the symposium ended in smoke.

The furniture arrived next day, and was soon bestowed;
for the principal property of the community consisted in books.
To this rare library was devoted the best room in the house,
and the few busts and pictures that still survived many flit-
tings were added to beautify the sanctuary, for here the family
was to meet for amusement, instruction, and worship.

Any housewife can imagine the emotions of Sister Hope,
when she took possession of a large, dilapidated kitchen, containing an old stove and the peculiar stores out of which food

184

was to be evolved for her little family of eleven. Cakes of
maple sugar, dried peas and beans, barley and hominy,
meal of all sorts, potatoes, and dried fruit. No milk, butter, cheese, tea, or meat, appeared. Even salt was considered a useless luxury and spice entirely forbidden by
these lovers of Spartan simplicity. A ten years' experience
of vegetarian vagaries had been good training for this new
freak, and her sense of the ludicrous supported her through
many trying scenes.

Unleavened bread, porridge, and water for breakfast;
bread, vegetables, and water for dinner; bread, fruit, and
water for supper was the bill of fare ordained by the elders.
No teapot profaned that sacred stove, no gory steak cried
aloud for vengeance from her chaste gridiron; and only a
brave woman's taste, time, and temper were sacrificed on
that domestic altar.

The vexed question of light was settled by buying a
quantity of bayberry wax for candles; and, on discovering
that no one knew how to make them, pine knots were introduced, to be used when absolutely necessary. Being summer, the evenings were not long, and the weary fraternity
found it no great hardship to retire with the birds. The inner light was sufficient for most of them. But Mrs. Lamb
rebelled. Evening was the only time she had to herself, and
while the tired feet rested the skilful hands mended torn
frocks and little stockings, or anxious heart forgot its burden in a book.

So "mother's lamp" burned steadily, while the philosophers built a new heaven and earth by moonlight; and through
all the metaphysical mists and philanthropic pyrotechnics of
that period Sister Hope played her own little game of "throwing light," and none but the moths were the worse for it.

Such farming probably was never seen before since
Adam delved. The band of brothers began by spading garden and field; but a few days of it lessened their ardor
amazingly. Blistered hands and aching backs suggested the
expediency of permitting the use of cattle till the workers
were better fitted for noble toil by a summer of the new life.

Brother Moses brought a yoke of oxen from his farm,
--at least, the philosophers thought so till it was discovered
that one of the animals was a cow; and Moses confessed that
he "must be let down easy, for he could n't live on garden
sarse entirely."

Great was Dictator Lion's indignation at this lapse from virtue. But time pressed, the work must be done; so the meek cow was permitted to wear the yoke and the recreant brother continued to enjoy forbidden draughts in the barn, which dark proceeding caused the children to regard him as one set apart for destruction.

The sowing was equally peculiar, for, owing to some mistake, the three brethren, who devoted themselves to this graceful task, found when about half through the job that each had been sowing a different sort of grain in the same field; a mistake which caused much perplexity, as it could not be remedied; but, after a long consultation and a good deal of laughter, it was decided to say nothing and see what would come of it.

The garden was planted with a generous supply of useful roots and herbs; but, as manure was not allowed to profane the virgin soil, few of these vegetable treasures ever came up. Purslane reigned supreme, and the disappointed planters ate it philosophically, deciding that Nature knew what was best for them, and would generously supply their needs, if they could only learn to digest her "sallets" and wild roots.

The orchard was laid out, a little grafting done, new trees and vines set, regardless of the unfit season and entire ignorance of the husbandmen, who honestly believed that in the autumn they would reap a bounteous harvest.

Slowly things got into order, and rapidly rumors of the new experiment went abroad, causing many strange spirits to flock thither, for in those days communities were the fashion and transcendentalism raged wildly. Some came to look on and laugh, some to be supported in poetic idleness, a few to believe sincerely and work heartily. Each member was allowed to mount his favorite hobby and ride it to his heart's content. Very queer were some of the riders, and very rampant some of the hobbies.

One youth, believing that language was of little consequence if the spirit was only right, startled new-comers by blandly greeting them with "good morning, damn you," and other remarks of an equally mixed order. A second irrepressible being held that all the emotions of the soul should be freely expressed, and illustrated his theory by antics that would have sent him to a lunatic asylum, if, as an unregenerate wag said, he had not already been in one. When his

spirit soared, he climbed trees and shouted; when doubt assailed him, he lay upon the floor and groaned lamentably.
At joyful periods, he raced, leaped, and sang; when sad, he
wept aloud; and when a great thought burst upon him in the
watches of the night, he crowed like a jocund cockerel, to
the great delight of the children and the great annoyance of
the elders.   One musical brother fiddled whenever so moved,
sang sentimentally to the four little girls, and put a music-
box on the wall when he hoed corn.

Brother Pease ground away at his uncooked food, or
browsed over the farm on sorrel, mint, green fruit, and
new vegetables.   Occasionally he took his walks abroad,
airily attired in an unbleached cotton poncho, which was the
nearest approach to the primeval costume he was allowed to
indulge in.   At midsummer he retired to the wilderness, to
try his plan where the woodchucks were without prejudices
and huckleberry-bushes were hospitably full.   A sunstroke
unfortunately spoilt his plan, and he returned to semi-
civilization a sadder and wiser man.

Forest Absalom preserved his Pythagorean silence,
cultivated his fine dark locks, and worked like a beaver,
setting an excellent example of brotherly love, justice, and
fidelity by his upright life.   He it was who helped overworked
Sister Hope with her heavy washes, kneaded the endless suc-
cession of batches of bread, watched over the children, and
did the many tasks left undone by the brethren, who were so
busy discussing and defining great duties that they forgot to
perform the small ones.

Moses White placidly plodded about, "chorin' raound,"
as he called it, looking like an old-time patriarch, with his
silver hair and flowing beard, and saving the community from
many a mishap by his thrift and Yankee shrewdness.

Brother Lion domineered over the whole concern; for,
having put the most money into the speculation, he was resolved to make it pay,--as if anything founded on an ideal
basis could be expected to do so by any but enthusiasts.

Abel Lamb simply revelled in the Newness, firmly believing that his dream was to be beautifully realized, and in
time not only little Fruitlands, but the whole earth, be turned
into a Happy Valley.   He worked with every muscle of his
body, for he was in deadly earnest.   He taught with his whole
head and heart; planned and sacrificed, preached and prophe-

sied, with a soul full of the purest aspirations, most unselfish purposes, and desires for a life devoted to God and man, too high and tender to bear the rough usage of this world.

It was a little remarkable that only one woman ever joined this community. Mrs. Lamb merely followed wheresoever her husband led,--"as ballast for his balloon," as she said, in her bright way.

Miss Jane Gage was a stout lady of mature years, sentimental, amiable, and lazy. She wrote verses copiously, and had vague yearnings and graspings after the unknown, which led her to believe herself fitted for a higher sphere than any she had yet adorned.

Having been a teacher, she was set to instructing the children in the common branches. Each adult member took a turn at the infants; and, as each taught in his own way, the result was a chronic state of chaos in the minds of these much-afflicted innocents.

Sleep, food, and poetic musings were the desires of dear Jane's life, and she shirked all duties as clogs upon her spirit's wings. Any thought of lending a hand with the domestic drudgery never occurred to her; and when to the question, "Are there any beasts of burden on the place?" Mrs. Lamb answered, with a face that told its own tale, "Only one woman!" the buxom Jane took no shame to herself, but laughed at the joke, and let the stout-hearted sister tug on alone.

Unfortunately, the poor lady hankered after the fleshpots, and endeavored to stay herself with private sips of milk, crackers, and cheese, and on one dire occasion she partook of fish at a neighbor's table.

One of the children reported this sad lapse from virtue, and poor Jane was publicly reprimanded by Timon.

"I only took a little bit of the tail," sobbed the penitent poetess.

"Yes, but the whole fish had to be tortured and slain that you might tempt your carnal appetite with that one taste of the tail. Know ye not, consumers of flesh meat, that ye are nourishing the wolf and tiger in your bosoms?"

At this awful question and the peal of laughter which arose from some of the younger brethren, tickled by the ludicrous contrast between the stout sinner, the stern judge, and the naughty satisfaction of the young detective, poor Jane fled from the room to pack her trunk, and return to a world where fishes' tails were not forbidden fruit.

Transcendental wild oats were sown broadcast that year, and the fame thereof has not yet ceased in the land; for, futile as this crop seemed to outsiders, it bore an invisible harvest, worth much to those who planted in earnest. As none of the members of this particular community have ever recounted their experiences before, a few of them may not be amiss, since the interest in these attempts has never died out and Fruitlands was the most ideal of all these castles in Spain.

A new dress was invented, since cotton, silk, and wool were forbidden as the product of slave-labor, worm-slaughter, and sheep-robbery. Tunics and trowsers of brown linen were the only wear. The women's skirts were longer, and their straw hat-brims wider than the men's, and this was the only difference. Some persecution lent a charm to the costume, and the long-haired, linen-clad reformers quite enjoyed the mild martyrdom they endured when they left home.

Money was abjured, as the root of all evil. The produce of the land was to supply most of their wants, or be exchanged for the few things they could not grow. This idea had its inconveniences; but self-denial was the fashion, and it was surprising how many things one can do without. When they desired to travel, they walked, if possible, begged the loan of a vehicle, or boldly entered car or coach, and, stating their principles to the officials, took the consequences. Usually their dress, their earnest frankness, and gentle resolution won them a passage; but now and then they met with hard usage, and had the satisfaction of suffering for their principles.

On one of these penniless pilgrimages they took passage on a boat, and, when fare was demanded, artlessly offered to talk, instead of pay. As the boat was well under way and they actually had not a cent, there was no help for it. So Brothers Lion and Lamb held forth to the assembled passengers in their most eloquent style. There must have been something effective in this conversation, for the listeners were moved to take up a contribution for these inspired lunatics, who preached peace on earth and good-will to man so earnestly, with empty pockets. A goodly sum was collected; but when the captain presented it the reformers proved that they were consistent even in their madness, for not a penny would they accept, saying, with a look at the group about them, whose indifference or contempt had changed to interest and respect, "You see how well we get on without money"; and so went serenely on their way, with their linen blouses flapping airily in the cold October wind.

They preached vegetarianism everywhere and resisted all temptations of the flesh, contentedly eating apples and bread at well-spread tables, and much afflicting hospitable hostesses by denouncing their food and taking away their appetites, discussing the "horrors of shambles," the "incorporation of the brute in man," and "on elegant abstinence the sign of a pure soul." But, when the perplexed or offended ladies asked what they should eat, they got in reply a bill of fare consisting of "bowls of sunrise for breakfast," "solar seeds of the sphere," "dishes from Plutarch's chaste table," and other viands equally hard to find in any modern market.

Reform conventions of all sorts were haunted by these brethren, who said many wise things and did many foolish ones. Unfortunately, these wanderings interfered with their harvest at home; but the rule was to do what the spirit moved, so they left their crops to Providence and went a-reaping in wider and, let us hope, more fruitful fields than their own.

Luckily, the earthly providence who watched over Abel Lamb was at hand to glean the scanty crop yielded by the "uncorrupted land," which, "consecrated to human freedom," had received "the sober culture of devout men."

About the time the grain was ready to house, some call of the Oversoul wafted all the men away. An easterly storm was coming up and the yellow stacks were sure to be ruined. Then Sister Hope gathered her forces. Three little girls, one boy (Timon's son), and herself, harnessed to clothes-baskets and Russia-linen sheets, were the only teams she could command; but with these poor appliances the indomitable woman got in the grain and saved food for her young, with the instinct and energy of a motherbird with a brood of hungry nestlings to feed.

This attempt at regeneration had its tragic as well as well as comic side, though the world only saw the former.

190

With the first frosts, the butterflies, who had sunned themselves in the new light through the summer, took flight, leaving the few bees to see what honey they had stored for winter use. Precious little appeared beyond the satisfaction of a few months of holy living.

At first it seemed as if a chance to try holy dying also was to be offered them. Timon, much disgusted with the failure of the scheme, decided to retire to the Shakers, who seemed to be the only successful community going.

"What is to become of us?" asked Mrs. Hope, for Abel was heart-broken at the bursting of his lovely bubble.

"You can stay here, if you like, till a tenant is found. No more wood must be cut, however, and no more corn ground. All I have must be sold to pay the debts of the con-cern, as the responsibility is mine," was the cheering reply.

"Who is to pay us for what we have lost? I gave all I had, --furniture, time, strength, six months of my chil-dren's lives, --and all are wasted. Abel gave himself body and soul, and is almost wrecked by hard work and disappoint-ment. Are we to have no return for this, but leave to starve and freeze in an old house, with winter at hand, no money, and hardly a friend left, for this wild scheme has alienated nearly all we had. You talk much about justice. Let us have a little, since there is nothing else left."

But the woman's appeal met with no reply but the old one: "It was an experiment. We all risked something, and must bear our losses as we can."

With this cold comfort, Timon departed with his son, and was absorbed into the Shaker brotherhood, where he soon found that the order of things was reversed, and it was all work and no play.

Then the tragedy began for the forsaken little family. Desolation and despair fell upon Abel. As his wife said, his new beliefs had alienated many friends. Some thought him mad, some unprincipled. Even the most kindly thought him a visionary, whom it was useless to help till he took more practical views of life. All stood aloof, saying: "Let him work out his own ideas, and see what they are worth."

He had tried, but it was a failure. The world was

not ready for Utopia yet, and those who attempted to found it
only got laughed at for their pains.   In other days, men could
sell all and give to the poor, lead lives devoted to holiness
and high thought, and, after the persecution was over, find
themselves honored as saints or martyrs.   But in modern
times these things are out of fashion.   To live for one's
principles, at all costs, is a dangerous speculation; and the
failure of an ideal, no matter how humane and noble, is
harder for the world to forgive and forget than bank robbery
or the grand swindles of corrupt politicans.

Deep waters now for Abel, and for a time there seemed
no passage through.   Strength and spirits were exhausted by
hard work and too much thought.   Courage failed when, looking about for help, he saw no sympathizing face, no hand outstretched to help him, no voice to say cheerily, --

"We all make mistakes, and it takes many experiences
to shape a life.   Try again, and let us help you."

Every door was closed, every eye averted, every heart
cold, and no way open whereby he might earn bread for his
children.   His principles would not permit him to do many
things that others did; and in the few fields where conscience
would allow him to work, who would employ a man who had
flown in the face of society, as he had done?

Then this dreamer, whose dream was the life of his
life, resolved to carry out his idea to the bitter end.   There
seemed no place for him here, --no work, no friend.   To go
begging conditions was as ignoble as to go begging money.
Better perish of want than sell one's soul for the sustenance
of his body.   Silently he lay down upon his bed, turned his
face to the wall, and waited with pathetic patience for death
to cut the knot which he could not untie.   Days and nights
went by, and neither food nor water passed his lips.   Soul
and body were dumbly struggling together, and no word of
complaint betrayed what either suffered.

His wife, when tears and prayers were unavailing, sat
down to wait the end with a mysterious awe and submission;
for in this entire resignation of all things there was an eloquent significance to her who knew him as no other human being did.

"Leave all to God," was his belief; and in this crisis
the loving soul clung to this faith, sure that the All-wise

Father would not desert this child who tried to live so near to Him. Gathering her children about her, she waited the issue of the tragedy that was being enacted in that solitary room, while the first snow fell outside, untrodden by the footprints of a single friend.

But the strong angels who sustain and teach perplexed and troubled souls came and went, leaving no trace without, but working miracles within. For, when all other sentiments had faded into dimness, all other hopes died utterly; when the bitterness of death was nearly over, when body was past any pang of hunger or thirst, and soul stood ready to depart, the love that outlives all else refused to die. Head had bowed to defeat, hand had grown weary with too heavy tasks, but heart could not grow cold to those who lived in its tender depths, even when death touched it.

"My faithful wife, my little girls, --they have not forsaken me, they are mine by ties that none can break. What right have I to leave them alone? What right to escape from the burden and the sorrow I have helped to bring? This duty remains to me, and I must do it manfully. For their sakes, the world will forgive me in time; for their sakes, God will sustain me now."

Too feeble to rise, Abel groped for the food that always lay within his reach, and in the darkness and solitude of that memorable night ate and drank what was to him the bread and wine of a new communion, a new dedication of heart and life to the duties that were left him when the dreams fled.

In the early dawn, when that sad wife crept fearfully to see what change had come to the patient face on the pillow, she found it smiling at her, saw a wasted hand outstretched to her, and heard a feeble voice cry bravely, "Hope!"

What passed in that little room is not to be recorded except in the hearts of those who suffered and endured much for love's sake. Enough for us to know that soon the wan shadow of a man came forth, leaning on the arm that never failed him, to be welcomed and cherished by the children, who never forgot the experiences of that time.

"Hope" was the watchword now; and, while the last logs blazed on the hearth, the last bread and apples covered the table, the new commander, with recovered courage, said to her husband, --

"Leave all to God--and me.   He has done his part;
now I will do mine."

"But we have no money, dear."

"Yes, we have.   I sold all we could spare, and have
enough to take us away from this snowbank."

"Where can we go?"

"I have engaged four rooms at our good neighbor,
Lovejoy's.   There we can live cheaply till spring.   Then
for new plans and a home of our own, please God."

"But, Hope, your little store won't last long, and we
have no friends."

"I can sew and you can chop wood.   Lovejoy offers
you the same pay as he gives his other men; my old friend,
Mrs. Truman, will send me all the work I want; and my
blessed brother stands by us to the end.   Cheer up, dear
heart, for while there is work and love in the world we shall
not suffer."

"And while I have my good angel Hope, I shall not
despair, even if I wait another thirty years before I step beyond the circle of the sacred little world in which I still have
a place to fill."

So one bleak December day, with their few possessions
piled on an ox-sled, the rosy children perched atop, and the
parents trudging arm in arm behind, the exiles left their
Eden and faced the world again.

"Ah, me! my happy dream.   How much I leave behind
that never can be mine again," said Abel, looking back at the
lost Paradise, lying white and chill in its shroud of snow.

"Yes, dear; but how much we bring away," answered
brave-hearted Hope, glancing from husband to children.

"Poor Fruitlands!   The name was as great a failure
as the rest!" continued Abel, with a sigh, as a frost-bitten
apple fell from a leafless bough at his feet.

But the sigh changed to a smile as his wife added, in
a half-tender, half-satirical tone, --

194

"Don't you think Apple Slump would be a better name for it, dear?"

LETTERS TO THE WOMAN'S JOURNAL

Editors Journal:--As other towns report their first experience of women at the polls, Concord should be heard from, especially as she has distinguished herself by an unusually well conducted and successful town meeting.

Twenty-eight women intended to vote, but owing to the omission of some formality several names could not be put upon the lists. Three or four were detained at home by family cares and did not neglect their domestic duties to rush to the polls as has been predicted. Twenty, however, were there, some few coming alone, but mostly with husbands, fathers or brothers as they should; all in good spirits and not in the least daunted by the awful deed about to be done.

Our town meetings I am told are always orderly and decent, this one certainly was; and we found it very like a lyceum lecture only rather more tedious than most, except when gentlemen disagreed and enlivened the scene with occasional lapses into bad temper or manners, which amused but did not dismay the women-folk, while it initiated them into the forms and courtesies of parliamentary debate.

Voting for school committee did not come till about three, and as the meeting began at one, we had ample time to learn how the mystic rite was performed, so, when at last our tickets were passed to us we were quite prepared to follow our leader without fear.

Mr. Alcott with a fatherly desire to make the new step as easy as possible for us, privately asked the moderator when the women were to vote, and on being told that they could take their chance with the men or come later, proposed that they should come first as a proper token of respect and for the credit of the town. One of the selectmen said "By all means"; and proved himself a tower of strength by seconding the philosopher on this momentous occasion.

The moderator (who is also the registrar and has most kindly and faithfully done his duty to the women in spite of his own difference of opinion) then announced that the ladies would prepare their votes and deposit them before the men did. No one objected, we were ready, and filed out in good order, dropping our votes and passing back to our seats as quickly and quiety as possible, while the assembled gentlemen watched us in solemn silence.

No bolt fell on our audacious heads, no earthquake shook the town, but a pleasing surprise created a general outbreak of laughter and applause, for, scarcely were we seated when Judge Hoar rose and proposed that the polls be closed. The motion was carried before the laugh subsided, and the polls were closed without a man's voting; a perfectly fair proceeding we thought since we were allowed no voice on any other question.

The superintendent of schools expressed a hope that the whole town would vote, but was gracefully informed that it made no difference as the women had all voted as the men would.

Not quite a correct statement by the way, as many men would probably have voted for other candidates, as tickets were prepared and some persons looked disturbed at being deprived of their rights. It was too late, however, for the joke became sober earnest, and the women elected the school committee for the coming year, feeling satisfied, with one or two exceptions, that they had secured persons whose past services proved their fitness for the office.

The business of the meeting went on, and the women remained to hear the discussion of ways and means, and see officers elected with neatness and dispatch by the few who appeared to run the town pretty much as they pleased.

At five the housewives retired to get tea for the exhausted gentlemen, some of whom certainly looked as if they would need refreshment of some sort after their labors. It was curious to observe as the women went out how the faces which had regarded them with disapproval, derision or doubt when they went in now smiled affably, while several men hoped the ladies would come again, asked how they liked it, and assured them that there had not been so orderly a meeting for years.

One of the pleasant sights to my eyes was a flock of school-boys watching with great interest their mothers, aunts and sisters, who were showing them how to vote when their own emancipation day came. Another was the spectacle of women sitting beside their husbands, who greatly enjoyed the affair though many of them differed in opinion and had their doubts about the Suffrage question.

Among the new voters were descendents of Major Buttrick of Concord fight renown, two of Hancock and Quincy, and others whose grandfathers or great grandfathers had been among the first settlers of the town. A goodly array of dignified and earnest women, though some of the "first families" of the historic town were conspicuous by their absence.

But the ice is broken, and I predict that next year our ranks will be fuller, for it is the first step that counts, and when the timid or indifferent, several of whom came to look on, see that we still live, they will venture to express publicly the opinions they held or have lately learned to respect and believe.

L. M. A.

Concord, March 30, 1880

Editors Woman's Journal: There is very little to report about the woman's vote at Concord Town Meeting, as only eight were there in time to do the one thing permitted them.

With the want of forethought and promptness which shows how much our sex have yet to learn in the way of business habits, some dozen delayed coming till the vote for school committee was over. It came third on the warrant, and a little care in discovering this fact would have spared us much disappointment. It probably made no difference in the choice of officers, as there is seldom any trouble about the matter, but it is to be regretted that the women do not give more attention to the duty which they really care for, yet fail, as yet, to realize the importance of, small as it is at present.

Their delay shows, however, that home affairs are not neglected, for the good ladies remained doubtless to give the men a comfortable dinner and set their houses in order before going to vote.

Next time I hope they will leave the dishes till they get home, as they do when in a hurry to go to the sewing-society, Bible-class, or picnic. A hasty meal once a year will not harm the digestion of the lords of creation, and the women need all the drill they can get in the new duties that are surely coming to widen their sphere, sharpen their wits, and strengthen their wills, teaching them the courage, intelligence and independence all should have, and many sorely need in a world of vicissitudes. A meeting should be called before the day for action comes, to talk over matters, to get posted as to time, qualification of persons, and the good of the schools; then the women can act together, know what they are doing, and keep up the proper interest all should feel in so important a matter.

"I come, but I'm lukewarm," said one lady, and that is the spirit of too many.

"We ought to have had a meeting, but you were not here to call it, so no one did," said another, as if it were not a very simple thing to open any parlor and ask the twenty-eight women voters to come and talk an hour.

It was a good lesson, and we hope there will be energy and foresight enough in Concord to register more names, have a quiet little caucus, and send a goodly number of earnest, wide-awake ladies to town-meeting next year.

Louisa M. Alcott

Concord, May 8, 1884

ELIZABETH STUART PHELPS WARD

(1844-1911)

Elizabeth Stuart Phelps Ward was born in Boston in 1844.
Her father was a Congregational minister in that city, and
her mother, Elizabeth Stuart Phelps, was a successful writer of sentimental fiction. When Elizabeth was four years
old, her family moved to Andover, where her father had
been appointed to a professorship in the Calvinistic Andover
Theological Seminary. When Elizabeth was eight, her mother died, a devastating blow to the young girl. She attended
private schools in Andover, receiving an education equivalent
to that obtainable at most colleges at that time. Needless to
say her religious indoctrination was strict and orthodox and
remained a major influence throughout her life. Following
her mother's example, she aspired to be an author and when
only twenty published a resounding best-seller, Gates Ajar
(1864), which purported to reveal the heavenly joys awaiting
one after death. Many other books in many genres--fifty-
seven in all--followed. When she was forty-five, she married Herbert D. Ward, who was seventeen years younger
than she and also a writer. An inveterate reformer, she
attached herself to many causes, among them temperance,
feminism, and antivivisection. Her "A Woman's Pulpit" (Atlantic Monthly, July 1870), which follows, is typical of her
better work. In a way Ward supports the cause unsuccess-
fully defended by Anne Hutchinson two hundred and forty
years earlier--the competence and right of a woman to teach
and preach Christian doctrine.

     For additional material on Ward, see her autobio-
graphical Chapters from a Life (1896) and Mary Angela Ben-
nett, Elizabeth Stuart Phelps (1939).

198

"A WOMAN'S PULPIT," Atlantic Monthly, July 1870

I fell to regretting to-day, for the first time in my life, that I am an old maid; for this reason: I have a very serious, long, religious story to tell, and a brisk matrimonial quarrel would have been such a vivacious, succinct, and secular means of introducing it.

But when I said, one day last winter, "I want some change," it was only Mädchen who suggested, "Wait for specie payment."

And when I said, for I felt sentimental, and it was Sunday too, "I will offer myself as a missionary in Boston," I received no more discouraging reply than, "I think I see you! You'd walk in and ask if anything could be done for their souls to-day? And if they said No, you'd turn around and come out!"

And when I urged, "The country heathen requires less courage; I will offer myself in New Vealshire," I was met by no louder lion than the insinuation, "Perhaps I meant to turn Universalist, then?"

"Mädchen!" said I, "you know better!"

"Yes," said Mädchen.

"And you know I could preach as well as anybody!"

"Yes," said Mädchen.

"Well!" said I.

"Well!" said Mädchen.

So that was all that was said about it. For Mädchen is a woman and minds her own business.

It should be borne in mind, that I am a woman "myself, Mr. Copperfull," and that the following correspondence, now for the first time given to the public, was accordingly finished and filed, before Mädchen ever saw or thought of it.

This statement is not at all to the point of my purpose, further than that it may have, as I suppose, some near or remote bearings, movable on springs to demand, upon the business abilities--by which, as nearly as I can make out, is meant the power of holding one's tongue--of the coming woman, and that I am under stress of oath never to allow an opportunity to escape me, of strewing my garments in the way of her distant, royal feet.

"To be sparing," as has been said, "of prefatory, that is to say, of condemnatory remarking," I append at once an accurate vellum copy of the valuable correspondence in question.

> Hercules, February 28, 18--
> Secretary of the New Vealshire
> Home Missionary Society

Reverend and Dear Sir:--I am desirous of occupying one of your vacant posts of ministerial service: place and time entirely at your disposal. I am not a college graduate, nor have I yet applied for license to preach. I am, however, I believe, the possessor of a fair education, and of some slight experience in usefulness of a kind akin to that which I seek under your auspices, as well as of an interest in the neglected portions of New England, which ought to warrant me success in an attempt to serve their religious welfare.

For confirmation of these statements I will refer you, if you like, to the Rev. Dr. Dagon of Dagonsville, and to Professor Tacitus of Sparta.

An answer at your earliest convenience, informing me if you are disposed to accept my services, and giving me details of terms and times, will oblige,

> Yours respectfully,
> J. W. Bangs

> Harmony, N. V., March 5, 18--
> J. W. Bangs, Esq.

My Dear Sir:--Your lack of collegiate education is an objection to your filling one of our stations, but not an insurmountable one. I like your letter, and am inclined to think favorably of the question of accepting your services. I should probably send

you among the Gray Hills, and in March.   We pay
six dollars a week and "found."   Will this be satisfactory?   Let me hear from you again.
    Truly yours,
            Z. Z. Zangrow,
            Sect. N. V. H. M. S.

    P. S.   I have been too busy as yet to pursue your
recommendations, but have no doubt that they are
satisfactory.

                            Hercules, March 9, 18--
Rev. Dr. Zangrow.

    Dear Sir:--Yours of the 5th is at hand.   Terms
are satisfactory.   I neglected to mention in my
last that I am a woman.
    Yours truly,
            Jerusha W. Bangs

                    Harmony, N. V., March 9, 18--
Jerusha W. Bangs.

    Dear Madam:--You have played me an admirable
joke.   Regret that I have no time to return it.
    Yours very sincerely,
            Z. Z. Zangrow, Sect.

                            Hercules, March 11th

    Dear Sir:--I was never more in earnest in my
life.
    Yours,
            J. W. Bangs

                        Harmony, March 14th

    Dear Madam:--I am sorry to hear it.
    Yours,
            Z. Z. Zangrow

Hercules, March 15, 18--

Rev. Dr. Zangrow.

My Dear Sir:--After begging your pardon for
encroaching again upon your time and patience,
permit me to inquire if you are not conscious of
some slight--we will call it by its mildest possible cognomen--inconsistency in your recent correspondence with me? By your own showing, I am
individually and concretely qualified for the business in question; I am generally and abstractly beyond its serious recognition. As an educated
American Christian, I am capable, by the word
that goeth forth out of my mouth, of saving the
Vealshire Mountain soul. As an educated American Christian woman, I am remanded by the piano
and the crochet-needle to the Hercules parlor soul.
You will--or you would, if it fell to your lot--
send me under the feminine truce flag of "teacher"
into Virginia to speak on Sabbath mornings to a
promiscuous audience of a thousand negroes: you
forbid me to manage a score of White-Mountaineers.
Mr. Spurgeon's famous lady parishioner may preach
to a "Sabbath-school class" of seven hundred men:
you would deny her the scanty hearing of your mission pulpits.
My dear sir, to crack a hard argument, you
have, in the words of Sir William the logical, "mistaken the associations of thought for the connections
of existence." If you will appoint me a brief meeting at your own convenience in your own office in
Harmony, I shall not only be very much in debt to
your courtesy, but I shall convince you that you
ought to send me into New Vealshire.
Meantime I am
Sincerely yours,
J. W. Bangs

Harmony, March 18, 18--

My Dear Miss Bangs:--You are probably aware
that, while it is not uncommon in the Universalist
pulpit to find the female preacher, she is a specimen of humanity quite foreign to Orthodox ecclesi-
astical society.
I will confess to you, however (since you are

determined to have your own way), that I have expressed in our hurried correspondence rather a de-
nominational and professional than an individual
opinion.

I can give you fifteen minutes on Tuesday next
at twelve o'clock in my office, No. 41 Columbia
Street.

It will at least give me the pleasure to make
your personal acquaintance, whether I am able or
not to gratify your enthusiastic and somewhat ec-
centric request.

I am, my dear madam,
Cordially yours,
Z. Z. Zangrow, Sect.

I went, I saw, I conquered. I stayed fifteen minutes,
just. I talked twelve of them. The secretary sat and
drummed meditatively upon the table for the other three.
He was a thin man in a white cravat. Two or three other
thin men in white cravats came in as I was about to leave.
The secretary whispered to them; they whispered to the secretary: they and the secretary looked at me. Somebody
shook his head: somebody else shook his head. The secretary, drumming, smiled. Drumming and smiling, he
bowed me out, merely remarking that I should hear from
him in the course of a few days.

In the course of a few days I heard from him. I
have since acquired a vague suspicion, which did not dawn
at the time upon my broadest imagination, that the secretary
sent me into New Vealshire as a private, personal, metaphysical speculation upon the woman question, and that the
New Vealshire Home Missionary Society would sooner have
sent me to heaven.

However that may be, I received from the secretary
the following:--

Harmony, N.V., March 23, 18--

Dear Miss Bangs:--I propose to send you as
soon as possible to the town of Storm, New Vealshire, to occupy on trial, for a few weeks, a
small church long unministered to, nearly extinct.
You will be met at the station by a person of the
name of Dobbins, with whom I shall make all necessary arrangements for your board and introduction.

204

When can you go?
Yours, etc.,
  Z. Z. Zangrow, <u>Sect</u>.

Hercules, March 24, 18--

My Dear Dr. Zangrow:--I can go to-morrow.
Yours, etc.,
  J. W. Bangs

A telegram from the secretary, however, generously allowed me three days "to pack." If I had been less kindly entreated at his hands, I should have had nothing to pack but my wounded dignity. I <u>always</u> travel in a bag. Did he expect me to preach out a Saratoga trunkful of flounces? I explosively demanded of Mädchen?

"He is a man," said Mädchen, soothingly, "and he has n't behaved in the least like one. Don't be hard upon him."

I relented so far as to pack a lace collar and an extra paper of hairpins. Mädchen suggested my best bonnet. I am sorry to say that I locked her out of the room.

For the benefit of any of my sex who may feel induced to follow in my footsteps, I will here remark that I packed one dress, Barnes on Matthew, Olshausen on something else, a Tischendorff Testament, Mädchen's little English Bible, Jeremy Taylor (Selections), and my rubber boots. Also, that my bag was of the large, square species, which gapes from ear to ear.

"It is n't here," said Mädchen, patiently, as I locked the valise.

"Mädchen," said I, severely, "if you mean my Florentine, I am perfectly aware of it. I am going to preach in black ties, --always!"

"Storm!" said Mädchen, concisely. As that was precisely what I was doing, to the best of my abilities, I regarded Mädchen confusedly, till I saw the Pathfinder on her knees, her elbows on the Pathfinder, and her chin in her hands.

"It is n't here," repeated Mädchen, "nor anything
nearer to it than Whirlwind.   That's in the eastern part of
Connecticut. "

I think the essentially feminine fancy will before this
have dwelt upon the fact that the secretary's letter was not,
to say the least of it, opulent in directions for reaching the
village of Storm.   I do not think mine is an essentially feminine fancy.   I am sure this never had occurred to me.

When it comes to Railway Guides, I am not, nor did
I ever profess to be, strong-minded.   When I trace, never
so patiently, the express to Kamtschatka, I am let out of the
Himalaya, Saturday-night accommodation.   If I aim at a
morning call in the Himalayas, I am morally sure to be
landed on the southern peak of Patagonia.   Mädchen, you
understand, would leave her card in the Himalayas, if she
had to make the mountains when she got there.

So, when Mädchen closed the Pathfinder with a snap
of despair, I accepted her fiat without the wildest dream of
disputing it, simply remarking that perhaps the conductor
would know.

"Undoubtedly," said Mädchen, with her scientific smile.
"Tell him you are going to see Mr. Dobbin of New Vealshire.
He cannot fail to set you down at his back door. "

He did, or nearly.   If I cannot travel on paper, I can
on iron.   Although in the Pathfinder's index I am bewildered,
routed, non est inventus, "a woman and an idiot," I can master the patois of brakemen and the hearts of conductors with
unerring ease.   I am sure I don't know how I got to Storm,
and when I got there I was sure I did n't know how I was to
get back again; but the fact remains that I got there.   I repeat it with emphasis.   I beg especially to call the masculine
attention to it.   I desire the future historian of "Woman in
the Sacred Desk," as he playfully skims the surface of antiquated opposition to this then long-established phase of civilization, to make a note of it, that there was a woman, and
she at the disadvantage of a pioneer, who got there.

Before proceeding to a minute account of my clerical
history, I should like to observe, for the edification of the
curious as well as for the instruction of the imitative, that
I labored under the disadvantage of ministering to two sepa-

rate and distinct parishes, which it was as impossible to
reconcile as hot coals and parched corn. These were the
Parish Real and the Parish Ideal. At their first proximity
to each other, my ideal parish hopped in the corn-popper of
my startled imagination, and, as nearly as I can testify,
continued in active motion till the popper was full.

Let us, then, in the first place, briefly consider (you
will bear, I am sure, under the circumstances, with my "po-
rochial" style)

The Parish Ideal

It was "in the wilderness astray," but it abounded in
fresh meat and canned vegetables. Its inhabitants were
heathen, of a cultivated turn of mind. Its opportunities were
infinite, its demands delicately considerate; its temper was
amiable, its experience infantine. It numbered a score or
so of souls, women and children for the most part; with a
few delightful old men, whose white hairs would go down in
sorrow to the grave, should they miss, in the afternoon of
life, the protecting shade of my ministrations. I collected
my flock in some rude tenement, --a barn perhaps, or antiquated school-house,--half exposed to the fury of the elements, wholly picturesque and poetical. Among them, but
not of them, at a little table probably, with a tallow candle,
I sat and talked, as the brooks run, as the clouds fly, as
waves break; smoothly, as befitted a kind of New Vealshire
conversazione; eloquently, as would Wesley, as would Whit-
field, as would Chalmers, Spurgeon, Beecher.

Royally but modestly, I ruled their stormy hearts.
(N. B. No pun intended.) Their rude lives opened, paved
with golden glories, to my magic touch. Hearts, which
masculine wooing would but have intrenched in their shells
of ignorance and sin, bowed, conquered, and chained to their
own well-being and the glory of God--or their minister--by
my woman's fingers. I lived among them as their idol, and
died--for I would die in their service--as their saint. Mädchen might stay at home and make calls. For me, I had
found the arena worthy of my possibilities, and solely created for my happiness.

I wish to say just here, that, according to the best
information which I can command, there was nothing particularly uncommon, certainly nothing particularly characteristic

of my sex, in this mental pas seul through which I tripped.
I suspect that I was no more interested in myself, and as
much interested in my parishioners, as most young clergymen.   The Gospel ministry is a very poor business investment, but an excellent intellectual one.   Your average pastor must take care of his own horse, dress his daughter in
her rich relations' cast-off clothing, and never be able to
buy the new Encyclopaedia, as well at the end of twenty
years as of two.   But he bounds from his recitation-room
into a position of unquestioned and unquestionable official
authority and public importance, in two months.   No other
profession offers him this advantage.   To be sure, no other
profession enfolds the secret, silent, tremendous struggles
and triumphs, serving and crowning of the Christian minister,--a struggle and service which no patent business motive
can touch at arm's length; a triumph and crown which it is
impossible to estimate by the tests of the bar, the bench,
the lecture-room.   But as it is perfectly well known that
this magazine is never read on Sundays, and that the introduction of any but "week-day holiness" into it would be the
ruin of it, I refrain from pursuing my subject in any of its
finer, inner lights, such as you can bear, you know, after
church, very comfortably; and have only to bespeak your patience for my delay in introducing you to

The Parish Real

        I arrived there on Saturday night, at the end of the
day, a ten miles' stage-ride, and a final patch of crooked
railway, in a snow-storm.   Somebody who lectures has
somewhere described the unique sensations of hunting in a
railway station for a "committee" who never saw you, and
whom you never saw.   He should tell you how I found Mr.
Dobbin, for I am sure I cannot.   I found myself landed in
a snow-drift--I suppose there was a platform under it, but
I never got so far--with three other women.   The three women had on waterproofs; I had on a waterproof.   There
were four men and a half, as nearly as I could judge, in
slouched hats, to be seen in or about the little crazy station.
One man, one of the whole ones, was a ticketed official of
some kind; the other two were lounging against the station
walls, making a spittoon of my snow-drift; the half-man was
standing with his hands in his pockets.

        "Was you lookin' for anybody in partikkelar?" said
one of the waterproofs, thoughtfully, or curiously, as I stood
dismally regarding the prospect.

"Thank you. Yes. Can you tell me if Mr. Do--"

"obbins," said the half-man at this juncture, "Bangs?"

"Yes, sir."

"New parson?"

"Yes, sir."

"That's the talk!" said Mr. Dobbins. "Step right round here, ma'am!"

"Right round here," brought us up against an old buggy sleigh, and an old horse with patient ears. "Hold on a spell," said Mr. Dobbins, "I'll put ye in."

Now Mr. Dobbins was not, as I have intimated, a large man. Whether he were actually a dwarf, or whether he only got so far and stopped, I never satisfactorily discovered. But at all events, I could have "put" Mr. Dobbins into anything twice as comfortably as I could support the reversal of the process; to say nothing of the fact that the ascent of a sleigh is not at most a superhuman undertaking. However, not wishing to wound his feelings, I submitted to the situation, and Mr. Dobbins handed me in and tucked me up, with consummate gallantry. I mention this circumstance, not because I was prepared for, or expected, or demanded, in my ministerial capacity, any peculiar deference to my sex, but because it is indicative of the treatment which, throughout my ministerial experience, I received.

"Comfortable?" asked Mr. Dobbins after a pause, as we turned our faces eastward, towards a lonely landscape of billowy gray and white, and in the jaws of the storm; "'cause there's four miles and three quarters of this. Tough for a lady."

I assured him that I was quite comfortable, and that if the weather were tough for a lady, I was too.

"You don't!" said Mr. Dobbins.

Another pause followed, after which Mr. Dobbins delivered himself of the following:--

"Been at the trade long?"

"Of preaching?   Not long."

"Did n't expect it, you know" (confidentially).   "Not such a young un.   Never thought on 't."

Not feeling called upon to make any reply to this, I made none, and we braved in silence the great gulps of mountain wind that wellnigh swept the buggy sleigh over.

"Nor so good lookin', neither," said Mr. Dobbins, when we had ridden perhaps half a mile.

This was discouraging.   A vision of Mädchen scientifically smiling, of the Rev. Dr. Z. Z. Zangrow dubiously drumming, of the New Vealshire Home Missionary Society shaking its head, drifted distinctly by me, in the wild white whirlpool over Mr. Dobbins's hat.

Were my professional prospects to be gnawed at the roots by a dispensation of Providence for which I was, it would be admitted by the most prejudiced, not in the least accountable?   Were the Universalist clergywomen never young and "good lookin'?"

I did not ask Mr. Dobbins the question, but his next burst of eloquence struck athwart it thus:--

"Had 'em here in spots, ye see; Spiritooalist and sech. There 's them as thinks 't ain't scriptooral in women folks to hev a hand in the business, noway.   Then ag'in there 's them as feels very like the chap whose wife took to beatin' of him; 'It amuses her, and it don't hurt me.'   Howsomever, there 's them as jest as lieves go to meetin' as not, when there 's nothin' else goin' on.   Last one brought her baby, and her husband he sat with his head ag'in the door, and held it."

To these consoling observations Mr. Dobbins added, I believe, but two others in the course of our four miles and three quarters' drive; these were equally cheering:--

"S'pose you know you 're ticketed to Samphiry's."

I was obliged to admit that I had never so much as heard a rumor of the existence of Samphiry.

"Cousin of mine," explained Mr. Dobbins, "on the

mother's side. Children got the mumps down to her place.
Six on 'em. "

It will be readily inferred that Mr. Dobbins dropped
me in the drifts about Samphiry's front door, in a subdued
state of mind. Samphiry greeted me with a sad smile. She
was a little yellow woman in a red calico apron. Six children, in various picturesque stages of the disease which Mr.
Dobbins had specified, hung about her.

"Law me, child!" said Samphiry, when she had got
me in by the fire, taken my dripping hat and cloak, and
turned me full in the dying daylight and living firelight.
"Why, I don't believe you 're two year older than Mary Ann!"

Mary Ann, an overgrown child of perhaps seventeen,
in short dresses buttoned up behind, sat with her mouth open,
and looked at me during the expression of this encouraging
comparison.

I assumed my severest ministerial gravity and silence,
but my heart was sinking.

I had salt-pork and barley bread for supper, and
went to bed in a room where the ice stood on my hair all
night, where I wrapped it around my throat as a preventive
of diphtheria. I was prepared for hardship, however, and
bore these little physical inconveniences bravely; but when
one of Mary Ann's brothers, somewhere in the extremely
small editions, cried aloud from midnight to five A. M. , and
Samphiry apologized for the disturbance the next morning on
this wise: "--Hope you was n't kept awake last night, I'm
sure. They generally cry for a night or two before they get
through with it. If you 'd been a man-minister now, I don't
s'pose I should have dared to undertake the keep of you,
with mumps in the house; but it's so different with a woman;
she's got so much more fellow-feeling for babies; I thought
you would n't mind!"--I confess that my heart dropped "deeper than did ever plummet sound. " For about ten minutes I
would rather have been in Hercules making calls than in New
Vealshire preaching the Gospel.

I was aroused from this brief state of despair, however, by the remembrance of my now near-approaching professional duties; and after a hot breakfast (of salt-pork and
barley bread), I retired to my icy room to prepare my mind
appropriately for my morning's discourse.

The storm had bent and broken since early dawn. The
sun and the snow winked blindly at each other. The great
hills lifted haughty heads out of wraps of ermine and gold.
Outlines in black and gray of awful fissures and caverns
gaped through the mass of wealthy color which they held.
Little shy, soft clouds fled over these, frightened, one
thought; now and then a row of ragged black teeth snapped
them up; I could see them struggle and sink. Which was
the more relentless, the beauty or the power of the sight,
it were difficult choosing. But I, preparing to preach my
first sermon, and feeling in myself (I hope) the stillness
and smallness of the very valley of humiliation, did not try
to choose. I could only stand at my window and softly say,
"Before the mountains were brought forth, THOU art."

I do not know whether Mary Ann heard me, but when
she appeared at that crisis with my "shaving-water," and
blushed scarlet, transfixed in the middle of the room, with
her mouth open, to beg pardon for the mistake, but "she 'd
got kinder used to it with the last minister, and never thought
till she opened the door and see my crinoline on the chair!"
I continued, with a gentle enthusiasm:--

"That is a grand sight, my dear, over there. It
ought to make one very good, I think, to live in the face of
such hills as those."

"I want to know!" said Mary Ann, coming and gaping
over my shoulder. "Why, I get as used to 'em as I do to
washing-day!"

I had decided upon extempore preaching as best
adapted to the needs of my probable audience, and, with my
icy hands in the warm "shaving-water" and my eyes on the
icy hills, was doing some rambling thinking about the Lord's
messages and messengers, --a subject which the color and
dazzle and delight of the morning had touched highly to my
fancy; but wondering, through my slicing of introduction,
firstly, secondly, a, b, c, d, and conclusion, if the rural
tenement in which we should worship possessed a dinnerbell,
or a gong, or anything of that sort, which could be used as
summons to assemble, and if it were not quite time to hear
the sound, when Mary Ann introduced herself upon the scene
again, to signify that Mr. Dobbins awaited my pleasure down
stairs. Somewhat confused by this sudden announcement, I
seized my Bible and my hat, and presented myself promptly
but palpitating.

"Morning," said Mr. Dobbins, with a pleasant smile.
"Rested yet?"

I thanked him, and was quite rested.

"You don't!" said Mr. Dobbins. "Wal, you see I
come over to say that meetin' 's gin up for to-day."

"Given up!"

"Wal, yes. Ye see there 's such a heft of snow, and
no paths broke, and seein' it was a gal as was goin' to
preach, me and the other deacon we thought she 'd get her
feet wet, or suthin', and so we 'greed we would n't ring the
bell! Thought ye 'd be glad to be let off, after travellin'
all day yesterday, too!"

I looked at Mr. Dobbins. Mr. Dobbins looked at me.
There was a pause.

"Will your paths be broken out by night?" I asked,
with a terrible effort at self-control.

"Wal, yes. In spots; yes; middlin' well."

"Will my audience be afraid of wetting their feet,
after the paths are broken?"

"Bless you, no!" said Mr. Dobbins, staring, "they
're used to 't."

"Then you will please to appoint an evening service,
and ring your bell at half past six precisely. I shall be
there, and shall preach, if there is no one but the sexton
to hear me. And next Sabbath you will oblige me by proceeding with the regular services, whatever the weather,
without the least anxiety for my feet."

"If you was n't a minister, I should say you was
spunky," said Mr. Dobbins, thoughtfully. He regarded me
for some moments with disturbed interest, blindly suspicious
that somebody was offended, but whether pastor or parishioner
he could not make out. He was still undecided, when he took
to his hat, and I to my "own sweet thoughts."

This incident vitally affected my programme for the
day. It was harrowing, but it was stimulative. There was

the inspiration of the rack about it.   The animus of the stake
was upon me.   I could die, but I would not surrender.   I
would gain the respect of my parishioners, whether--well,
yes--whether I gained their souls or not; I am not ashamed
to say it now, partly because of the true, single, gnawing
hunger for usefulness for usefulness' sake, and for higher
than usefulness' sake, which came to me afterwards, and
which, you remember, is all left out for the Sunday magazines; partly because the acquisition of my people's respect
was a necessary antecedent to that of their salvation.

So by help of a fire which I cajoled from Samphiry,
and the shaving-water which was warmer than the fire, I
contrived to employ the remainder of the Sabbath in putting
my first sermon upon paper.

The bell rang, as I had directed, at half past six.   It
did not occur to me at the time that it sounded less like a
dinner-gong than a church-bell of average size and respectability.   I and my sermon were both quite ready for it, and
I tramped off bravely (in my rubber boots), with Mary Ann
as my guide, through the drifted and drifting paths.   Once
more, for the benefit of my sex, I may be permitted to mention that I wore a very plain street suit of black, no crimps,
a white collar of linen, and a black tie; and that I retained
my outside garment--a loose sack--in the pulpit.

"Here we are," said Mary Ann, as I floundered up
half blinded from the depths of a three-feet drift.   Here we
were indeed.   If Mary Ann had not been with me I should
have sat down in the drift, and--no, I do not think I should
have cried, but I should have gasped a little.   Why I should
have been horribly unprepared for the sight of a commodious
white church, with a steeple, and a belfry and stone steps,
and people going up the steps in the latest frill and the stove-
pipe hat, the reader who has ever tried to patronize an
American seamstress, or give orders to an American servant, or ask an American mechanic if he sees a newspaper,
must explain.   The citizens of Storm might be heathen, but
they were Yankees; what more could be said?   Sentence a
Yankee into the Desert of Sahara for life, and out of the
"sandwiches there" he would contrive means to live like
"other folks."

However, I did not sit down in the drift, but went on,
with meeting-house and worshippers all in an unnatural light
like stereoscopic figures, and sat down in the pulpit; a course

of conduct which had at least one advantage,--it saved me a cold.

Mr. Dobbins, it should be noted, met me at the church door, and conducted me, with much respect, up the pulpit stairs. When he left me, I removed my hat and intrenched my beating heart behind a hymn-book.

It will be understood that, while I was not unpractised in Sabbath-school teaching, mission prayer-meeting exhortation, "remarks" at sewing-schools, and other like avenues of religious influence, of the kind considered suitable for my sex, I had never engaged in anything which could be denominated public speech; and that, when the clear clang of the bell hushed suddenly, and the pause on the faces of my audience--there may have been forty of them--warned me that my hour had come, I was in no wise more ready to meet it than any Miss A, B, or C, who would be content to employ life in making sofa-pillows, but would be quite safe from putting it to the outré purpose of making sermons.

So I got through my introductory exercises with a grim desperation, and made haste to my sermon. Once with the manuscript in my hands, I drew breath. Once having looked my audience fairly in the eye, I was prepared to conquer or be conquered by it. There should be no half-way work between us. So I held up my head and did my best.

The criticism of that sermon would be, I suspect, a choice morning's work for any professor of homiletics in the country. Its divisions were numerous and startling; its introduction occurred just where I thought it would sound best, and its conclusion was adjusted to the clock. I reasoned of righteousness and judgment to come, in learned phrase. Theology and metaphysics, exegesis and zoölogy, poetry and botany, were impressed liberally into its pages. I quoted Sir William Hamilton, Strauss, Aristotle, in liberal allowance. I toyed with the names of Schleiermacher and Copernicus. I played battledoor and shuttlecock with "views" of Hegel and Hobbes. As nearly as I can recollect, that sermon was a hash of literature in five syllables, with a seasoning of astronomy and Adam.

I had the satisfaction of knowing, when I read as modestly, reverently, and as much like an unanointed church-member as I knew how, a biblical benediction, and sat down again on the pulpit cushions, that if I had not preached the

Gospel, I had at least subdued the church-going population of Storm.

Certain rough-looking fellows, upon whom I had had my eye since they came in,--there were several of them, grimy and glum, with keen eyes; men who read Tom Paine, you would say, and had come in "to see the fun,"--while I must admit that they neither wept nor prayed, left the house in a respectful, stupid way that was encouraging.

"You gin it to us!" said Mr. Dobbins, enthusiastically. "Folks is all upsot about ye. That there was an eloquent discourse, marm. Why, they don't see but ye know jest as much as if ye was n't a woman!"

And when I touched Mary Ann upon the shoulder to bring her home, I found her sitting motionless, not quite strangled stiff. She had made such a cavern of her mouth, during my impassioned peroration, that an irreligious boy somewhere within good aim had snapped an India-rubber ball into it, which had unfortunately stuck.

Before night, I had reason to feel assured from many sources that I had "made a hit" in my corner of New Vealshire. But before night I had locked myself into the cool and dark, and said, as was said of the Charge of the Six Hundred: "It is magnificent; but it is not war!"

But this is where the Sunday part of my story comes in again, so it is of no consequence to us. Suffice it to say that I immediately appointed a little prayer-meeting, very much after the manner of the ideal service, for the following Wednesday night, in the school-house, with a little table, and a tallow candle, too. The night was clear, and the room packed. The men who read Tom Paine were there. There were some old people present who lived out of walking distance of the church. There were a few young mothers with very quiet children. I succeeded in partially ventilating the room, and chanced on a couple of familiar hymns. It needed only a quiet voice to fill and command the quiet place. I felt very much like a woman, quite enough like a lady, a little, I hope, like a Christian too. Like the old Greek sages, I "was not in haste to speak; I said only that which I had resolved to say." The people listened to me, and prayed as if they felt the better for it. My meeting was full of success and my heart of hope.

Arrived at this point in my narrative, I feel myself
in strong sympathy with the famous historian of Old Mother
Morey. For, when "my story 's just begun, " why, "now, my
story 's done. "

"Ce n'est pas la victoire, mais le combat, " which is
as suitable for autobiographical material, as to "make the
happiness of noble hearts. "

From the time of that little Wednesday-evening meeting my life in Storm was a triumph and a joy, in all the better meanings that triumph and joy can hold. My people respected me first and loved me afterwards. I taught them a
little, and they taught me a great deal. I brightened a few
weeks of their dulled, drowsy, dejected life: they will gild
years of mine.

I desire especially to record that all sense of personal embarrassment and incongruity to the work rapidly left
me. My people at once never remembered and never forgot
that I was a woman. The rudest of the readers of the "Age
of Reason" tipped his hat to me, and read "Ecce Homo" to
gratify me, and after that the Gospel of John to gratify himself.

Every Sabbath morning I read a plain-spoken but carefully written sermon, which cost me perhaps three days of
brain-labor. Every Sabbath afternoon I talked of this and
that, according to the weather and the audience. Every Wednesday night I sat in the school-house, behind the little table and
the tallow candle, with the old people and the young mothers,
and the hush, and the familiar hymns, and lines of hungry
faces down before me that made my heart ache at one look
and bound at the next. It used to seem to me that the mountains had rather starved than fed them. They were pinched,
compressed, shut-down, shut-in faces. All their possibilities
and developments of evil were those of the dwarf, not of the
giant. They were like the poor little Chinese monsters,
moulded from birth in pitchers and vases; all the crevices
and contortions of life they filled, stupidly. Whether it was
because, as Mary Ann said, they "got as used to the mountains as they did to washing-day, " and the process of blunt-
ing to one grandeur dulled them to all others, I can only con-
jecture; but of this my New Vealshire experience convinced
me: the temptations to evil of the city of Paris will bear no
comparison to those of the grandest solitude that God ever
made. It is in repression, not in extension, that the danger

of disease lies to an immortal life. No risks equal those
of ignorance. Daniel Webster may or may not escape the
moral shipwrecks of life, but what chance has an idiot beside him?

"It 's enough to make a man wish he 'd been born a
horse in a treadmill and done with it!" said Happen to me
one day. Happen was a poor fellow on whom I made my
first "parish call"; and I made a great many between Sunday
and Sunday. He lived five miles out of the village, at the
end of an inexpressible mountain road, in a gully which lifted
a pinched, purple face to the great Harmonia Range. I made,
with difficulty, a riding-skirt out of my waterproof, and three
miles an hour out of Mr. Dobbins's horse, and got to him.

The road crawled up a hill into his little low brown
shanty, and there stopped. Here he had "farmed it, man
and boy," till the smoke of Virginia battles puffed over the
hills into his straightforward brown young eyes.

"So I up and into it, marm, two years on 't tough;
then back again to my hoe and my wife and my baby, to say
nothing of the old lady,--you see her through the door there,
bedridden this dozen year,--and never a grain of salt too
much for our porridge, I can tell ye, when one day I 'm
out to cut and chop, ten mile deep in the furrest,--alon' too,
--and first I know I 'm hit and down with the trunk of a
great hickory lyin' smash! along this here leg. Suffer?
Well; it was a day and a half before they found me; and another half-day afore you can get the nighest doctor, you see,
over to East Storm. Well, mebbe he did his best by me, but
mebbe he did n't know no more how to set a bone nor you do.
He vowed there was n't no fracture there. Fracture! it was
jelly afore his eyes. So he ties it up and leaves a tumbler
of suthin', and off. Mortified? Yes. Been here ever since
--on this sofy--yes. Likely to be here--bless you, yes! My
wife, she tends the farm and the baby and the old lady and
me. Sometimes we have two meals a day, and again we
don't. When you come to think as your nighest neighbor 's
five mile off, and that in winter-time,--why, I can see, a-
lookin' from my sofy six feet of snow drifted across that
there road to town,--and nought but one woman in gunshot
of you, able to stir for you if you starve; why, you feel,
sometimes, now, marm, beggin' your pardon, you feel like
hell! There 's summer-folks in their kerridges comes riding
by to see them there hills,--and kind enough to me some of
'em is, I 'll say that for 'em,--and I hear them a-talking and

chattering among themselves, about 'the grand sight,' says
they. 'The d--d sight,' says I; for I lie on my sofy and
look over their heads, marm, at things they never see,--
lines and bars like, over Harmonia, red-hot, and criss-
cross like prison grates. Which comes mebbe of layin' and
lookin' so long, and fanciful. They say, I 'd stand a chance
to the hospital to New York or Boston, mebbe. I hain't gin
it up yet. I 've hopes to go and try my luck some day. But
I suppose it costs a sight. And my wife, she 's set her
heart on the leg's coming to of itself, and so we hang along.
Sometimes folks send me down books and magazines and such
like. I got short o' reading this winter and read the Bible
through; every word, from 'In the beginning' to 'Amen.' It 's
quite a pretty little story-book, too. True? I don't know
about that. Most stories set up to be true. I s'pose if I
was a parson, and a woman into the bargain, I should think
so."

Among my other parochial discoveries, I learned one
day, to my exceeding surprise, that Samphiry--who had been
reticent on her family affairs--was the widow of one of my
predecessors. She had married him when she was young and
pretty, and he was young and ambitious,--"Fond of his book,
my dear," she said, as if she had been talking of some dead
child, "but slow in speech, like Aaron of old. And three
hundred and fifty dollars was tight living for a family like
ours. And his heart ran out, and his people, and maybe his
sermons, too. So the salary kept a-dropping off, twenty-five
dollars at a time, and he could n't take a newspaper, besides
selling the library mostly for doctor's bills. And so he grew
old and sick and took to farming here, without the salary,
and baptized babies and prayed with sick folks free and willing, and never bore anybody a grudge. So he died year before last, and half the valley turned out to bury him. But
that did n't help it any, and I know you 'd never guess me
to be a minister's widow, as well as you do, my dear. I 'm
all washed out and flattened in. And I can't educate my children, one of them. If you 'll believe it, I don't know enough
to tell when they talk bad grammar half the time, and I 'd
about as lieves they 'd eat with their knives as not. If they
get anything to eat, it 's all I 've got heart to care. I 've
got an aunt down in Massachusetts, but it 's such a piece of
work to get there. So I suppose we shall live and die here,
and I don't know but it 's just as well."

What a life it was! I felt so young, so crude, so
blessed and bewildered beside it, that I gave out that night,

at evening prayers, and asked Samphiry to "lead" for herself and me. But I felt no older, no more finished, no less blessed or bewildered, when she had done so.

I should not neglect to mention that I conducted several funerals while I was in Storm. I did not know how, but I knew how to be sorry, which seemed to answer the same purpose; at least they sought me out for the object from far and near. On one occasion I was visited by a distant neighbor, with the request that I would bury his wife. I happened to know that the dead woman had been once a member of the Methodist church in East Storm, whose pastor was alive, active, and a man.

"Would it not be more suitable," I therefore suggested, "at least more agreeable to the feelings of Brother Hand, if you were to ask him to conduct either the whole or a part of the service?"

"Waal, ye see, marm," urged the widower, "the cops was partikelar sot on hevin' you, and as long as I promised her afore she drawed her last that you should conduct the business, I think we 'd better perceed without any reference to Brother Hand. I 've been thinking of it over, and I come to the conclusion that he could n't take offence on so slight an occasion!"

I had ministered "on trial" to the people of Storm, undisturbed by Rev. Dr. Zangrow, who, I suspect, was in private communication of some sort with Mr. Dobbins, for a month, --a month of pouting, spring weather, and long, lazy walks for thinking, and brisk, bright ones for doing; of growing quite fond of salt-pork and barley bread; of calling on old, bedridden women, and hunting up neglected girls, and keeping one eye on my Tom Paine friends; of preaching and practising, of hoping and doubting, of struggling and succeeding, of finding my heart and hands and head as full as life could hold; of feeling that there was a place for me in the earnest world, and that I was in my place; of feeling thankful every day and hour that my womanhood and my work had hit and fitted; of a great many other things which I have agreed not to mention here, --when one night the stage brought me a letter which ran:--

Hercules, April 28, 18--

My Dear:--I have the measles.
Mädchen

Did ever a woman try to do anything, that some of the children did not have the measles?

I felt that fate was stronger than I. I bowed my head submissively, and packed my valise shockingly. Some of the people came in a little knot that night to say good by. The women cried and the men shook hands hard. It was very pleasant and very heartbreaking. I felt a dismal foreboding that, once in the clutches of Hercules and Mädchen, I should never see their dull, dear faces again. I left my sorrow and my Jeremy Taylor for Happen, and my rubber-boots for Samphiry. I tucked the lace collar and the spare paper of hairpins into Mary Ann's upper drawer. I begged Mr. Dobbins's acceptance of Barnes on Matthew, with the request that he would start a Sunday school.

In the gray of the early morning the patient horse trotted me over, with lightened valise and heavy heart, to the crazy station. When I turned my head for a farewell look at my parish, the awful hills were crossed with Happen's red-hot bars, and Mary Ann, with her mouth open, stood in her mother's crumbling door.

SARAH ORNE JEWETT

(1849-1909)

Sarah Orne Jewett was born in South Berwick, southern Maine, in 1849, the second of three daughters of Theodore H. and Frances (Perry) Jewett. Her father was a country doctor, whom Sarah often accompanied on his calls into the countryside, thus gaining a firsthand knowledge of the rural and coastal folk, who figure in much of her fiction. She was educated in a local grammar school and in Berwick Academy. She gave up an early ambition to be a physician, feeling that as a woman she would be handicapped in the profession. A voracious reader, she began in her teens to write and publish stories, one of the earliest of which appeared in the Atlantic Monthly in 1868. The family mansion in South Berwick remained her home, and a very dear one, throughout her life; but after her father's death in 1878, and as her literary efforts prospered, she spent much time in Boston and Manchester-by-the-Sea with her intimate friend Annie Fields, the wife of the prominent Boston publisher James T. Fields. At the Fieldses' Boston home, 148 Charles Street, she became a part of the contemporary literary scene, for here the publisher and his wife entertained many of the outstanding authors of Europe and America. At 148 Charles Street also, she first became the friend and mentor of Willa Cather, then a beginning writer, who later credited Jewett with giving her advice that led to her own literary success.

Jewett is among the two or three best writers of New England local-color fiction. Her accurate observation of settings and character and her sensitive ear for dialect place her squarely and prominently in the realistic tradition of the late nineteenth century. Though she occasionally verges on the sentimental, she does not gloss over the spiritual and physical rigors and deprivations of life in the back country and along the coast. That her characters, especially her women, frequently transcend the restrictions of environment attests to her Emersonian belief in the power of self-reliance.

221

Jewett's first book was Deephaven (1877), a collection of tales and sketches laid in a decaying Maine seaport. Other collections and novels followed, among them A White Heron and Other Stories (1886), in which "Marsh Rosemary," the tale that follows, is included. Her best-known book is The Country of the Pointed Firs (1896), a somewhat loosely connected series of narratives and vignettes centered in a Down East fishing village. Two fine studies of Jewett's life and work are F. O. Matthiessen, Sarah Orne Jewett (1929), and Richard Cary, Sarah Orne Jewett (1962). Perry D. Westbrook, Acres of Flint: Sarah Orne Jewett and Her Contemporaries, rev. ed. (1981) considers Jewett as representative of New England literary regionalism.

From A WHITE HERON AND OTHER STORIES

Marsh Rosemary

I

One hot afternoon in August, a single moving figure might have been seen following a straight road that crossed the salt marshes of Walpole. Everybody else had either stayed at home or crept into such shade as could be found near at hand. The thermometer marked at least ninety degrees. There was hardly a fishing-boat to be seen on the glistening sea, only far away on the hazy horizon two or three coasting schooners looked like ghostly flying Dutchmen, becalmed for once and motionless.

Ashore, the flaring light of the sun brought out the fine, clear colors of the level landscape. The marsh grasses were a more vivid green than usual, the brown tops of those that were beginning to go to seed looked almost red, and the soil at the edges of the tide inlets seemed to be melting into a black, pitchy substance like the dark pigments on a painter's palette. Where the land was higher the hot air flickered above it dizzily. This was not an afternoon that one

would naturally choose for a long walk, yet Mr. Jerry Lane
stepped briskly forward, and appeared to have more than
usual energy. His big boots trod down the soft carpet of
pussy-clover that bordered the dusty, whitish road. He
struck at the stationary procession of thistles with a little
stick as he went by. Flight after flight of yellow butterflies
fluttered up as he passed, and then settled down again to
their thistle flowers, while on the shiny cambric back of
Jerry's Sunday waistcoat basked at least eight large green-
headed flies in complete security.

It was difficult to decide why the Sunday waistcoat
should have been put on that Saturday afternoon. Jerry had
not thought it important to wear his best boots or best trou-
sers, and had left his coat at home altogether. He smiled
as he walked along, and once when he took off his hat, as
a light breeze came that way, he waved it triumphantly before he put it on again. Evidently this was no common errand that led him due west, and made him forget the hot
weather, and caused him to shade his eyes with his hand,
as he looked eagerly at a clump of trees and the chimney
of a small house a little way beyond the boundary of the
marshes, where the higher ground began.

Miss Ann Floyd sat by her favorite window, sewing,
twitching her thread less decidedly than usual, and casting
a wistful glance now and then down the road or at the bees
in her gay little garden outside. There was a grim expression overshadowing her firmly-set, angular face, and the
frown that always appeared on her forehead when she sewed
or read the newspaper was deeper and straighter than usual.
She did not look as if she were conscious of the heat, though
she had dressed herself in an old-fashioned skirt of sprigged
lawn and a loose jacket of thin white dimity with out-of-date
flowing sleeves. Her sandy hair was smoothly brushed; one
lock betrayed a slight crinkle at its edge, but it owed nothing
to any encouragement of Nancy Floyd's. A hard, honest,
kindly face this was, of a woman whom everybody trusted,
who might be expected to give of whatever she had to give,
good measure, pressed down and running over. She was a
lonely soul; she had no near relatives in the world. It
seemed always as if nature had been mistaken in not planting her somewhere in a large and busy household.

The little square room, kitchen in winter and sitting-
room in summer, was as clean and bare and thrifty as one

would expect the dwelling-place of such a woman to be. She
sat in a straight-backed, splint-bottomed kitchen chair, and
always put back her spool with a click on the very same spot
on the window-sill. You would think she had done with youth
and with love affairs, yet you might as well expect the ancient cherry-tree in the corner of her yard to cease adven-
turing its white blossoms when the May sun shone! No woman in Walpole had more bravely and patiently borne the
burden of loneliness and lack of love. Even now her outward behavior gave no hint of the new excitement and delight
that filled her heart.

"Land sakes alive!" she says to herself presently,
"there comes Jerry Lane. I expect, if he sees me settin'
to the winder, he 'll come in an' dawdle round till supper
time!" But good Nancy Floyd smooths her hair hastily as
she rises and drops her work, and steps back toward the
middle of the room, watching the gate anxiously all the time.
Now, Jerry, with a crestfallen look at the vacant window,
makes believe that he is going by, and takes a loitering step
or two onward, and then stops short; with a somewhat sheepish smile he leans over the neat picket fence and examines
the blue and white and pink larkspur that covers most of the
space in the little garden. He takes off his hat again to cool
his forehead, and replaces it, without a grand gesture this
time, and looks again at the window hopefully.

There is a pause. The woman knows that the man is
sure she is there; a little blush colors her thin cheeks as she
comes boldly to the wide-open front door.

"What do you think of this kind of weather?" asks
Jerry Lane, complacently, as he leans over the fence, and
surrounds himself with an air of self-sacrifice.

"I call it hot," responds the Juliet from her balcony,
with deliberate assurance, "but the corn needs sun, everybody says. I should n't have wanted to toil up from the
shore under such a glare, if I had been you. Better come
in and set a while, and cool off," she added, without any
apparent enthusiasm. Jerry was sure to come, any way.
She would rather make the suggestion than have him.

Mr. Lane sauntered in, and seated himself opposite
his hostess, beside the other small window, and watched her
admiringly as she took up her sewing and worked at it with

great spirit and purpose. He clasped his hands together and leaned forward a little. The shaded kitchen was very comfortable, after the glaring light outside, and the clean orderliness of the few chairs and the braided rugs and the table under the clock, with some larkspur and asparagus in a china vase for decoration, seemed to please him unexpectedly. "Now just see what ways you women folks have of fixing things up smart!" he ventured gallantly.

Nancy's countenance did not forbid further compliment; she looked at the flowers herself, quickly, and explained that she had gathered them a while ago to send to the minister's sister, who kept house for him. "I saw him going by, and expected he 'd be back this same road. Mis' Elton 's be'n havin' another o' her dyin' spells this noon, and the deacon went by after him hot foot. I 'd souse her well with stone-cold water. She never sent for me to set up with her; she knows better. Poor man, 't was likely he was right into the middle of tomorrow's sermon. 'T ain't considerate of the deacon, and when he knows he 's got a fool for a wife, he need n't go round persuading other folks she 's so suffering as she makes out. They ain't got no larkspur this year to the parsonage, and I was going to let the minister take this over to Amandy; but I see his wagon over on the other road, going towards the village, about an hour after he went by here."

It seemed to be a relief to tell somebody all these things after such a season of forced repression, and Jerry listened with gratifying interest. "How you do see through folks!" he exclaimed in a mild voice. Jerry could be very soft spoken if he thought best. "Mis' Elton 's a die-away lookin' creatur'. I heard of her saying last Sunday, comin' out o' meetin', that she made an effort to git there once more, but she expected 't would be the last time. Looks as if she eat well, don't she?" he concluded, in a meditative tone.

"Eat!" exclaimed the hostess, with snapping eyes. "There ain't no woman in town, sick or well, can lay aside the food that she does. 'T ain't to the table afore folks, but she goes seeking round in the cupboards half a dozen times a day. An' I 've heard her remark 't was the last time she ever expected to visit the sanctuary as much as a dozen times within five years."

"Some places I 've sailed to they 'd have hit her over

the head with a club long ago," said Jerry, with an utter
lack of sympathy that was startling. "Well, I must be get-
tin' back again. Talkin' of eatin' makes us think o' supper
time. Must be past five, ain't it? I thought I 'd just step
up to see if there wa'n't anything I could lend a hand about,
this hot day."

Sensible Ann Floyd folded her hands over her sewing,
as it lay in her lap, and looked straight before her without
seeing the pleading face of the guest. This moment was a
great crisis in her life. She was conscious of it, and knew
well enough that upon her next words would depend the course
of future events. The man who waited to hear what she had
to say was indeed many years younger than she, was shift-
less and vacillating. He had drifted to Walpole from nobody
knew where, and possessed many qualities which she had
openly rebuked and despised in other men. True enough,
he was good-looking, but that did not atone for the lacks of
his character and reputation. Yet she knew herself to be
the better man of the two, and since she had surmounted
many obstacles already she was confident that, with a push
here and a pull there to steady him, she could keep him in
good trim. The winters were so long and lonely; her life
was in many ways hungry and desolate in spite of its thrift
and conformity. She had laughed scornfully when he stopped,
one day in the spring, and offered to help her weed her garden; she had even joked with one of the neighbors about it.
Jerry had been growing more and more friendly and pleasant
ever since. His ease-loving careless nature was like a comfortable cushion for hers, with its angles, its melancholy anticipations and self-questionings. But Jerry liked her, and
if she liked him and married him, and took him home, it
was nobody's business; and in that moment of surrender to
Jerry's cause she arrayed herself at his right hand against
the rest of the world, ready for warfare with any and all of
its opinions.

She was suddenly aware of the sunburnt face and light,
curling hair of her undeclared lover, at the other end of the
painted table with its folded leaf. She smiled at him vacantly
across the larkspur; then she gave a little start, and was
afraid that her thoughts had wandered longer than was seemly.
The kitchen clock was ticking faster than usual, as if it were
trying to attract attention.

"I guess I 'll be getting home," repeated the visitor
ruefully, and rose from his chair, but hesitated again at an
unfamiliar expression upon his companion's face.

"I don't know as I 've got anything extra for supper,
but you stop, " she said, "an' take what there is.   I would
n't go back across them marshes right in this heat. "

Jerry Lane had a lively sense of humor, and a queer
feeling of merriment stole over him now, as he watched the
mistress of the house.   She had risen, too; she looked so
simple and so frankly sentimental, there was such an incon-
gruous coyness added to her usually straightforward, angular
appearance, that his instinctive laughter nearly got the better
of him, and might have lost him the prize for which he had
been waiting these many months.   But Jerry behaved like a
man: he stepped forward and kissed Ann Floyd; he held her
fast with one arm as he stood beside her, and kissed her
again and again.   She was a dear good woman.   She had a
fresh young heart, in spite of the straight wrinkle in her
forehead and her work-worn hands.   She had waited all her
days for this joy of having a lover.

II

Even Mrs. Elton revived for a day or two under the tonic of
such a piece of news.   That was what Jerry Lane had hung
round for all summer, everybody knew at last.   Now he would
strike work and live at his ease, the men grumbled to each
other; but all the women of Walpole deplored most the weakness and foolishness of the elderly bride.   Ann Floyd was
comfortably off, and had something laid by for a rainy day;
she would have done vastly better to deny herself such an
expensive and utterly worthless luxury as the kind of husband
Jerry Lane would make.   He had idled away his life.   He
earned a little money now and then in seafaring pursuits,
but was too lazy, in the shore parlance, to tend lobsterpots.
What was energetic Ann Floyd going to do with him?   She
was always at work, always equal to emergencies, and entirely opposed to dullness and idleness and even placidity.
She liked people who had some snap to them, she often
avowed scornfully, and now she had chosen for a husband
the laziest man in Walpole.   "Dear sakes, " one woman said
to another, as they heard the news, "there 's no fool like an
old fool !"

The days went quickly by, while Miss Ann made her
plain wedding clothes.   If people expected her to put on airs
of youth they were disappointed.   Her wedding bonnet was the
same sort of bonnet she had worn for a dozen years, and one
disappointed critic deplored the fact that she had spruced up

so little, and kept on dressing old enough to look like Jerry
Lane's mother. As her acquaintances met her they looked
at her with close scrutiny, expecting to see some outward
trace of such a silly, uncharacteristic departure from good
sense and discretion. But Miss Floyd, while she was still
Miss Floyd, displayed no silliness and behaved with dignity,
while on the Sunday after a quiet marriage at the parsonage
she and Jerry Lane walked up the side aisle to their pew,
the picture of middle-aged sobriety and respectability. Their
fellow parishoners, having recovered from their first aston-
ishment and amusement, settled down to the belief that the
newly married pair understood their own business best, and
that if anybody could make the best of Jerry and get any
work out of him, it was his capable wife.

"And if she undertakes to drive him too hard he can
slip off to sea, and they 'll be rid of each other," commented
one of Jerry's 'longshore companions, as if it were only reasonable that some refuge should be afforded to those who
make mistakes in matrimony.

There did not seem to be any mistake at first, or for
a good many months afterward. The husband liked the comfort that came from such good housekeeping, and enjoyed a
deep sense of having made a good anchorage in a well-
sheltered harbor, after many years of thriftless improvi-
dence and drifting to and fro. There were some hindrances
to perfect happiness: he had to forego long seasons of gossip with his particular friends, and the outdoor work which
was expected of him, though by no means heavy for a person
of his strength, fettered his freedom not a little. To chop
wood, and take care of a cow, and bring a pail of water now
and then, did not weary him so much as it made him practically understand the truth of weakly Sister Elton's remark
that life was a constant chore. And when poor Jerry, for
lack of other interest, fancied that his health was giving way
mysteriously, and brought home a bottle of strong liquor to
be used in case of sickness, and placed it conveniently in
the shed, Mrs. Lane locked it up in the small chimney cupboard where she kept her camphor bottle and her opodeldoc
and the other family medicines. She was not harsh with her
husband. She cherished him tenderly, and worked diligently
at her trade of tailoress, singing her hymns gayly in summer weather; for she never had been so happy as now, when
there was somebody to please beside herself, to cook for and
sew for, and to live with and love. But Jerry complained

more and more in his inmost heart that his wife expected too much of him. Presently he resumed an old habit of resorting to the least respected of the two country stores of that neighborhood, and sat in the row of loafers on the outer steps. "Sakes alive," said a shrewd observer one day, "the fools set there and talk and talk about what they went through when they follered the sea, till when the womenfolks comes tradin' they are obleeged to climb right over 'em."

But things grew worse and worse, until one day Jerry Lane came home a little late to dinner, and found his wife unusually grim-faced and impatient. He took his seat with an amiable smile, and showed in every way his determination not to lose his temper because somebody else had. It was one of the days when he looked almost boyish and entirely irresponsible. His hair was handsome and curly from the dampness of the east wind, and his wife was forced to remember how, in the days of their courtship, she used to wish that she could pull one of the curling locks straight, for the pleasure of seeing it fly back. She felt old and tired, and was hurt in her very soul by the contrast between herself and her husband. "No wonder I am aging, having to lug everything on my shoulders," she thought. Jerry had forgotten to do whatever she had asked him for a day or two. He had started out that morning to go lobstering, but he had returned from the direction of the village.

"Nancy," he said pleasantly, after he had begun his dinner, a silent and solitary meal, while his wife stitched busily by the window, and refused to look at him, --"Nancy, I 've been thinking a good deal about a project."

"I hope it ain't going to cost so much and bring in so little as your other notions have, then," she responded, quickly; though somehow a memory of the hot day when Jerry came and stood outside the fence, and kissed her when it was settled he should stay to supper, --a memory of that day would keep fading and brightening in her mind.

"Yes," said Jerry, humbly, "I ain't done right, Nancy. I ain't done my part for our livin'. I 've let it sag right on to you, most ever since we was married. There was that spell when I was kind of weakly, and had a pain acrost me. I tell you what it is: I never was good for nothin' ashore, but now I 've got my strength up I 'm going to show ye what I can do. I 'm promised to ship with Cap'n Low's brother, Skipper Nathan, that sails out o' Eastport in the coasting trade, lumber and so on. I shall get good wages, and you shall keep the whole on 't 'cept what I need for clothes."

"You need n't be so plaintive," said Ann, in a sharp voice. "You can go if you want to. I have always been able to take care of myself, but when it comes to maintainin' two, 't ain't so easy. When be you goin'?"

"I expected you would be sorry," mourned Jerry, his face falling at this outbreak. "Nancy, you need n't be so quick. 'T ain't as if I had n't always set everything by ye, if I be wuthless."

Nancy's eyes flashed fire as she turned hastily away. Hardly knowing where she went, she passed through the open doorway, and crossed the clean green turf of the narrow side yard, and leaned over the garden fence. The young cabbages and cucumbers were nearly buried in weeds, and the currant bushes were fast being turned into skeletons by the ravaging worms. Jerry had forgotten to sprinkle them with hellebore, after all, though she had put the watering-pot into his very hand the evening before. She did not like to have the whole town laugh at her for hiring a man to do his work; she was busy from early morning until late night, but she could not do everything herself. She had been a fool to marry this man, she told herself at last, and a sullen discontent and rage that had been of slow but certain growth made her long to free herself from this unprofitable hindrance for a time, at any rate. Go to sea? Yes, that was the best thing that could happen. Perhaps when he had worked hard a while on schooner fare, he would come home and be good for something!

Jerry finished his dinner in the course of time, and then sought his wife. It was not like her to go away in this silent fashion. Of late her gift of speech had been proved sufficiently formidable, and yet she had never looked so resolutely angry as to-day.

"Nancy," he began, --"Nancy, girl! I ain't goin' off to leave you, if your heart 's set against it. I 'll spudge up and take right holt."

But the wife turned slowly from the fence and faced him. Her eyes looked as if she had been crying. "You need n't stay on my account," she said. "I 'll go right to work an' fit ye out. I 'm sick of your meechin' talk, and I don't want to hear no more of it. Ef I was a man"--

Jerry Lane looked crestfallen for a minute or two;
but when his stern partner in life had disappeared within the
house, he slunk away among the apple-trees of the little orchard, and sat down on the grass in a shady spot.   It was
getting to be warm weather, but he would go round and hoe
the old girl's garden stuff by and by.   There would be something goin' on aboard the schooner, and with delicious anti-
cipation of future pleasure this delinquent Jerry struck his
knee with his hand, as if he were clapping a crony on the
shoulder.   He also winked several times at the same fancied
companion.   Then, with a comfortable chuckle, he laid himself down, and pulled his old hat over his eyes, and went to
sleep, while the weeds grew at their own sweet will, and the
currant worms went looping and devouring from twig to twig.

III

Summer went by, and winter began, and Mr. Jerry Lane did
not reappear.   He had promised to return in September,
when he parted from his wife early in June, for Nancy had
relented a little at the last, and sorrowed at the prospect of
so long a separation.   She had already learned the vacilla-
tions and uncertainties of her husband's character; but though
she accepted the truth that her marriage had been in every
way a piece of foolishness, she still clung affectionately to
his assumed fondness for her.   She could not believe that
his marriage was only one of his makeshifts, and that as
soon as he grew tired of the constraint he was ready to
throw the benefits of respectable home life to the four winds.
A little sentimental speech-making and a few kisses the morning he went away, and the gratitude he might well have shown
for her generous care-taking and provision for his voyage
won her soft heart back again, and made poor, elderly,
simple-hearted Nancy watch him cross the marshes with
tears and foreboding.   If she could have called him back
that day, she would have done so and been thankful.   And
all summer and winter, whenever the wind blew and thrashed
the drooping elm boughs against the low roof over her head,
she was as full of fears and anxieties as if Jerry were her
only son and making his first voyage at sea.   The neighbors
pitied her for her disappointment.   They liked Nancy; but
they could not help saying, "I told you so."   It would have
been impossible not to respect the brave way in which she
met the world's eye, and carried herself with innocent un-
consciousness of having committed so laughable and unrewarding a folly.   The loafers on the store steps had been unwont-

edly diverted one day, when Jerry, who was their chief wit
and spokesman, rose slowly from his place, and said in pious tones, "Boys, I must go this minute. Grandma will
keep dinner waiting." Mrs. Ann Lane did not show in her
aging face how young her heart was, and after the schooner
Susan Barnes had departed she seemed to pass swiftly from
middle life and an almost youthful vigor to early age and a
look of spent strength and dissatisfaction. "I suppose he did
find it dull," she assured herself, with wistful yearning for
his rough words of praise, when she sat down alone to her
dinner, or looked up sadly from her work, and missed the
amusing though unedifying conversation he was wont to offer
occasionally on stormy winter nights. How much of his ad-
venturing was true she never cared to ask. He had come
and gone, and she forgave him his shortcomings, and longed
for his society with a heavy heart.

One spring day there was news in the Boston paper
of the loss of the schooner Susan Barnes with all on board,
and Nancy Lane's best friends shook their sage heads, and
declared that as far as regarded Jerry Lane, that idle vagabond, it was all for the best. Nobody was interested in any
other member of the crew, so the misfortune of the Susan
Barnes seemed of but slight consequence in Walpole, she
having passed out of her former owners' hands the autumn
before. Jerry had stuck by the ship; at least, so he had
sent word then to his wife by Skipper Nathan Low. The
Susan Barnes was to sail regularly between Shediac and Newfoundland, and Jerry sent five dollars to Nancy, and promised to pay her a visit soon. "Tell her I 'm layin' up somethin' handsome," he told the skipper with a grin, "and I 've
got some folks in Newfoundland I 'll visit with on this voyage,
and then I 'll come ashore for good and farm it."

Mrs. Lane took the five dollars from the skipper as
proudly as if Jerry had done the same thing so many times
before that she hardly noticed it. The skipper gave the messages from Jerry, and felt that he had done the proper thing.
When the news came long afterward that the schooner was
lost, that was the next thing that Nancy knew about her wandering mate; and after the minister had come solemnly to in-
form her of her bereavement, and had gone away again, and
she sat down and looked her widowhood in the face, there
was not a sadder nor a lonelier woman in the town of Walpole.

All the neighbors came to condole with our heroine,

and, though nobody was aware of it, from that time she was really happier and better satisfied with life than she had ever been before. Now she had an ideal Jerry Lane to mourn over and think about, to cherish and admire; she was day by day slowly forgetting the trouble he had been and the bitter shame of him, and exalting his memory to something near saintliness. "He meant well," she told herself again and again. She thought nobody could tell so good a story; she felt that with her own bustling, capable ways he had no chance to do much that he might have done. She had been too quick with him, and alas, alas! how much better she would know how to treat him if she only could see him again! A sense of relief at his absence made her continually assure herself of her great loss, and, false even to herself, she mourned her sometime lover diligently, and tried to think herself a broken-hearted woman. It was thought among those who knew Nancy Lane best that she would recover her spirits in time, but Jerry's wildest anticipations of a proper respect to his memory were more than realized in the first two years after the schooner Susan Barnes went to the bottom of the sea. She mourned for the man he ought to have been, not for the real Jerry, but she had loved him in the beginning enough to make her own love a precious possession for all time to come. It did not matter much, after all, what manner of man he was; she had found in him something on which to spend her hoarded affection.

IV

Nancy Lane was a peaceable woman and a good neighbor, but she never had been able to get on with one fellow townswoman, and that was Mrs. Deacon Elton. They managed to keep each other provoked and teased from one year's end to the other, and each good soul felt herself under a moral microscope, and understood that she was judged by a not very lenient criticism and discussion. Mrs. Lane clad herself in simple black after the news came of her husband's timely death, and Mrs. Elton made one of her farewell pilgrimages to church to see the new-made widow walk up the aisle.

"She need n't tell me she lays that affliction so much to heart," the deacon's wife sniffed faintly, after her exhaustion had been met by proper treatment of camphor and a glass of currant wine, at the parsonage, where she rested a while after service. "Nancy Floyd knows she 's well over with such a piece of nonsense. If I had had my health, I should

have spoken with her and urged her not to take the step in
the first place. She has n't spoken six beholden words to
me since that vagabond came to Walpole. I dare say she
may have heard something I said at the time she married.
I declare for 't, I never was so outdone as I was when the
deacon came home and told me Nancy Floyd was going to
be married. She let herself down too low to ever hold the
place again that she used to have in folks' minds. And it
's my opinion," said the sharp-eyed little woman, "she ain't
got through with her pay yet."

But Mrs. Elton did not know with what unconscious
prophecy her words were freighted.

The months passed by: summer and winter came
and went, and even those few persons who were misled by
Nancy Lane's stern visage and forbidding exterior into forgetting her kind heart were at last won over to friendliness
by her renewed devotion to the sick and old people of the
rural community. She was so tender to little children that
they all loved her dearly. She was ready to go to any household that needed help, and in spite of her ceaseless industry
with her needle she found many a chance to do good, and
help her neighbors to lift and carry the burdens of their
lives. She blossomed out suddenly into a lovely, painstaking
eagerness to be of use; it seemed as if her affectionate
heart, once made generous, must go on spending its wealth
wherever it could find an excuse. Even Mrs. Elton herself
was touched by her old enemy's evident wish to be friends,
and said nothing more about poor Nancy's looking as savage
as a hawk. The only thing to admit was the truth that her
affliction had proved a blessing to her. And it was in a
truly kind and compassionate spirit that, after hearing an
awful piece of news, the deacon's hysterical wife forbore to
spread it far and wide through the town first, and went down
to the Widow Lane's one September afternoon. Nancy was
stitching busily upon the deacon's new coat, and looked up
with a friendly smile as her guest came in, in spite of an
instinctive shrug as she had seen her coming up the yard.
The dislike of the poor souls for each other was deeper than
their philosophy could reach.

Mrs. Elton spent some minutes in the unnecessary en-
deavor to regain her breath, and to her surprise found she
must make a real effort before she could tell her unwelcome
news. She had been so full of it all the way from home that

she had rehearsed the whole interview; now she hardly knew
how to begin. Nancy looked serener than usual, but there
was something wistful about her face as she glanced across
the room, presently, as if to understand the reason of the
long pause. The clock ticked loudly; the kitten clattered a
spool against the table-leg, and had begun to snarl the thread
around her busy paws, and Nancy looked down and saw her;
then the instant consciousness of there being some unhappy
reason for Mrs. Elton's call made her forget the creature's
mischief, and anxiously lay down her work to listen.

"Skipper Nathan Low was to our house to dinner," the
guest began. "He 's bargaining with the deacon about some
hay. He 's got a new schooner, Skipper Nathan has, and is
going to build up a regular business of freighting hay to Boston by sea. There 's no market to speak of about here, unless you haul it way over to Downer, and you can't make but
one turn a day."

"'T would be a good thing," replied Nancy, trying to
think that this was all, and perhaps the deacon wanted to
hire her own field another year. He had underpaid her once,
and they had not been on particularly good terms ever since.
She would make her own bargains with Skipper Nathan, she
thanked him and his wife!

"He 's been down to the provinces these two or three
years back, you know," the whining voice went on, and
straightforward Ann Lane felt the old animosity rising within
her. "At dinner time I was n't able to eat much of anything,
and so I was talking with Cap'n Nathan, and asking him some
questions about them parts; and I spoke something about the
mercy 't was his life should ha' been spared when that
schooner, the Susan Barnes, was lost so quick after he sold
out his part of her. And I put in a word, bein' 's we were
neighbors, about how edifyin' your course had be'n under affliction. I noticed then he 'd looked sort o' queer whilst I
was talkin', but there was all the folks to the table, and you
know he 's a very cautious man, so he spoke of somethin'
else. 'T wa'n't half an hour after dinner, I was comin' in
with some plates and cups, tryin' to help what my stren'th
would let me, and says he, 'Step out a little ways into the
piece with me, Mis' Elton. I want to have a word with ye.'
I went, too, spite o' my neuralgy, for I saw he 'd got somethin' on his mind. 'Look here,' says he, 'I gathered from
the way you spoke that Jerry Lane's wife expects he 's dead.'
Certain, says I, his name was in the list o' the Susan Barnes's

crew, and we read it in the paper. 'No,' says he to me, 'he ran away the day they sailed; he was n't aboard, and he 's livin' with another woman down to Shediac.' Them was his very words."

Nancy Lane sank back in her chair, and covered her horror-stricken eyes with her hands. "'T ain't pleasant news to have to tell," Sister Elton went on mildly, yet with evident relish and full command of the occasion. "He said he seen Jerry the morning he came away. I thought you ought to know it. I 'll tell you one thing, Nancy: I told the skipper to keep still about it, and now I 've told you, I won't spread it no further to set folks a-talking. I 'll keep it secret till you say the word. There ain't much trafficking betwixt here and there, and he 's dead to you, certain, as much as if he laid up here in the burying-ground."

Nancy had bowed her head upon the table; the thin sandy hair was streaked with gray. She did not answer one word; this was the hardest blow of all.

"I 'm much obliged to you for being so friendly," she said after a few minutes, looking straight before her now in a dazed sort of way, and lifting the new coat from the floor, where it had fallen. "Yes, he 's dead to me,--worse than dead, a good deal," and her lip quivered. "I can't seem to bring my thoughts to bear. I 've got so used to thinkin'-- No, don't you say nothin' to the folks, yet. I 'd do as much for you." And Mrs. Elton knew that the smitten fellow-creature before her spoke the truth, and forebore.

Two or three days came and went, and with every hour the quiet, simple-hearted woman felt more grieved and unsteady in mind and body. Such a shattering thunderbolt of news rarely falls into a human life. She could not sleep; she wandered to and fro in the little house, and cried until she could cry no longer. Then a great rage spurred and excited her. She would go to Shediac, and call Jerry Lane to account. She would accuse him face to face; and the woman whom he was deceiving, as perhaps he had deceived her, should know the baseness and cowardice of this miserable man. So, dressed in her respectable Sunday clothes, in the gray bonnet and shawl that never had known any journeys except to meeting, or to a country funeral or quiet holiday-making, Nancy Lane trusted herself for the first time to the bewildering railway, to the temptations and dangers of the wide world outside the bounds of Walpole.

Two or three days later still, the quaint, thin figure familiar in Walpole highways flitted down the street of a provincial town. In the most primitive region of China this woman could hardly have felt a greater sense of foreign life and strangeness. At another time her native good sense and shrewd observation would have delighted in the experiences of this first week of travel, but she was too sternly angry and aggrieved, too deeply plunged in a survey of her own calamity, to take much notice of what was going on about her. Later she condemned the unworthy folly of the whole errand, but in these days the impulse to seek the culprit and confront him was irresistible.

The innkeeper's wife, a kindly creature, had urged this puzzling guest to wait and rest and eat some supper, but Nancy refused, and without asking her way left the brightly lighted, flaring little public room, where curious eyes already offended her, and went out into the damp twilight. The voices of the street boys sounded outlandish, and she felt more and more lonely. She longed for Jerry to appear for protection's sake; she forgot why she sought him, and was eager to shelter herself behind the flimsy bulwark of his manhood. She rebuked herself presently with terrible bitterness for a womanish wonder whether he would say, "Why, Nancy, girl!" and be glad to see her. Poor woman, it was a work-laden, serious girlhood that had been hers at any rate. The power of giving her whole self in unselfish, enthusiastic, patient devotion had not belonged to her youth only; it had sprung fresh and blossoming in her heart as every new year came and went.

One might have seen her stealing through the shadows, skirting the edge of a lumber-yard, stepping among the refuse of the harbor side, asking a question timidly now and then of some passer-by. Yes, they knew Jerry Lane,--his house was only a little way off; and one curious and compassionate Scotchman, divining by some inner sense the exciting nature of the errand, turned back, and offered fruitlessly to go with the stranger. "You know the man?" he asked. "He is his own enemy, but doing better now that he is married. He minds his work, I know that well; but he 's taken a good wife." Nancy's heart beat faster with honest pride for a moment, until the shadow of the ugly truth and reality made it sink back to heaviness, and the fire of her smouldering rage was again kindled. She would speak to Jerry face to face before she slept, and a horrible contempt and scorn were ready for him, as with a glance either way along the road she entered the narrow yard, and went noiselessly toward

the window of a low, poor-looking house, from whence a
bright light was shining out into the night.

Yes, there was Jerry, and it seemed as if she must
faint and fall at the sight of him. How young he looked still!
The thought smote her like a blow. They never were mates
for each other, Jerry and she. Her own life was waning;
she was an old woman.

He never had been so thrifty and respectable before;
the other woman ought to know the savage truth about him,
for all that! But at that moment the other woman stooped
beside the supper table, and lifted a baby from its cradle,
and put the dear, live little thing into its father's arms.
The baby was wide awake, and laughed at Jerry, who laughed
back again, and it reached up to catch at a handful of the
curly hair which had been poor Nancy's delight.

The other woman stood there looking at them, full of
pride and love. She was young, and trig, and neat. She
looked a brisk, efficient little creature. Perhaps Jerry would
make something of himself now; he always had it in him.
The tears were running down Nancy's cheeks; the rain, too,
had begun to fall. She stood there watching the little household sit down to supper, and noticed with eager envy how well
cooked the food was, and how hungrily the master of the house
ate what was put before him. All thoughts of ending the new
wife's sin and folly vanished away. She could not enter in
and break another heart; hers was broken already, and it
would not matter. And Nancy Lane, a widow indeed, crept
away again, as silently as she had come, to think what was
best to be done, to find alternate woe and comfort in the
memory of the sight she had seen.

The little house at the edge of the Walpole marshes
seemed full of blessed shelter and comfort the evening that
its forsaken mistress came back to it. Her strength was
spent; she felt much more desolate now that she had seen
with her own eyes that Jerry Lane was alive than when he
was counted among the dead. An uncharacteristic disregard
of the laws of the land filled this good woman's mind. Jerry
had his life to live, and she wished him no harm. She wondered often how the baby grew. She fancied sometimes the
changes and conditions of the far-away household. Alas! she
knew only too well the weakness of the man, and once, in a
grim outburst of impatience, she exclaimed, "I 'd rather she
should have to cope with him than me!"

But that evening, when she came back from Shediac, and sat in the dark for a long time, lest Mrs. Elton should see the light and risk her life in the evening air to bring unwelcome sympathy, --that evening, I say, came the hardest moment of all, when the Ann Floyd, tailoress, of so many virtuous, self-respecting years, whose idol had turned to clay, who was shamed, disgraced, and wronged, sat down alone to supper in the little kitchen.

She had put one cup and saucer on the table; she looked at them through bitter tears.   Somehow a consciousness of her solitary age, her uncompanioned future, rushed through her mind; this failure of her best earthly hope was enough to break a stronger woman's heart.

Who can laugh at my Marsh Rosemary, or who can cry, for that matter?   The gray primness of the plant is made up of a hundred colors, if you look close enough to find them.   This same Marsh Rosemary stands in her own place, and holds her dry leaves and tiny blossoms steadily toward the same sun that the pink lotus blooms for, and the white rose.

MARY E. WILKINS FREEMAN

(1852-1930)

Mary E. Wilkins Freeman was born in 1852 in Randolph, Massachusetts, a farming and shoemaking town twelve miles south of Boston. Her father, Warren Wilkins, a carpenter, and her mother, Eleanor Lothrop Wilkins, were both descended from seventeenth-century New England Puritans. Mary's early schooling was in Randolph; later, after the family moved to Brattleboro, Vermont, where her father opened a drygoods store, she attended the high school there, graduating in 1870. She then entered Mt. Holyoke Seminary, but because of ill health remained only one year. Aside from some courses at a seminary in West Brattleboro, her formal education had ended. When she was nineteen, she developed an attachment for a man of a prominent family in Brattleboro, but nothing came of it. In 1873 she made an unsuccessful attempt at school-teaching. Shortly after the death of her mother in 1880 Mary had her first success in writing, placing several poems in children's magazines. In 1880, when she sold a story to Harper's New Monthly, her career as an author began in earnest. And in 1883, after her father died in Florida on a construction job--his drygoods business had long since failed--there was nothing to hold her in Brattleboro, and she returned to her native Randolph. For the rest of her life her literary production was prolific. Among her many books the outstanding ones are A Humble Romance and Other Stories (1887) and A New England Nun and Other Stories (1891), from which "Louisa," the selection in this anthology, is taken, and the novels Jane Field (1893), Pembroke (1894), and The Portion of Labor (1901). In 1902, at the age of fifty, she married Dr. Charles Freeman of Metuchen, New Jersey. The alliance was an unfortunate one, ending in a legal separation in 1922. Following her marriage and her move to New Jersey, Freeman continued to write, but the quality of her work declined, as eventually did the quantity. However, in 1926 the American Academy of Letters awarded her the William Dean Howells

240

Gold Medal for Fiction, and in the same year the National Institute of Arts and Letters elected her to membership. She died in 1930 in Metuchen.

It is interesting to compare Freeman's Louisa with Alice Brown's Mandy in the final selection. Mandy needs a man to give her a reason to exist; Louisa is independent and proud and triumphs in the end.

Two biographical and critical studies of Freeman are Edward Foster, Mary E. Wilkins Freeman (1956), and Perry D. Westbrook, Mary Wilkins Freeman (1967).

From A NEW ENGLAND NUN AND OTHER STORIES

Louisa

"I don't see what kind of ideas you've got in your head for my part." Mrs. Britton looked sharply at her daughter Louisa, but she got no response.

Louisa sat in one of the kitchen chairs close to the door. She had dropped into it when she first entered. Her hands were all brown and grimy with garden-mould; it clung to the bottom of her old dress and her coarse shoes.

Mrs. Britton, sitting opposite by the window, waited, looking at her. Suddenly Louisa's silence seemed to strike her mother's will with an electric shock; she recoiled, with an angry jerk of her head. "You don't know nothin' about it. You'd like him well enough after you was married to him," said she, as if in answer to an argument.

Louisa's face looked fairly dull; her obstinacy seemed to cast a film over it. Her eyelids were cast down; she leaned her head back against the wall.

"Sit there like a stick if you want to!" cried her mother.

Louisa got up. As she stirred, a faint earthy odor diffused itself through the room. It was like a breath from a ploughed field.

Mrs. Britton's little sallow face contracted more forcibly. "I s'pose now you're goin' back to your potater patch," said she. "Plantin' potaters out there jest like a man, for all the neighbors to see. Pretty sight, I call it."

"If they don't like it, they needn't look," returned Louisa. She spoke quite evenly. Her young back was stiff with bending over the potatoes, but she straightened it rigorously. She pulled her old hat farther over her eyes.

There was a shuffling sound outside the door and a fumble at the latch. It opened, and an old man came in, scraping his feet heavily over the threshold. He carried an old basket.

"What you got in that basket, father?" asked Mrs. Britton.

The old man looked at her. His old face had the round outlines and naive grin of a child.

"Father, what you got in that basket?"

Louisa peered apprehensively into the basket. "Where did you get those potatoes, grandfather?" said she.

"Digged 'em." The old man's grin deepened. He chuckled hoarsely.

"Well, I'll give up if he ain't been an' dug up all them potaters you've been plantin'!" said Mrs. Britton.

"Yes, he has," said Louisa. "Oh, grandfather, didn't you know I'd jest planted those potatoes?"

The old man fastened his bleared blue eyes on her face, and still grinned.

"Didn't you know better, grandfather?" she asked again.

But the old man only chuckled. He was so old that he had come back into the mystery of childhood. His motives were hidden and inscrutable; his amalgamation with the human race was so much weaker.

"Land sakes! don't waste no more time talkin' to
him," said Mrs. Britton. "You can't make out whether he
knows what he's doin' or not. I've give it up. Father, you
jest set them pertaters down, an' you come over here an'
set down in the rockin'-chair; you've done about 'nough work
to-day."

The old man shook his head with slow mutiny.

"Come right over here."

Louisa pulled at the basket of potatoes. "Let me have
'em, grandfather," said she. "I've got to have 'em."

The old man resisted. His grin disappeared, and he
set his mouth. Mrs. Britton got up, with a determined air,
and went over to him. She was a sickly, frail-looking woman, but the voice came firm, with deep bass tones, from
her little lean throat.

"Now, father," said she, "you jest give her that basket, an' you walk across the room, and you set down in that
rockin'-chair."

The old man looked down into her little, pale, wedge-
shaped face. His grasp on the basket weakened. Louisa
pulled it away, and pushed past out of the door, and the old
man followed his daughter sullenly across the room to the
rocking-chair.

The Brittons did not have a large potato field; they
had only an acre of land in all. Louisa had planted two
thirds of her potatoes; now she had to plant them all over
again. She had gone to the house for a drink of water; her
mother had detained her, and in the meantime the old man
had undone her work. She began putting the cut potatoes
back in the ground. She was careful and laborious about it.
A strong wind, full of moisture, was blowing from the east.
The smell of the sea was in it, although this was some miles
inland. Louisa's brown calico skirt blew out in it like a sail.
It beat her in the face when she raised her head.

"I've got to get these in to-day somehow," she muttered. "It 'll rain to-morrow."

She worked as fast as she could, and the afternoon
wore on. About five o'clock she happened to glance at the
road--the potato field lay beside it--and she saw Jonathan

Nye driving past with his gray horse and buggy. She turned
her back to the road quickly, and listened until the rattle of
the wheels died away. At six o'clock her mother looked out
of the kitchen window and called her to supper.

"I'm comin' in a minute," Louisa shouted back. Then
she worked faster than ever. At half-past six she went into
the house, and the potatoes were all in the ground.

"Why didn't you come when I called you?" asked her
mother.

"I had to get the potatoes in."

"I guess you wa'n't bound to get 'em all in to-night.
It's kind of discouragin' when you work, an' get supper all
ready, to have it stan' an hour, I call it. An' you've worked
'bout long enough for one day out in this damp wind, I should
say."

Louisa washed her hands and face at the kitchen sink,
and smoothed her hair at the little glass over it. She had
wet her hair too, and made it look darker: it was quite a
light brown. She brushed it in smooth straight lines back
from her temples. Her whole face had a clear bright look
from being exposed to the moist wind. She noticed it herself, and gave her head a little conscious turn.

When she sat down to the table her mother looked at
her with admiration, which she veiled with disapproval.

"Jest look at your face," said she; "red as a beet.
You'll be a pretty-lookin' sight before the summer's out, at
this rate."

Louisa thought to herself that the light was not very
strong, and the glass must have flattered her. She could
not look as well as she had imagined. She spread some
butter on her bread very sparsely. There was nothing for
supper but some bread and butter and weak tea, though the
old man had his dish of Indian-meal porridge. He could not
eat much solid food. The porridge was covered with milk
and molasses. He bent low over it, and ate large spoonfuls
with loud noises. His daughter had tied a towel around his
neck as she would have tied a pinafore on a child. She had
also spread a towel over the tablecloth in front of him, and
she watched him sharply lest he should spill his food.

"I wish I could have somethin' to eat that I could relish the way he does that porridge and molasses," said she. She had scarcely tasted anything. She sipped her weak tea laboriously.

Louisa looked across at her mother's meagre little figure in its neat old dress, at her poor small head bending over the tea-cup, showing the wide parting in the thin hair.

"Why don't you toast your bread, mother?" said she. "I'll toast it for you."

"No, I don't want it. I'd jest as soon have it this way as any. I don't want no bread, nohow. I want somethin' to relish--a herrin', or a little mite of cold meat, or somethin'. I s'pose I could eat as well as anybody if I had as much as some folks have. Mis' Mitchell was sayin' the other day that she didn't believe but what they had butcher's meat up to Mis' Nye's every day in the week. She said Jonathan he went to Wolfsborough and brought home great pieces in a market-basket every week. I guess they have everything."

Louisa was not eating much herself, but now she took another slice of bread with a resolute air. "I guess some folks would be thankful to get this," said she.

"Yes, I s'pose we'd ought to be thankful for enough to keep us alive, anybody takes so much comfort livin'," returned her mother, with a tragic bitterness that sat oddly upon her, as she was so small and feeble. Her face worked and strained under the stress of emotion; her eyes were full of tears; she sipped her tea fiercely.

"There's some sugar," said Louisa. "We might have had a little cake."

The old man caught the word. "Cake?" he mumbled, with pleased inquiry, looking up, and extending his grasping old hand.

"I guess we ain't got no sugar to waste in cake," returned Mrs. Britton. "Eat your porridge, father, an' stop teasin'. There ain't no cake."

After supper Louisa cleared away the dishes; then she put on her shawl and hat.

"Where you goin'?" asked her mother.

"Down to the store."

"What for?"

"The oil's out. There wasn't enough to fill the lamps this mornin'. I ain't had a chance to get it before."

It was nearly dark. The mist was so heavy it was almost rain. Louisa went swiftly down the road with the oil-can. It was a half-mile to the store where the few staples were kept that sufficed the simple folk in this little settlement. She was gone a half-hour. When she returned, she had besides the oil-can a package under her arm. She went into the kitchen and set them down. The old man was asleep in the rocking-chair. She heard voices in the adjoining room. She frowned, and stood still, listening.

"Louisa!" called her mother. Her voice was sweet, and higher pitched than usual. She sounded the i in Louisa long.

"What say?"

"Come in here after you've taken your things off."

Louisa knew that Jonathan Nye was in the sitting-room. She flung off her hat and shawl. Her old dress was damp, and had still some earth stains on it; her hair was roughened by the wind, but she would not look again in the glass; she went into the sitting-room just as she was.

"It's Mr. Nye, Louisa," said her mother, with effusion.

"Good-evenin', Mr. Nye," said Louisa.

Jonathan Nye half arose and extended his hand, but she did not notice it. She sat down peremptorily in a chair at the other side of the room. Jonathan had the one rocking-chair; Mrs. Britton's frail little body was poised anxiously on the hard rounded top of the carpet-covered lounge. She looked at Louisa's dress and hair, and her eyes were stony with disapproval, but her lips still smirked, and she kept her voice sweet. She pointed to a glass dish on the table.

"See what Mr. Nye has brought us over, Louisa," said she.

Louisa looked indifferently at the dish.

"It's honey," said her mother; "some of his own bees made it. Don't you want to get a dish an' taste of it? One of them little glass sauce dishes."

"No, I guess not," replied Louisa. "I never cared much about honey. Grandfather 'll like it."

The smile vanished momentarily from Mrs. Britton's lips, but she recovered herself. She arose and went across the room to the china closet. Her set of china dishes was on the top shelves, the lower were filled with books and papers. "I've got somethin' to show you, Mr. Nye," said she.

This was scarcely more than a hamlet, but it was incorporated, and had its town books. She brought forth a pile of them, and laid them on the table beside Jonathan Nye. "There," said she, "I thought mebbe you'd like to look at these." She opened one and pointed to the school report. This mother could not display her daughter's accomplishments to attract a suitor, for she had none. Louisa did not own a piano or organ; she could not paint; but she had taught school acceptably for eight years--ever since she was sixteen --and in every one of the town books was testimonial to that effect, intermixed with glowing eulogy. Jonathan Nye looked soberly through the books; he was a slow reader. He was a few years older than Louisa, tall and clumsy, long-featured and long-necked. His face was a deep red with embarrassment, and it contrasted oddly with his stiff dignity of demeanor.

Mrs. Britton drew a chair close to him while he read. "You see, Louisa taught that school for eight year," said she; "an' she'd be teachin' it now if Mr. Mosely's daughter hadn't grown up an' wanted somethin' to do, an' he put her in. He was committee, you know. I dun' know as I'd ought to say so, an' I wouldn't want you to repeat it, but they do say Ida Mosely don't give very good satisfaction, an' I guess she won't have no reports like these in the town books unless her father writes 'em. See this one."

Jonathan Nye pondered over the fulsome testimony to

Louisa's capability, general worth, and amiability, while she
sat in sulky silence at the farther corner of the room. Once
in a while her mother, after a furtive glance at Jonathan,
engrossed in a town book, would look at her and gesticulate
fiercely for her to come over, but she did not stir. Her
eyes were dull and quiet, her mouth closely shut; she looked
homely. Louisa was very pretty when pleased and animated,
at other times she had a look like a closed flower. One
could see no prettiness in her.

Jonathan Nye read all the school reports; then he arose
heavily. "They're real good," said he. He glanced at Louisa
and tried to smile; his blushes deepened.

"Now don't be in a hurry," said Mrs. Britton.

"I guess I'd better be goin'; mother's alone."

"She won't be afraid; it's jest on the edge of the evenin'."

"I don't know as she will. But I guess I'd better be
goin'." He looked hesitatingly at Louisa.

She arose and stood with an indifferent air.

"You'd better set down again," said Mrs. Britton.

"No; I guess I'd better be goin'." Jonathan turned
towards Louisa. "Good-evenin'," said he.

"Good-evenin'."

Mrs. Britton followed him to the door. She looked
back and beckoned imperiously to Louisa, but she stood still.
"Now come again, do," Mrs. Britton said to the departing
caller. "Run in any time; we're real lonesome evenin's.
Father he sets an' sleeps in his chair, an' Louisa an' me
often wish somebody 'd drop in; folks round here ain't none
too neighborly. Come in any time you happen to feel like
it, an' we'll both of us be glad to see you. Tell your mother
I'll send home that dish to-morrer, an' we shall have a real
feast off that beautiful honey."

When Mrs. Britton had fairly shut the outer door upon
Jonathan Nye, she came back into the sitting-room as if her
anger had a propelling power like steam upon her body.

"Now, Louisa Britton, " said she, "you'd ought to be ashamed of yourself--ashamed of yourself! You've treated him like a--hog!"

"I couldn't help it. "

"Couldn't help it! I guess you could treat anybody decent if you tried. I never saw such actions! I guess you needn't be afraid of him. I guess he ain't so set on you that he means to ketch you up an' run off. There's other girls in town full as good as you an' better-lookin'. Why didn't you go an' put on your other dress? Comin' into the room with that old thing on, an' your hair all in a frowse! I guess he won't want to come again. "

"I hope he won't, " said Louisa, under her breath. She was trembling all over.

"What say?"

"Nothin'. "

"I shouldn't think you'd want to say anything, treatin' him that way, when he came over and brought all that beautiful honey! He was all dressed up, too. He had on a real nice coat--cloth jest as fine as it could be, an' it was kinder damp when he come in. Then he dressed all up to come over here this rainy night an' bring this honey." Mrs. Britton snatched the dish of honey and scudded into the kitchen with it. "Sayin' you didn't like honey after he took all that pains to bring it over!" said she. "I'd said I liked it if I'd lied up hill and down. " She set the dish in the pantry. "What in creation smells so kinder strong an' smoky in here?" said she, sharply.

"I guess it's the herrin'. I got two or three down to the store. "

"I'd like to know what you got herrin' for?"

"I thought maybe you'd relish 'em. "

"I don't want no herrin's, now we've got this honey. But I don't know that you've got money to throw away." She shook the old man by the stove into partial wakefulness, and steered him into his little bedroom off the kitchen. She herself slept in one off the sitting-rooms; Louisa's room was upstairs.

Louisa lighted her candle and went to bed, her mother's scolding voice pursuing her like a wrathful spirit. She cried when she was in bed in the dark, but she soon went to sleep. She was too healthfully tired with her out-door work not to. All her young bones ached with the strain of manual labor as they had ached many a time this last year since she had lost her school.

The Brittons had been and were in sore straits. All they had in the world was this little house with the acre of land. Louisa's meagre school money had bought their food and clothing since her father died. Now it was almost starvation for them. Louisa was struggling to wrest a little sustenance from their stony acre of land, toiling like a European peasant woman, sacrificing her New England dignity. Lately she had herself split up a cord of wood which she had bought of a neighbor, paying for it in instalments with work for his wife.

"Think of a school-teacher goin' into Mis' Mitchell's house to help clean!" said her mother.

She, although she had been of poor, hard-working people all her life, with the humblest surroundings, was a born aristocrat, with that fiercest and most bigoted aristocracy which sometimes arises from independent poverty. She had the feeling of a queen for a princess of the blood about her school-teacher daughter; her working in a neighbor's kitchen was as galling and terrible to her. The projected marriage with Jonathan Nye was like a royal alliance for the good of the state. Jonathan Nye was the only eligible young man in the place; he was the largest land-owner; he had the best house. There were only himself and his mother; after her death the property would all be his. Mrs. Nye was an older woman than Mrs. Britton, who forgot her own frailty in calculating their chances of life.

"Mis' Nye is considerable over seventy," she said often to herself; "an' then Jonathan will have it all."

She saw herself installed in that large white house as reigning dowager. All the obstacle was Louisa's obstinacy, which her mother could not understand. She could see no fault in Jonathan Nye. So far as absolute approval went, she herself was in love with him. There was no more sense, to her mind, in Louisa's refusing him than there would have been in a princess refusing the fairy prince and spoiling the story.

"I'd like to know what you've got against him," she said often to Louisa.

"I ain't got anything against him."

"Why don't you treat him different, then, I want to know?"

"I don't like him." Louisa said "like" shamefacedly, for she meant love, and dared not say it.

"Like! Well, I don't know nothin' about such likin's as some pretend to, an' I don't want to. If I see anybody is good an' worthy, I like 'em, an' that's all there is about it."

"I don't--believe that's the way you felt about--father," said Louisa, softly, her young face flushed red.

"Yes, it was. I had some common sense about it."

And Mrs. Britton believed it. Many hard middle-aged years lay between her and her own love-time, and nothing is so changed by distance as the realities of youth. She believed herself to have been actuated by the same calm reason in marrying young John Britton, who had had fair prospects, which she thought should actuate her daughter in marrying Jonathan Nye.

Louisa got no sympathy from her, but she persisted in her refusal. She worked harder and harder. She did not spare herself in doors or out. As the summer wore on her face grew as sunburnt as a boy's, her hands were hard and brown. When she put on her white dress to go to meeting on a Sunday there was a white ring around her neck where the sun had not touched it. Above it her face and neck showed browner. Her sleeves were rather short, and there were also white rings above her brown wrists.

"You look as if you were turnin' Injun by inches," said her mother.

Louisa, when she sat in the meeting-house, tried slyly to pull her sleeves down to the brown on her wrists; she gave a little twitch to the ruffle around her neck. Then she glanced across, and Jonathan Nye was looking at her. She thrust her hands, in their short-wristed, loose cotton gloves, as far out of the sleeves as she could; her brown wrists showed conspicuously on her white lap. She had never heard of the princess who destroyed her beauty that she might not be forced to wed the man whom she did not love, but she had something of the same feeling, although she did not have it for the sake of any tangible lover. Louisa had never seen anybody whom she would have preferred to Jonathan Nye. There was no other marriageable young man in the place. She had only her dreams, which she had in common with other girls.

That Sunday evening before she went to meeting her mother took some old wide lace out of her bureau drawer. "There," said she, "I'm goin' to sew this in your neck an' sleeves before you put your dress on. It 'll cover up a little; it's wider than the ruffle."

"I don't want it in," said Louisa.

"I'd like to know why not? You look like a fright. I was ashamed of you this mornin'."

Louisa thrust her arms into the white dress sleeves peremptorily. Her mother did not speak to her all the way to meeting. After meeting, Jonathan Nye walked home with them, and Louisa kept on the other side of her mother. He went into the house and stayed an hour. Mrs. Britton entertained him, while Louisa sat silent. When he had gone, she looked at her daughter as if she could have used bodily force, but she said nothing. She shot the bolt of the kitchen door noisily. Louisa lighted her candle. The old man's loud breathing sounded from his room; he had been put to bed for safety before they went to meeting; through the open windows sounded the loud murmur of the summer night, as if that, too, slept heavily.

"Good-night, mother," said Louisa, as she went upstairs; but her mother did not answer.

The next day was very warm. This was an exceptionally hot summer. Louisa went out early; her mother would not ask her where she was going. She did not come home until noon. Her face was burning; her wet dress clung to her arms and shoulders.

"Where have you been?" asked her mother.

"Oh, I've been out in the field."

"What field?"

"Mr. Mitchell's."

"What have you been doin' out there?"

"Rakin' hay."

"Rakin' hay with the men?"

"There wasn't anybody but Mr. Mitchell and Johnny.
Don't, mother!"

Mrs. Britton had turned white. She sank into a chair.
"I can't stan' it nohow," she moaned. "All the daughter I've
got."

"Don't, mother! I ain't done any harm. What harm
is it? Why can't I rake hay as well as a man? Lots of
women do such things, if nobody round here does. He's
goin' to pay me right off, and we need the money. Don't,
mother!" Louisa got a tumbler of water. "Here, mother,
drink this."

Mrs. Britton pushed it away. Louisa stood looking
anxiously at her. Lately her mother had grown thinner than
ever; she looked scarcely bigger than a child. Presently she
got up and went to the stove.

"Don't try to do anything, mother; let me finish getting
dinner," pleaded Louisa. She tried to take the pan of biscuits out of her mother's hands, but she jerked it away.

The old man was sitting on the door-step, huddled up
loosely in the sun, like an old dog.

"Come, father," Mrs. Britton called, in a dry voice,
"dinner's ready--what there is of it!"

The old man shuffled in, smiling.

There was nothing for dinner but the hot biscuits and
tea. The fare was daily becoming more meagre. All Louisa's little hoard of school money was gone, and her earnings
were very uncertain and slender. Their chief dependence for
food through the summer was their garden, but that had failed
them in some respects.

One day the old man had come in radiant, with his
shaking hands full of potato blossoms; his old eyes twinkled

over them like a mischievous child's. Reproaches were useless; the little potato crop was sadly damaged. Lately, in
spite of close watching, he had picked the squash blossoms,
piling them in a yellow mass beside the kitchen door. Still,
it was nearly time for the pease and beans and beets; they
would keep them from starvation while they lasted.

But when they came, and Louisa could pick plenty of
green food every morning, there was still a difficulty: Mrs.
Britton's appetite and digestion were poor; she could not live
upon a green-vegetable diet; and the old man missed his porridge, for the meal was all gone.

One morning in August he cried at the breakfast-table
like a baby, because he wanted his porridge, and Mrs. Britton pushed away her own plate with a despairing gesture.

"There ain't no use," said she. "I can't eat no more
garden-sauce nohow. I don't blame poor father a mite. You
ain't got no feelin' at all."

"I don't know what I can do; I've worked as hard as I
can," said Louisa, miserably.

"I know what you can do, and so do you."

"No, I don't, mother," returned Louisa, with alacrity.
"He ain't been here for two weeks now, and I saw him with
my own eyes yesterday carryin' a dish into the Moselys',
and I knew 'twas honey. I think he's after Ida."

"Carryin' honey into the Moselys'? I don't believe it."

"He was; I saw him."

"Well, I don't care if he was. If you're a mind to
act decent now, you can bring him round again. He was dead
set on you, an' I don't believe he's changed round to that
Mosely girl as quick as this."

"You don't want me to ask him to come back here, do
you?"

"I want you to act decent. You can go to meetin' to-
night, if you're a mind to--I sha'n't go; I ain't got strength
'nough--an' 'twouldn't hurt you none to hang back a little after
meetin', and kind of edge round his way. 'Twouldn't take
more'n a look."

"Mother!"

"Well, I don't care. 'Twouldn't hurt you none. It's the way more'n one girl does, whether you believe it or not. Men don't do all the courtin'--not by a long shot. 'Twon't hurt you none. You needn't look so scart."

Mrs. Britton's own face was a burning red. She looked angrily away from her daughter's honest, indignant eyes.

"I wouldn't do such a thing as that for a man I liked," said Louisa; "and I certainly sha'n't for a man I don't like."

"Then me an' your grandfather 'll starve," said her mother; "that's all there is about it. We can't neither of us stan' it much longer."

"We could--"

"Could what?"

"Put a--little mortgage on the house."

Mrs. Britton faced her daughter. She trembled in every inch of her weak frame. "Put a mortgage on this house, an' by-an'-by not have a roof to cover us! Are you crazy? I tell you what 'tis, Louisa Britton, we may starve, your grandfather an' me, an' you can follow us to the graveyard over there, but there's only one way I'll ever put a mortgage on this house. If you have Jonathan Nye, I'll ask him to take a little one to tide us along an' get your weddin' things."

"Mother, I'll tell you what I'm goin' to do."

"What?"

"I am goin' to ask Uncle Solomon."

"I guess when Solomon Mears does anythin' for us you'll know it. He never forgave your father about that wood lot, an' he's hated the whole of us ever since. When I went to his wife's funeral he never answered when I spoke to him. I guess if you go to him you'll take it out in goin'."

Louisa said nothing more. She began clearing away the breakfast dishes and setting the house to rights. Her mother was actually so weak that she could scarcely stand, and she recognized it. She had settled into the rocking-chair, and leaned her head back. Her face looked pale and sharp against the dark calico cover.

When the house was in order, Louisa stole up-stairs to her own chamber. She put on her clean old blue muslin and her hat, then she went slyly down and out the front way.

It was seven miles to her uncle Solomon Mears's, and she had made up her mind to walk them. She walked quite swiftly until the house windows were out of sight, then she slackened her pace a little. It was one of the fiercest dog-days. A damp heat settled heavily down upon the earth; the sun scalded.

At the foot of the hill Louisa passed a house where one of her girl acquaintances lived. She was going in the gate with a pan of early apples. "Hullo, Louisa," she called.

"Hullo, Vinnie."

"Where you goin'?"

"Oh, I'm goin' a little way."

"Ain't it awful hot? Say, Louisa, do you know Ida Mosely's cuttin' you out?"

"She's welcome."

The other girl, who was larger and stouter than Louisa, with a sallow, unhealthy face, looked at her curiously. "I don't see why you wouldn't have him," said she. "I should have thought you'd jumped at the chance."

"Should you if you didn't like him, I'd like to know?"

"I'd like him if he had such a nice house and as much money as Jonathan Nye," returned the other girl.

She offered Louisa some apples, and she went along the road eating them. She herself had scarcely tasted food that day.

It was about nine o'clock; she had risen early. She calculated how many hours it would take her to walk the seven

miles.   She walked as fast as she could to hold out.   The
heat seemed to increase as the sun stood higher.   She had
walked about three miles when she heard wheels behind her.
Presently a team stopped at her side.

"Good-mornin'," said an embarrassed voice.

She looked around.   It was Jonathan Nye, with his
gray horse and light wagon.

"Good-mornin'," said she.

"Goin' far?"

"A little ways."

"Won't you--ride?"

"No, thank you.   I guess I'd rather walk."

Jonathan Nye nodded, made an inarticulate noise in
his throat, and drove on.   Louisa watched the wagon bowling
lightly along.   The dust flew back.   She took out her handkerchief and wiped her dripping face.

It was about noon when she came in sight of her uncle
Solomon Mears's house in Wolfsborough.   It stood far back
from the road, behind a green expanse of untrodden yard.
The blinds on the great square front were all closed; it
looked as if everybody were away.   Louisa went around to
the side door.   It stood wide open.   There was a thin blue
cloud of tobacco smoke issuing from it.   Solomon Mears sat
there in the large old kitchen smoking his pipe.   On the table
near him was an empty bowl; he had just eaten his dinner of
bread and milk.   He got his own dinner, for he had lived
alone since his wife died.   He looked at Louisa.   Evidently
he did not recognize her.

"How do you do, Uncle Solomon?" said Louisa.

"Oh, it's John Britton's daughter!   How d'ye do?"

He took his pipe out of his mouth long enough to speak,
then replaced it.   His eyes, sharp under their shaggy brows,
were fixed on Louisa; his broad bristling face had a look of
stolid rebuff like an ox; his stout figure, in his soiled farmer
dress, surged over his chair.   He sat full in the doorway.

Louisa standing before him, the perspiration trickling over her burning face, set forth her case with a certain dignity. This old man was her mother's nearest relative. He had property and to spare. Should she survive him, it would be hers, unless willed away. She, with her unsophisticated sense of justice, had a feeling that he ought to help her.

The old man listened. When she stopped speaking he took the pipe out of his mouth slowly, and stared gloomily past her at his hay field, where the grass was now a green stubble.

"I ain't got no money I can spare jest now," said he. "I s'pose you know your father cheated me out of consider'ble once?"

"We don't care so much about money, if you have got something you could spare to--eat. We ain't got anything but garden-stuff."

Solomon Mears still frowned past her at the hay field. Presently he arose slowly and went across the kitchen. Louisa sat down on the door-step and waited. Her uncle was gone quite a while. She, too, stared over at the field, which seemed to undulate like a lake in the hot light.

"Here's some things you can take, if you want 'em," said her uncle, at her back.

She got up quickly. He pointed grimly to the kitchen table. He was a deacon, an orthodox believer; he recognized the claims of the poor, but he gave alms as a soldier might yield up his sword. Benevolence was the result of warfare with his own conscience.

On the table lay a ham, a bag of meal, one of flour, and a basket of eggs.

"I'm afraid I can't carry 'em all," said Louisa.

"Leave what you can't then." Solomon caught up his hat and went out. He muttered something about not spending any more time as he went.

Louisa stood looking at the packages. It was utterly impossible for her to carry them all at once. She heard her uncle shout to some oxen he was turning out of the barn. She

took up the bag of meal and the basket of eggs and carried
them out to the gate; then she returned, got the flour and
ham, and went with them to a point beyond. Then she returned for the meal and eggs, and carried them past the
others. In that way she traversed the seven miles home.
The heat increased. She had eaten nothing since morning
but the apples that her friend had given her. Her head was
swimming, but she kept on. Her resolution was as immovable under the power of the sun as a rock. Once in a while
she rested for a moment under a tree, but she soon arose
and went on. It was like a pilgrimage, and the Mecca at the
end of the burning, desert-like road was her own maiden independence.

It was after eight o'clock when she reached home.
Her mother stood in the doorway watching for her, straining
her eyes in the dusk.

"For goodness sake, Louisa Britton! where have you
been?" she began; but Louisa laid the meal and eggs down
on the step.

"I've got to go back a little ways," she panted.

When she returned with the flour and ham, she could
hardly get into the house. She laid them on the kitchen table,
where her mother had put the other parcels, and sank into a
chair.

"Is this the way you've brought all these things home?"
asked her mother.

Louisa nodded.

"All the way from Uncle Solomon's?"

"Yes."

Her mother went to her and took her hat off. "It's a
mercy if you ain't got a sunstroke," said she, with a sharp
tenderness. "I've got somethin' to tell you. What do you
s'pose has happened? Mr. Mosely has been here, an' he
wants you to take the school again when it opens next week.
He says Ida ain't very well, but I guess that ain't it. They
think she's goin' to get somebody. Mis' Mitchell says so.
She's been in. She says he's carryin' things over there the
whole time, but she don't b'lieve there's anything settled yet.

She says they feel so sure of it they're goin' to have Ida
give the school up. I told her I thought Ida would make him
a good wife, an' she was easier suited than some girls.
What do you s'pose Mis' Mitchell says? She says old Mis'
Nye told her that there was one thing about it: if Jonathan
had you, he wa'n't goin' to have me an' father hitched on to
him; he'd look out for that. I told Mis' Mitchell that I guess
there wa'n't none of us willin' to hitch, you nor anybody else.
I hope she'll tell Mis' Nye. Now I'm a-goin' to turn you out
a tumbler of milk--Mis' Mitchell she brought over a whole
pitcherful; says she's got more'n they can use--they ain't
got no pig now--an' then you go an' lay down on the sittin'-
room lounge, an' cool off; an' I'll stir up some porridge for
supper, an' boil some eggs. Father 'll be tickled to death.
Go right in there. I'm dreadful afraid you'll be sick. I
never heard of anybody doin' such a thing as you have."

Louisa drank the milk and crept into the sitting-room.
It was warm and close there, so she opened the front door
and sat down on the step. The twilight was deep, but there
was a clear yellow glow in the west. One great star had
come out in the midst of it. A dewy coolness was spreading
over everything. The air was full of bird calls and children's
voices. Now and then there was a shout of laughter. Louisa
leaned her head against the door-post.

The house was quite near the road. Some one passed
--a man carrying a basket. Louisa glanced at him, and recognized Jonathan Nye by his gait. He kept on down the road
toward the Moselys', and Louisa turned again from him to
her sweet, mysterious, girlish dreams.

ALICE BROWN
_____
(1856-1948)

Alice Brown was born in 1856 in Hampton Falls, New Hampshire, six miles from the ocean. Brought up on her family's farm, she attended high school in nearby Exeter. After graduation she taught school for a while, an occupation that she disliked intensely. Her real interest was in writing, and she soon began to place her stories. Thus encouraged, she moved to Boston to earn her living as an author and an editor. During her long life Brown wrote voluminously and in a variety of genres, including novels, short stories, travel books, drama, and biographies (e.g., a life of Mercy Warren--see above, pp. 46-52). Most readers agree that her stories of rural New Hampshire life, collected in Meadow-Grass (1895) and Tiverton Tales (1899) are her best work. Like Mary E. Wilkins Freeman and Sarah Orne Jewett she depicted, sometimes with a touch of sentimentality, the confined lives and hypertrophied wills of New England farm folk. The situation in "Told in a Poorhouse" (excerpted from Meadow-Grass) is not as fantastic or unrealistic as a modern reader might suppose. Note that in this story Brown employs a device used with great success by Mary Wilkins Freeman--the narrating of the tale in the words of a local gossip. Mandy's sole reason for existence is to meet her husband Josh's needs. Her excessive dependency, probably in the name of "love," has made her totally vulnerable to the attitudes and actions of her husband.

Dorothea Walker, Alice Brown (1974), is the only book-length study of Brown's life and work.

From MEADOW-GRASS

Told in the Poorhouse

"Le' me see, " said old Sally Flint, "was it fifty year ago,
or was it on'y forty? Some'er's betwixt 1825 an' '26 it must
ha' been when they were married, an' 'twas in '41 he died."

The other old women in the Poorhouse sitting-room
gathered about her. Old Mrs. Forbes, who dearly loved a
story, unwound a length of yarn with peculiar satisfaction,
and put her worn shoe up to the fire. Everybody knew when
Sally Flint was disposed to open her unwritten book of folk-
tales for the public entertainment; and to-day, having tied on
a fresh apron and bound a new piece of red flannel about her
wrist, she was, so to speak, in fighting trim. The other
members of the Poorhouse had scanty faith in that red flannel.
They were aware that Sally had broken her wrist, some twenty
years before, and that the bandage was consequently donned
on days when her "hand felt kind o' cold, " or was "burnin'
like fire embers"; but there was an unspoken suspicion that
it really served as token of her inability to work whenever
she felt bored by the prescribed routine of knitting and sweeping. No one had dared presume on that theory, however,
since the day when an untactful overseer had mentioned it,
to be met by such a stream of unpleasant reminiscence concerning his immediate ancestry that he had retreated in dismay, and for a week after, had served extra pieces of pie
to his justly offended charge.

"They were married in June, " continued Sally. "No,
'twa'n't; 'twas the last o' May. May thirty-fust--no, May
'ain't but thirty days, has it?"

"'Thirty days hath September,'" quoted Mrs. Giles,
with importance. "That's about all I 've got left o' my school-
in', Miss Flint. May's got thirty-one days, sure enough."

"Call it the thirty-fust, then. It's nigh enough, anyway. Well, Josh Marden an' Lyddy Ann Crane was married,
an' for nine year they lived like two kittens. Old Sperry
Dyer, that wanted to git Lyddy himself, used to call 'em cup

an' sasser. 'There they be,' he 'd say, when he stood outside the meetin'-house door an' they drove up; 'there comes
cup an' sasser.' Lyddy was a little mite of a thing, with
great black eyes; an' if Josh hadn't been as tough as tripe,
he 'd ha' got all wore out waitin' on her. He even washed
the potaters for her, made the fires, an' lugged water.
Scairt to death if she was sick! She used to have sick headaches, an' one day he stopped choppin' pine limbs near the
house 'cause the noise hurt Lyddy Ann's head. Another time,
I recollect, she had erysipelas in her face, an' I went in to
carry some elder-blows, an' found him readin' the Bible.
'Lord!' says I, 'Josh, that 's on'y Genesis! 'twon't do the
erysipelas a mite o' good for you to be settin' there readin'
the begats! You better turn to Revelation.' But 'twa'n't all
on his side, nuther. 'Twas give an' take with them. It used
to seem as if Lyddy Ann kind o' worshipped him. 'Josh' we
all called him; but she used to say 'Joshuay,' an' look at him
as if he was the Lord A'mighty."

"My! Sally!" said timid Mrs. Spenser, under her
breath; but Sally gave no heed, and swept on in the stream
of her recollections.

"Well, it went on for fifteen year, an' then 'Mandy
Knowles, Josh's second cousin, come to help 'em with the
work. 'Mandy was a queer creatur'. I 've studied a good
deal over her, an' I dunno 's I 've quite got to the bottom
of her yit. She was one o' them sort o' slow women, with
a fat face, an' she hadn't got over dressin' young, though
Lyddy an' the rest of us that was over thirty was wearin'
caps an' talkin' about false fronts. But she never 'd had no
beaux; an' when Josh begun to praise her an' say how nice
'twas to have her there, it tickled her e'en a'most to death.
She 'd lived alone with her mother an' two old-maid aunts,
an' she didn't know nothin' about men-folks; I al'ays thought
she felt they was different somehow, --kind o' cherubim an'
seraphim, --an' you 'd got to mind 'em as if you was the
Children of Isr'el an' they was Moses. Josh never meant
a mite o' harm, I 'll say that for him. He was jest man-
like, that 's all. There 's lots o' different kinds, --here,
Mis' Niles, you know; you 've buried your third, --an' Josh
was the kind that can't see more 'n one woman to a time.
He looked at 'Mandy, an' he got over seein' Lyddy Ann,
that 's all. Things would ha' come out all right--as right
as they be for most married folks--if Lyddy Ann hadn't been
so high-sperited; but she set the world by Joshuay, an' there
'twas. 'Ain't it nice to have her here?' he kep' on sayin'

over 'n' over to Lyddy, an' she 'd say 'Yes'; but byme-by,
when she found he was al'ays on hand to bring a pail o'
water for 'Mandy, or to throw away her suds, or even help
hang out the clo'es--I see 'em hangin' out clo'es one day
when I was goin' across their lot huckleberr'in', an' he did
look like a great gump, an' so did she--well, then, Lyddy
Ann got to seemin' kind o' worried, an' she had more sick
headaches than ever. 'Twa'n't a year afore that, I 'd been
in one day when she had a headache, an' he says, as if he
was perfessin' his faith in meetin', 'By gum! I wish I could
have them headaches for her!' an' I thought o' speakin' of it,
about now, when I run in to borrer some saleratus, an' he
hollered into the bedroom: 'Lyddy Ann, you got another
headache? If I had such a head as that, I 'd cut it off!'
An' all the time 'Mandy did act like the very Old Nick, jest
as any old maid would that hadn't set her mind on men-folks
till she was thirty-five. She bought a red-plaid bow an'
pinned it on in front, an' one day I ketched her at the lookin'-
glass pullin' out a gray hair.

"'Land, 'Mandy,' says I (I spoke right up), 'do you
pull 'em out as fast as they come? That 's why you ain't
no grayer, I s'pose. I was sayin' the other day, "'Mandy
Knowles is gittin' on, but she holds her own pretty well. I
dunno how she manages it, whether she dyes or not,"'
says I.

"An' afore she could stop herself, 'Mandy turned
round, red as a beet, to look at Josh an' see if he heard.
He stamped out into the wood-house, but Lyddy Ann never
took her eyes off her work. Them little spiteful things
didn't seem to make no impression on her. I 've thought
a good many times sence, she didn't care how handsome
other women was, nor how scrawny she was herself, if she
could on'y keep Josh. An' Josh he got kind o' fretful to her,
an' she to him, an' 'Mandy was all honey an' cream. Nothin'
would do but she must learn how to make the gingerbread he
liked, an' iron his shirts; an' when Lyddy Ann found he
seemed to praise things up jest as much as he had when she
done 'em, she give 'em up, an' done the hard things herself,
an' let 'Mandy see to Josh. She looked pretty pindlin' then,
mark my words; but I never see two such eyes in anybody's
head. I s'pose 'twas a change for Josh, anyway, to be with
a woman like 'Mandy, that never said her soul 's her own,
for Lyddy 'd al'ays had a quick way with her; but, land! you
can't tell about men, what changes 'em or what don't. If
you 're tied to one, you 've jest got to bear with him, an'

be thankful if he don't run some kind of a rig an' make you town-talk."

There was a murmur from gentle Lucy Staples, who had been constant for fifty years to the lover who died in her youth; but no one took any notice of her, and Sally Flint went on:

"It come spring, an' somehow or nuther 'Mandy found out the last o' March was Josh's birthday, an' nothin' would do but she must make him a present. So she walked over to Sudleigh, an' bought him a great long pocket-book that you could put your bills into without foldin' 'em, an' brought it home, tickled to death because she 'd been so smart. Some o' this come out at the time, an' some wa'n't known till arterwards; the hired man told some, an' a good deal the neighbors see themselves. An' I 'll be whipped if 'Mandy herself didn't tell the heft on 't arter 'twas all over. She wa'n't more 'n half baked in a good many things. It got round somehow that the pocket-book was comin', an' when I see 'Mandy walkin' home that arternoon, I ketched up my shawl an' run in behind her, to borrer some yeast. Nobody thought anything o' birthdays in our neighborhood, an' mebbe that made it seem a good deal more 'n 'twas; but when I got in there, I vow I was sorry I come. There set Josh by the kitchen table, sort o' red an' pleased, with his old pocket-book open afore him, an' he was puttin' all his bills an' papers into the new one, an' sayin', every other word, --

"'Why, 'Mandy, I never see your beat! Ain't this a nice one, Lyddy?'

"An' 'Mandy was b'ilin' over with pride, an' she stood there takin' off her cloud; she 'd been in such a hurry to give it to him she hadn't even got her things off fust. Lyddy stood by the cupboard, lookin' straight at the glass spoonholder. I thought arterwards I didn't b'lieve she see it; an' if she did, I guess she never forgot it.

"'Yes, it 's a real nice one,' says I.

"I had to say suthin', but in a minute, I was most scairt. Lyddy turned round, in a kind of a flash; her face blazed all over red, an' her eyes kind o' went through me. She stepped up to the table, an' took up the old pocket-book.

"'You 've got a new one,' says she. 'May I have this?'

"'Course you may,' says he.

"He didn't look up to see her face, an' her voice was
so soft an' still, I guess he never thought nothin' of it.
Then she held the pocket-book up tight ag'inst her dress
waist an' walked off into the bedroom.   I al'ays thought she
never knew I was there.   An' arterwards it come out that
that old pocket-book was one she 'd bought for him afore
they was married,--earned it bindin' shoes."

"'Twas kind o' hard," owned Mrs. Niles, bending forward, and, with hands clasped over her knees, peering into
the coals for data regarding her own marital experiences.
"But if 'twas all wore out--did you say 'twas wore?--well,
then I dunno 's you could expect him to set by it.   An' 'twa'n't
as if he 'd give it away; they 'd got it between 'em."

"I dunno; it 's all dark to me," owned Sally Flint.   "I
guess 'twould puzzle a saint to explain men-folks, anyway,
but I 've al'ays thought they was sort o' numb about some
things.   Anyway, Josh Marden was.   Well, things went on
that way till the fust part o' the summer, an' then they come
to a turnin'-p'int.   I s'pose they 'd got to, some time, an'
it might jest as well ha' been fust as last.   Lyddy Ann was
pretty miserable, an' she 'd been dosin' with thoroughwort
an' what all when anybody told her to; but I al'ays thought
she never cared a mite whether she lived to see another
spring.   The day I 'm comin' to, she was standin' over the
fire fryin' fish, an' 'Mandy was sort o' fiddlin' round, settin' the table, an' not doin' much of anything arter all.   I
dunno how she come to be so aggravatin', for she was al'ays
ready to do her part, if she had come between husband an'
wife.   You know how hard it is to git a fish dinner!   Well,
Lyddy Ann was tired enough, anyway.   An' when Josh come
in, 'Mandy she took a cinnamon-rose out of her dress, an'
offered it to him.

"'Here 's a flower for your button-hole,' says she,
as if she wa'n't more 'n sixteen.   An' then she set down in
a chair, an' fanned herself with a newspaper.

"Now that chair happened to be Lyddy Ann's at the
table, an' she see what was bein' done.   She turned right
round, with the fish-platter in her hand, an' says she, in
an awful kind of a voice,--

"'You git up out o' my chair!   You 've took my husband away, but you sha'n't take my place at the table!'

"The hired man was there, washin' his hands at the sink, an' he told it to me jest as it happened. Well, I guess they all thought they was struck by lightnin', an' Lyddy Ann most of all. Josh he come to, fust. He walked over to Lyddy Ann.

"'You put down that platter!' says he. An' she begun to tremble, an' set it down.

"I guess they thought there was goin' to be murder done, for 'Mandy busted right out cryin' an' come runnin' over to me, an' the hired man took a step an' stood side o' Lyddy Ann. He was a little mite of a man, Cyrus was, but he wouldn't ha' stood no violence.

"Josh opened the door that went into the front entry, an' jest p'inted. 'You walk in there,' he says, 'an' you stay there. That 's your half o' the house, an' this is mine. Don't you dast to darken my doors!'

"Lyddy Ann she walked through the entry an' into the fore-room, an' he shet the door."

"I wouldn't ha' done it!" snorted old Mrs. Page, who had spent all her property in lawsuits over a right of way. "Ketch me!"

"You would if you 'd 'a' been Lyddy Ann!" said Sally Flint, with an emphatic nod. Then she continued: "I hadn't more 'n heard 'Mandy's story afore I was over there; but jest as I put my foot on the door-sill, Josh he come for'ard to meet me.

"'What 's wanted?' says he. An' I declare for 't I was so scairt I jest turned round an' cut for home. An' there set 'Mandy, wringin' her hands.

"'What be I goin' to do?' says she, over 'n' over. 'Who ever 'd ha' thought o' this?'

"'The thing for you to do,' says I, 'is to go straight home to your mother, an' I 'll harness up an' carry you. Don't you step your foot inside that house ag'in. Maybe ma'am will go over an' pack up your things. You 've made mischief enough.' So we got her off that arternoon, an' that was an end of her.

"I never could see what made Josh think so quick that

day. We never thought he was brighter 'n common; but jest see
how in that flash o' bein' mad with Lyddy Ann he 'd planned
out what would be most wormwood for her! He gi'n her the
half o' the house she 'd furnished herself with hair-cloth
chairs an' a what-not, but 'twa'n't the part that was fit to
be lived in. She stayed pretty close for three or four days,
an' I guess she never had nothin' to eat. It made me kind
o' sick to think of her in there settin' on her hair-cloth sofy,
an' lookin' at her wax flowers an' the coral on the what-not,
an' thinkin' what end she 'd made. It was of a Monday she
was sent in there, an' Tuesday night I slipped over an' put
some luncheon on the winder-sill; but 'twas there the next
day, an' Cyrus see the old crower fly up an' git it. An'
that same Tuesday mornin', Josh had a j'iner come an' begin a partition right straight through the house. It was all
rough boards, like a high fence, an' it cut the front entry in
two, an' went right through the kitchen--so 't the kitchen
stove was one side on 't, an' the sink the other. Lyddy
Ann's side had the stove. I was glad o' that, though I
s'pose she 'most had a fit every day to think o' him tryin'
to cook over the airtight in the settin'-room. Seemed kind
o' queer to go to the front door, too, for you had to open it
wide an' squeeze round the partition to git into Lyddy Ann's
part, an' a little mite of a crack would let you into Josh's.
But they didn't have many callers. It was a good long while
afore anybody dared to say a word to her; an' as for Josh,
there wa'n't nobody that cared about seein' him but the tax-
collector an' pedlers.

"Well, the trouble Josh took to carry out that mad
fit! He split wood an' laid it down at Lyddy Ann's door, an'
he divided the eggs an' milk, an' shoved her half inside. He
bought her a separate barrel o' flour, an' all the groceries
he could think on; they said he laid money on her winder-sill.
But, take it all together, he was so busy actin' like a crazed
one that he never got his 'taters dug till 'most time for the
frost. Lyddy Ann she never showed her head among the
neighbors ag'in. When she see she 'd got to stay there,
she begun to cook for herself; but one day, one o' the neighbors
heard her pleadin' with Josh, out in the cow-yard, while he
was milkin'.

"'O Joshuay,' she kep' a-sayin' over 'n' over, 'you
needn't take me back, if you 'll on'y let me do your work!
You needn't speak to me, an' I 'll live in the other part; but
I shall be crazy if you don't let me do your work. O Joshuay!
O Joshuay!' She cried an' cried as if her heart would break,
but Josh went on milkin', an' never said a word.

"I s'pose she thought he 'd let her, the old hunks, for the next day, she baked some pies an' set 'em on the table in his part. She reached in through the winder to do it. But that night, when Josh come home, he hove 'em all out into the back yard, an' the biddies eat 'em up. The last time I was there, I see them very pieces o' pie-plate, white an' blue-edged, under the syringa bush. Then she kind o' give up hope. I guess-- But no! I 'm gittin' ahead o' my story. She did try him once more. Of course his rooms got to lookin' like a hog's nest--"

"My! I guess when she see him doin' his own washin', she thought the pocket-book was a small affair," interpolated Mrs. Niles.

"She used to go round peerin' into his winders when he wa'n't there, an' one day, arter he 'd gone off to trade some steers, she jest spunked up courage an' went in an' cleaned all up. I see the bed airin', an' went over an' ketched her at it. She hadn't more 'n got through an' stepped outside when Josh come home, an' what should he do but take the wheelbarrer an', beat out as he was drivin' oxen five mile, go down to the gravel-pit an' get a barrerful o' gravel. He wheeled it up to the side door, an' put a plank over the steps, an' wheeled it right in. An' then he dumped it in the middle o' his clean floor. That was the last o' her tryin' to do for him on the sly.

"I should ha' had some patience with him if 'twa'n't for one thing he done to spite her. Seemed as if he meant to shame her that way afore the whole neighborhood. He wouldn't speak to her himself, but he sent a painter by trade to tell her he was goin' to paint the house, an' to ask her what color she 'd ruther have. The painter said she acted sort o' wild, she was so pleased. She told him yaller; an' Josh had him go right to work on 't next day. But he had her half painted yaller, an' his a kind of a drab, I guess you 'd call it. He sold a piece o' ma'sh to pay for 't. Dr. Parks said you might as well kill a woman with a hatchet, as the man did down to Sudleigh, as put her through such treatment. My! ain't it growin' late? Here, let me set back by the winder. I want to see who goes by, to-day. An' I 'll cut my story short.

"Well, they lived jest that way. Lyddy Ann she looked like an old woman, in a month or two. She looked every minute as old as you do, Mis' Gridley. Ain't you sixty-nine? Well, she wa'n't but thirty-six. Her hair turned gray, an' she was all stooped over. Sometimes I thought she wa'n't jest right. I used to go in to see if she 'd go coltsfootin' with me, or plummin'; but she never 'd make me no answer. I recollect two things she said. One day, she set rockin' back'ards an' for'ards in a straight chair, holdin' her hands round her knees, an' she says, --

"'I 'ain't got no pride, Sally Flint! I 'ain't got no pride!'

"An' once she looked up kind o' pitiful an' says, 'Ain't it queer I can't die?' But, poor creatur', I never thought she knew what she was sayin'. She 'd ha' been the last one to own she wa'n't contented if she 'd had any gover'ment over her words.

"Well, Josh he 'd turned the hired man away because he couldn't do for him over the airtight stove, an' he got men to help him by days' works. An' through the winter, he jest set over the fire an' sucked his claws, an' thought how smart he was. But one day 'twas awful cold, an' we 'd been tryin' out lard, an' the fat ketched fire, an' everything was all up in arms, anyway. Cyrus he was goin' by Josh's, an' he didn't see no smoke from the settin'-room stove. So he jest went to the side door an' walked in, an' there set Josh in the middle o' the room. Couldn't move hand nor foot! Cyrus didn't stop for no words, but he run over to our house, hollerin', 'Josh Marden 's got a stroke!' An' ma'am left the stove all over fat an' run, an' I arter her. I guess Lyddy Ann must ha' seen us comin', for we hadn't more 'n got into the settin'-room afore she was there. The place was cold as a barn, an' it looked like a hurrah's nest. Josh never moved, but his eyes follered her when she went into the bedroom to spread up the bed.

"'You help me, Cyrus,' says she, kind o' twittery-like, but calm. 'We 'll carry him in here. I can lift.'

"But our men-folks got there jest about as they was tryin' to plan how to take him, an' they h'isted him onto the bed. Cyrus harnessed up our horse an' went after Dr. Parks, an' by the time he come, we 'd got the room so 's to look decent. An'--if you 'll b'lieve it!--Lyddy Ann was in the bedroom tryin' to warm Josh up an' make him take some hot drink; but when I begun to sweep up, an' swop towards that gravel-pile in the middle o' the floor, she come hurryin' up, all out o' breath. She ketched the broom right out o' my hand.

"'I 'll sweep, byme-by,' says she. 'Don't you touch that gravel, none on ye!' An' so the gravel laid there, an' we walked round it, watchers an' all.

"She wouldn't have no watcher in his bedroom, though; she was determined to do everything but turn him an' lift him herself, but there was al'ays one or two settin' round to keep the fires goin' an' make sure there was enough cooked up. I swan, I never see a woman so happy round a bed o' sickness as Lyddy Ann was! She never made no fuss when Josh was awake, but if he shet his eyes, she 'd kind o' hang over the bed an' smooth the clo'es as if they was kittens, an' once I ketched her huggin' up the sleeve of his old barn coat that hung outside the door. If ever a woman made a fool of herself over a man that wa'n't wuth it, 'twas Lyddy Ann Marden!

"Well, Josh he hung on for a good while, an' we couldn't make out whether he had his senses or not. He kep' his eyes shet most o' the time; but when Lyddy Ann's back was turned, he seemed to know it somehow, an' he 'd open 'em an' foller her all round the room. But he never spoke. I asked the doctor about it.

"'Can't he speak, doctor?' says I. 'He can move that hand a leetle to-day. Don't you s'pose he could speak, if he 'd a mind to?'

"The doctor he squinted up his eyes--he al'ays done that when he didn't want to answer--an' he says, --

"'I guess he 's thinkin' on 't over.'

"But one day, Lyddy Ann found she was all beat out, an' she laid down in the best bedroom an' went to sleep. I set with Josh. I was narrerin' off, but when I looked up, he was beckonin' with his well hand. I got up, an' went to the bed.

"'Be you dry?' says I. He made a little motion, an' then he lifted his hand an' p'inted out into the settin'-room.

"Do you want Lyddy Ann?' says I. 'She 's laid down.' No, he didn't want her. I went to the settin'-room door an' looked out, an'--I dunno how 'twas--it all come to me.

"'Is it that gravel-heap?' says I. 'Do you want it carried off, an' the floor swop up?' An' he made a motion

to say 'Yes.' I called Cyrus, an' we made short work o'
that gravel. When I 'd took up the last mite on 't, I went
back to the bed.

"'Josh Marden,' says I, 'can you speak, or can't you?'
But he shet his eyes, an' wouldn't say a word.

"When Lyddy Ann come out, I told her what he 'd
done, an' then she did give way a little mite. Two tears
come out o' her eyes, an' jest rolled down her cheeks, but
she didn't give up to 'em.

"'Sally,' says she, sort o' peaceful, 'I guess I 'll have
a cup o' tea.'

"Well, there was times when we thought Josh would git
round ag'in, if he didn't have another stroke. I dunno whether
he did have another or not, but one night, he seemed to be
sort o' sinkin' away. Lyddy Ann she begun to turn white, an'
she set down by him an' rubbed his sick hand. He looked at
her,--fust time he had, fair an' square,--an' then he begun
to wobble his lips round an' make a queer noise with 'em.
She put her head down, an' then she says, 'Yes, Joshuay!
yes, dear!' An' she got up an' took the pocket-book 'Mandy
had gi'n him off the top o' the bureau, an' laid it down on
the bed where he could git it. But he shook his head, an'
said the word ag'in, an' a queer look--as if she was scairt
an' pleased--flashed over Lyddy Ann's face. She run into
the parlor, an' come back with that old pocket-book he 'd
give up to her, an' she put it into his well hand. That was
what he wanted. His fingers gripped it up, an' he shet his
eyes. He never spoke ag'in. He died that night."

"I guess she died, too!" said Lucy Staples, under her
breath, stealthily wiping a tear from her faded cheek.

"No, she didn't, either!" retorted Sally Flint, hastily,
getting up to peer from the window down the country road.
"She lived a good many year, right in that very room he 'd
drove her out on, an' she looked as if she owned the airth.
I 've studied on it consid'able, an' I al'ays s'posed 'twas because she 'd got him, an' that was all she cared for. There 's
the hearse now, an' two carriages, step an' step."

"Land! who's dead?" exclaimed Mrs. Forbes, getting
up in haste, while her ball rolled unhindered to the other end
of the room.

"It 's Lyddy Ann Marden," returned Sally Flint, with the triumphant quiet of one first at the goal.   "I see it this mornin' in the 'County Democrat,' when I was doin' up my wrist, an' you was all so busy."

BIBLIOGRAPHICAL NOTE

In their introductions to many of the selections in this anthology the editors name additional writings by and about the
authors. For some of the authors, however, very little biographical or critical writing exists. For information and
comment concerning them, the reader is referred to Notable
American Women 3 vols. (1971), Dictionary of American Biography 20 vols. (1929-1936), and Literary History of the
United States, 3rd ed., 3 vols. (1963), especially Vol. 3,
which is devoted entirely to bibliography. In addition, Lewis
Leary's three-volume Articles on American Literature (1954,
1970, and 1979) covering the periods 1900-1950, 1950-1967,
and 1968-1975, respectively, and the annual bibliographies of
the Modern Language Association of America are invaluable
aids in finding material on American writers. Useful general
studies of New England literature and culture in the nineteenth
century are Van Wyck Brooks, The Flowering of New England
(1936) and New England: Indian Summer (1940), and Perry D.
Westbrook, Acres of Flint: Sarah Orne Jewett and Her Contemporaries, rev. ed. (1981). A standard history of early
American writing is Moses Coit Tyler, A History of American Literature During the Colonial Period, 1607-1765 (1978).
Edmund S. Morgan, The Puritan Family (1944), provides information concerning the position of women in seventeenth-
century New England, and Marle Springer, ed., What Manner
of Woman: Essays on American and English Literature and
Life (1977), surveys the status of women as presented in literature from the Middle Ages to the present; of especial interest in that volume are essays by Ann Stanford, Nina Baym,
and Martha Banta dealing with American literature from Colonial times to World War I. Eleanor Flexner, Century of
Struggle: The Woman's Rights Movement in the United States
(1959), is a readable and authoritative treatment of its subject from earliest colonial times to the present.